A GENEALOGY OF QUEER THEORY

06

01

In the series

American Subjects

edited by Robert Dawidoff

A GENEALOGY OF QUEER THEORY

William B. Turner

Temple University Press

PHILADELPHIA

Temple University Press, Philadelphia 19122
Copyright © 2000 by Temple University
All rights reserved
Published 2000
Printed in the United States of America

Library of Congress Cataloging-in-Publication Data

Turner, William B. (William Benjamin), 1964–
  A genealogy of queer theory / William B. Turner.
      p. cm. — (American subjects)
  Included bibliographic references and index.
  ISBN 1-56639-786-3 (cloth : alk. paper) — ISBN 1-56639-787-1 (pbk. : alk paper)
      1. Homosexuality—Philosophy.   2. Lesbianism—Philosophy.   3. Gays—Identity.
  4. Lesbians—Identity.   I. Title.   II. Series.

HQ76.25.T775 2000
306.76'4'01—dc21   00-025422

Lyric on p. 172 reprinted from *SILENT LEGACY,* by Melissa Etheridge
© 1993 M.L.E. Music (ASCAP)
All Rights Administered by Almo Music Corp. (ASCAP)
All Rights Reserved   Used by Permission
WARNER BROS. PUBLICATIONS U.S. INC., Miami, FL 33014

For my parents

Contents

Series Foreword

Robert Dawidoff

One of the most challenging features of contemporary academic intellectual life in the humanities has been the importance of theory. "Theory" usually refers to a diverse body of work, predominantly French in origin, that subjects writing and thinking to a variety of analytical techniques. These techniques are meant to expose the ideologies and discordances of the things readers habitually take for granted. It is notoriously difficult to generalize about this approach to the study of what its adherents call "texts"; its methods are complicated, and its language is purposefully distant from the assumption-laden common language that it scrutinizes.

Many of the most respected theorists are now American, and the theoretical approach has received its most enthusiastic embrace in U.S. universities and colleges—especially but not exclusively in faculties of literature. The bulk of its American adherents first encountered theory as students, piecemeal and in translation. This most sophisticated of approaches has not always been warmly welcomed by those whose practices it would supplant and whose claims it has subverted and disputed. The history of theory's contentious reception has perhaps redoubled its already esoteric and self-referential tendencies. Except in caricature, Foucault, Derrida, Lacan, and other founders of this approach are still surpisingly unfamiliar to many educated readers who ought to know them. Theory has been an all too convenient occasion for academic and journalistic side taking in the unedifying and seemingly unending culture wars.

Queer theory is probably the most notorious theory of all. The term "queer theory" refers to the writing that has taken sexuality as its subject and has specifically addressed the ways in which lesbians, gays, and transsexuals raise questions about conventional understandings of sex and the sexes and, perforce, gender. Queer theory excites controversy among both the theoretically inclined and the theoretically challenged. It has been repugnant or threatening to some "straight" and some gay and lesbian academics and writers. Some activists have employed queer theory as an agenda. But queer theory remains counterintuitive in our sexphobic and homophobic public culture, and—because it is not easily accessible—it is all too easy to dismiss.

What we have missed is an account of queer theory that reliably introduces the reader to its texts and contexts. William B. Turner's *A Genealogy of Queer Theory* does this and more. Turner approaches the subject as a historian of ideas who is steeped in the writing and insights that he discusses. His work is historical in a number of ways: It tells us what queer theory is, it shows us where queer theory came from, and it introduces us to some of the most important thinkers and controversies that have marked the emergence of queer theory. With this book, Turner also makes his own decided and stimulating entry into the arguments about sexuality, and especially gay sexuality, that queer theory requires. He is a historical controversialist who is not content to turn what is a contested discourse about real people and their deepest desires into a placid, if interesting, historical account.

I respect and have learned from queer theory, but I am by temperament and, I fear, conviction less inclined than Turner and so many others from whom I have learned, in the theoretical direction. I have and continue to read such material and, with some exceptions, must confess that I continue to find it hard going. It would have been a great help to me if I had had Turner's strong and illuminating book many years ago, when I realized, that—given my own interests and those of my colleagues and students—I would have to read extensively in the body of writing that Turner introduces here. It would have helped me place and also pick and choose among this material. Turner's emphasis on Foucault, for instance, seems to me exactly right and especially well grounded. Too, his training in intellectual history gives this book an authority that inspires confidence. Turner makes it possible to distinguish between his general "genealogy" of ideas and his own theoretical and political views.

Turner does not, as others have done, take advantage of the shifting (and sometimes shifty) positioning that contemporary theory has made possible. His historical arguments and his prose resist the temptations of the common and willful obscurity that co-opts the urgent agendas of queer theory for those of the individual academic who is too often not up to the theoretical task.

Turner quickly establishes that queer theory is a subject we do want to know about and that he is a writer who understands that we need to enter this world by stages. He does not write as a reporter—even on the culture beat—but neither does he write as a theorist. Rather, he has written this book as an activist in the best sense, someone for whom political and cultural issues are not dead issues but ones that require attention and action. He has also written this as a reader, someone who has read and reread the theorists that he discusses partly because their thinking must inform activism; he has made a translation for activist purposes. *A Genealogy of Queer Theory* is also a historian's book—Turner writes as a historian of ideas who has been influenced by the theoretical writers he so ably dissects. He has written both the best first book one wants to read about this challenging subject, and a book that takes its place in the discourse to which it guides us.

Acknowledgments

A central contention of this book is that individuals' identities are the result of their historical experiences. Because I take that argument seriously, and because this project began as my dissertation, I feel compelled to offer unusually comprehensive acknowledgments. This is, in many ways, a very personal book. Thus while I remain solely responsible for its flaws, very many people contributed in very many different ways to whatever virtues it can claim.

First and foremost, I thank my parents and my four siblings for their unending patience and willingness to encourage me in the odd things that I do. My dear friends Paul Thompson, Jack Wozniak, and Don Hanks contributed to this work by demonstrating the potential health and happiness of gay men. My dearest friend, Becky Rhodes, and her family have helped me more than they know and in more ways than I can count.

In graduate school, Elisabeth Isreals Perry taught me my most important lessons about how to be a historian; all of my subsequent work will rest on the foundation that she laid. Charles Scott and Jay Clayton provided important help and encouragement at the beginning of my dissertation research. Valerie Traub taught me feminist theory. I learned much about the daily practice, as well as the theory, of feminism from Lee Meier Rice (and Jackson), Sarah Goodfellow (and Brando), Emily Walker Cook, and Claudia Baracchi. With her battles and her brilliance, Associate Professor of Philosophy Idit Dobbs-Weinstein stands as an inspiration to anyone who values intellectual work at Vanderbilt University.

My dissertation committee was unusually large but uniformly helpful. In addition to Professor Traub, Elisabeth Rose, Jim Epstein, Hugh Davis Graham, and Michael Bess provided thoughtful comments and practical advice. Many other professors who taught in the History Department during my years at Vanderbilt helped me in various ways. I thank Joel Harrington, Paul Freedman, Yoshi Igarashi, Eva Moskowitz, Sam McSeveney, Jimmie Franklin, David Carlton, Frank Wcislo, Don Winters, Margo Todd, Joyce Chaplin, Arleen Tuchman, Lewis Perry, and Don Doyle. I owe my greatest intellectual debt to Distinguished Professor of History Emeritus Paul K. Conkin. This project is vastly improved for his meticulous, cheerful shredding of it early on.

The History Department at Middle Tennessee State University (MTSU) has provided me with a welcome and congenial haven in four years of teaching there. I especially thank Jim Williams, Thaddeus Smith, Mary Hofschwelle, Nancy Rupprecht, and Susan Myers-Shirk for their help and encouragement. Professors affiliated with women's studies exemplify the extraordinary dedication to teaching and scholarship common at MTSU. I especially thank Jackie Eller, Candace Rosovsky, and Elyce Helford for opportunities to participate in feminist scholarship and activism there. I finished the revisions to this project only because time weighed heavily on my hands after the delightful Nora Sturges had the temerity to take a tenure-track job in Maryland—our loss is Maryland's gain. As the peculiarities of my historical writing attest, I also have considerable affinity for my colleagues in philosophy, who constitute what John McDermott has justly called the best small Philosophy Department in the nation. I am especially grateful for the intellectual companionship of Michael Principe, Ron Bombardi, Robert Hood, Jack Purcell, Michael Hinz, Clarence Johnson, and the ever fabulous feminist Mary Magada-Ward, who read and commented on important parts of the manuscript for this book.

Queer theory raises questions about the relationship between scholarship and politics. For their unfailing cooperation and good will, I thank the many lesbian, gay, bisexual, and transgender activists whom I have worked with during my ten years in Middle Tennessee, especially my compatriots in the Lesbian and Gay Coalition for Justice: Kathleen Maloy, Lon Thrasher, Horace Griffin, Richard Bird, Bob Conley, Terry Childress, Calpernia Addams, Norman Beaty, Gary McCullough, and Jamie Miner. LGCJ would have collapsed beneath me without the indefatigable Carter Witt, V. Our new treasurer, Nancy Reece, also earned my gratitude by helping secure permission for the snippet of Melissa Etheridge lyric that serves as epigraph for the conclusion. But I reserve my greatest affection and admiration for my hugely dedicated, irrepressible Co-chair, Rhonda White.

Finally, I am also grateful to Robert Dawidoff. I originally called him to discuss another project. He was too busy with his own series at Temple University Press, he said, but he enthusiastically offered to read my manuscript for possible inclusion in his series. He sounded only mildly disappointed when I told him it was about queer theory. "Is it in English?" he asked. If it is, he and Janet Francendese at Temple deserve credit, and my enormous thanks, for helping me turn the manuscript into a book.

Introduction

The Proliferation of Queers

The object was to learn to what extent the effort to think
one's own history can free thought from what it silently
thinks, and so enable it to think differently.

—Michel Foucault

ntroducing the topic of queer theory is as simple as pointing to violence. After a century of civil rights work by and
for African Americans and nearly a half-century of civil rights
work by and for queers, including some significant gains in
public policy, the culture of liberalism in the United States
leaves ample permission for the most hideous forms of violence against racial and sexual minorities. Three murders
within a year—James Byrd, dragged behind a pickup truck
in Texas; Matthew Shepard, pistol-whipped and left hanging
from a fence in Wyoming; and Billy Jack Gaither, beaten
and immolated on a pyre of tires in Alabama—illustrate the
point well enough.[1] In October 1999, around the first
anniversary of the death of gay college student Matthew
Shepard, the National Coalition of Anti-Violence Projects
compiled a partial list of lesbian, gay, bisexual, and transgender persons who had died as the result of anti-queer violence in the intervening year.[2] Simply by asking around
among constituent organizations, the organization compiled

1

a list of twenty instances, including that of a thirteen-year-old boy who had died of a beating inflicted by a fellow student at a school bus stop. All of the perpetrators face some significant punishment for their actions, but the question remains—why, when persons engage in violent rampages, do they so frequently choose their victims on the basis of racial or sexual difference? This is not to suggest that their attacks would be acceptable if they chose the victims using some different criteria. It is, rather, to ask how certain forms of difference become acceptable bases for the most violent expressions of prejudice while others do not. In other words, what sorts of differences matter?

This is a question about categories, about representation, about the process of attaching individuals to their identities as much as it is a question about politics and law conventionally defined. No example better illustrates the potential complexities of queer theory and politics than the murder of Barry Winchell. Winchell died on July 5, 1999 from wounds he suffered when a fellow soldier attacked him with a baseball bat as he slept in the barracks at Fort Campbell, an Army base that straddles the Kentucky-Tennessee border. He had beaten his attacker, Calvin Glover, in a fist fight the night before. Glover vowed, "I'm not going to let any faggot kick my ass." Although initial Army reports characterized the incident as an ordinary altercation between two soldiers, by the time of the trial in December 1999, the Army prosecutor refused to accept a plea of unpremeditated murder because he found overwhelming evidence that Glover had premeditated the murder out of hatred for Winchell's sexual orientation.[3]

But it is not clear that Winchell was gay. At the time of his death, he was dating Calpernia Addams, a male-to-female transgender veteran whose stint in the Navy included service in the Gulf War. Winchell met Addams when he went to the gay bar in Nashville where Addams worked as a cabaret performer. Many nongay Fort Campbell soldiers visited that gay bar regularly, however, and Winchell found himself attracted to Addams before discovering that she was not entirely female. Ultimately it matters little whether Winchell was "really" gay or not. What matters is that Calvin Glover believed that Winchell was gay; that Glover believed murder was an acceptable response to the unacceptable possibility that a faggot could kick his ass; and that the Army contributed to this belief by continuing, in defiance of all empirical evidence and reason, to enforce the proposition that openly lesbian and gay soldiers will undermine the combat worthiness of the armed forces.[4] What peculiar stew of anxiety, masculinity, heterosexism, nationalism, and other unnoticed elements combined to produce the impressively intractable belief that sexuality matters so desperately for military service in the United States? Why does this difference matter?

Or, to put the question in the terms of queer theory, why do some bodies matter more than others? Leading queer theorist Judith Butler titled one of her books *Bodies That Matter: On the Discursive Limits of "Sex."*[5] The basic approach, central to queer theory, is the investigation of foundational, seemingly indisputable concepts, such as "matter." Queer theorists perform those investigations with an eye to tracing the historical development of those concepts and their contributions to definitions of "sex" and "gender" such that differences of power along those axes of identity pervade our culture at a level that resists fulsomely the ministrations of political action conventionally defined. Could it be that effective resistance to violence, much less meaningful access to Life, Liberty, and the Pursuit of Happiness, requires not merely more legislation, however necessary legislation may be, but also a fundamental reconceptualization of the political, beginning with our understanding of individual identity as the foundation of political organization and action?

Queer theory results from a particular conceptual break that has occurred unevenly in western Europe and the United States since World War II. It is probably impossible to explain that break in any causal sense. Perhaps the disillusionment that came from recognizing the moral and political bankruptcy of Nazism had something to do with it. Certainly the economic and political changes that have allowed growing numbers of women, lesbian or not, to enter colleges and universities, and the increased openness of the gay men who have always been there, have been crucial. Whatever the cause, in 1999 a large and rapidly growing body of scholarly literature exists under the rubric of "queer" and "queer theory." The chapters of this book reflect a particular effort to account in some way for this proliferation of queer scholarship. They do not attempt to catalog that proliferation—I make no claim to exhaustiveness in my coverage.

Avatars of queer theory would be pleased to learn that the field remains conceptually slippery, that it is difficult to summarize what queer theory is about in a sentence, or even a paragraph. The remainder of this introduction offers a broad overview of the political and intellectual terrain that produced queer theory and in which queer theory operates. Then Chapter One summarizes the work of French philosopher Michel Foucault from the perspective of his impact on queer theorists. Chapters Two and Three describe gay male and feminist scholarship that provided the intellectual context for queer theoretical work in the United States, especially evidence of significant historical variation in the definitions of gender and sexuality as identity categories. Chapters Four and Five offer detailed discussions of specific queer theorists and their ideas. Just as queer theory itself entails a thoroughgoing questioning of existing categories, and even of the very process of categorization, so this book fails to fit neatly any existing disciplinary category. Consequently, the order of procession is not well established. If the tone and structure of what follows sometimes give the appearance that I am groping my way, that is because I am. But I believe this book demonstrates that, by following where queer theorists lead, I keep bumping into significant issues and controversies and that those issues and controversies are worth writing about.

Contesting Scholarship and Politics

Queer theory has sifted into the popular press. In January 1998, the *New York Times* ran a long article by Dinitia Smith on another leading queer theorist—Eve Kosofsky Sedgwick. An admirable effort to reduce abstruse academic debates to terms accessible to nonspecialists, Smith's article still illustrated the problems of translation that queer theory poses. No one who has read carefully Volume 1 of Michel Foucault's *History of Sexuality*,[6] or any of Sedgwick's major works, would state of Sedgwick that "like Foucault, she sees desire and repression as being at the root of all politics."[7] Instead, the relationships among desire, repression, and politics become matters for scrutiny. But even this is too simple, for—as Sedgwick insists in the same article—one cannot understand desire and repression without understanding gender, which in our culture is inextricably related to sexual practice and sexual identity. All of the above, in turn, have meaning for humans only via particular practices of language and representation, which add further complications. None of these domains—politics, desire, gender, sexuality, representation—is primary, determining all the rest. Their very unpredictability creates the fascination, and the importance, of these topics for queer theorists. But it is clear, at least to queer theorists, that we cannot fully understand any of these domains except as we understand how they interact.

Smith's article identifies Sedgwick and Butler as the founding mothers of queer theory, but it was feminist film theorist Teresa de Lauretis who first used the term "queer" in 1991 to describe her intellectual endeavors. Lauretis came to queer theory via questions about the ability of women to speak about and otherwise represent themselves using a language and conceptual framework that men had created in a social and political order that took little account of women, except as commodities for exchange. It is impossible to understand queer theory fully without first understanding something about the specifically and emphatically feminist concerns that motivated Lauretis, Sedgwick, Butler, and others. Often in what follows I shift, without explanation or remark, between queer theory and feminist theory. I do so not because the two are the same—clearly they are not—but because the concerns of queer theorists for sexuality, gender, and the relationships between the two, as well as their political and intellectual ramifications, grow distinctly out of feminist political and scholarly activity as much as, if not more than,out of gay political and scholarly activity. Or, more precisely, what often motivated Lauretis and Butler was the concern to maintain the specificity of lesbian experience against the tendency for lesbian lives, voices, and stories to disappear by subsumption into the categories "woman" and "gay or homosexual."

The exigencies of writing on newspaper deadlines explain the oversimplifications in Smith's account of queer theory. That the presence of uncontrolled queers continues to threaten in places where it should not becomes obvious in the responses of scholars who should have more time to reflect carefully before they write. Queer theorists suspect, however, that the scholarly ideal of dispassionate reflection, with reason as one's only guide, entails a refusal to recognize the multiple ways in which cultural and psychological factors influence what we think and write. Rather than assuming identities grounded in rational, dispassionate reflection as the basis for scholarship and politics, queer theorists wish to ask how we produce such identities. Gender and sexuality are only two of the myriad elements that constitute a given individual's identity. But, especially where they seem ambiguous or undisciplined, gender and sexuality provoke the greatest anxieties. Such anxieties, in turn, surface around queers, queerness, and the work of queer theorists.

Historian Lisa Duggan addressed this topic, somewhat obliquely, in her article on the "theory wars." Duggan pointed to feminist defenses of the famous hoax in which the journal *Social Text* unwittingly published a parody of "postmodern" scholarship. She noted how denunciations of allegedly apolitical "theory" tended to rely on sweeping, unevidenced generalizations and a failure to recognize the extent to which the supposed absurdities of the theory-addled actually resembled concepts that radical and progressive activists and scholars of the 1960s and 1970s had relied on heavily—especially arguments for the nonessentialism of identities and the dubious character of totalizing theory. But perhaps Duggan's most important point for present purposes was the "almost magical power" that critics seem to ascribe to Butler "to destroy progressive activism" and the possibility that the specifically queer character of much recent theory and activism, rather than Theory *tout court*, may be what disturbs critics.[8]

As if made to order, feminist philosopher Martha Nussbaum published a review of Butler's four books on sex and gender in the *New Republic* in early 1999. The importance of Nussbaum's review is not so much the specific claims she makes about Butler's work, although she does offer a succinct and accessible catalog of the complaints that various critics have lodged against Butler. The importance is the care with which Nussbaum defines feminist scholarship and activism at the beginning of her essay—such that Butler's work cannot count. Nussbaum rehearses the major accomplishments in public policy of feminist politics since roughly 1965, arguing that in their work most feminist scholars have strived to remain close to political battles and the lives of ordinary women, even leaving academics altogether in some cases. With her difficult explorations of the linguistic and other representational codes of gender and sex, Butler has completely abandoned these important, concrete topics in favor of "hip defeatism."[9]

According to Nussbaum's review of Butler's work, only one way to practice politics exists—the way other feminist scholars, such as Catharine McKinnon, have practiced it. Nussbaum would allow feminists to acknowledge that "the circumstances of women are often unjust," but they must also believe "that law and political action can make them more nearly just."[10] She knows precisely, and without fear of contradiction, what feminist scholars in the 1990s should be doing with the legal and political freedoms that feminist scholars/activists of the 1970s gained for them, and the list of permissible activities does not include reading or thinking seriously about Butler's work. Apparently we may not ask how it is that, after decades of feminist activism, much of it quite successful, discrimination on the basis of gender persists—

that, if we take the Promise Keepers, the Taliban, and other manifestations of crusading fundamentalism as indicators, discrimination may even be resurgent. We may not wonder if limits exist to the efficacy of reform via legislation and politics traditionally defined. We may not inquire into the ways that language and institutional practice serve to foreclose political possibilities by the way they define what constitutes a problem and what solutions seem possible. Nussbaum would forbid us to wonder if perhaps gender and sexuality are embedded in our every thought, word, and deed and if, as a result, some of us might productively try to think about where those thoughts, words, and deeds come from; how they interact; and why they are so remarkably persistent.

Where Butler began *Bodies That Matter* by interrogating the process through which "matter" became a foundational concept for western ontology and epistemology, Nussbaum accuses Butler of a "virtually complete turning from the material side of life." Nussbaum here deploys "the material" against Butler as an unexamined concept, as the defining characteristic of women's lives that Butler supposedly ignored in her allegedly dangerous feminism. As I explain in Chapter Four, I think Butler failed to follow through effectively with her genealogy of "matter." What she did brilliantly, however, especially in *The Psychic Life of Power*, was to articulate a fundamental problem for both feminists and queers: Why do people remain attached to their identities even when those identities leave them subject to discrimination, harassment, and violence? Nussbaum might reply that women cannot simply cease to be women because they suffer discrimination, although queers increasingly face the proposition that they can become "ex-gay" in order to "escape the gay lifestyle."

But the supposed immutability of identity will not suffice as a reply. This is not only because of growing empirical evidence indicating that definitions of identity, especially gender and sexual identity, vary considerably depending on race, ethnicity, class, geography, and time—the subject of Chapters Two and Three. For Nussbaum, feminist activism is, in principle, quite simple: "Men and women could decide, understanding the unhappy consequences of these habits, that they will henceforth do things differently; and changes in laws and institutions can assist in such decisions."[11] This account of Nancy Chodorow's psychoanalytic feminism may stand plausibly for what Nussbaum likes about all of the feminists whom she approves of, and there is no doubt that some men and women actually act this way.

Many, however, do not. What Nussbaum's account cannot answer is that age-old quandary: Why are not all women feminists, and why are not all queers activists (why are not all oppressed people everywhere activists, for that matter)? The ideal of smart, self-actualized, rational persons choosing to eliminate destructive and unhealthful practices from their lives is a shining vision that motivates lots of liberal politics. But what about those women who see nothing wrong with existing gender roles? What about those who actively defend the status quo? Butler has not addressed this question directly, but she has created conceptual space within which we can begin to ask it in terms of the constitution of identity. Beginning with gender and sexuality, Butler, Lauretis, Sedgwick, and others have begun to wonder how we adopt our genders and sexualities, how those categories come to have the specific meanings that they do, what symbolic and institutional practices contribute to our sense of ourselves as selves, and how those practices both enable and constrain us.

Contesting Categories

Could it be that everyone is queer? Queerness indicates merely the failure to fit precisely within a category, and surely all persons at some time or other find themselves discomfited by the bounds of the categories that ostensibly contain their identities.

Or could it be that this generalization violates the wish of queer theorists to avoid making universal claims? Sedgwick has suggested that the only definitive indicator of queerness is the inclination of an individual so to designate her- or himself. Instead of simply challenging the content of the categories, this move raises questions about the status of categories per se. Our language, and our philosophical tradition, encourages us to believe that valid categories possess some universality. If we wish to call something a "tree," then we must be able to adduce those qualities that make any given tree sufficiently like all other trees to justify creating the category and slapping a noun on it.

But the characteristic intellectual and political impulse of the late twentieth century has been to complain—not to say whine—about the inadequacy of categories, especially identity categories: "I'm not just a ————. I'm so much more than my ————." Many individuals find that the particularities of their own experiences do not fit well into the expectations that other persons bring with the categories that we all, usually without thinking, apply to one another daily. They also find that their relationship to those categories varies depending on whom they happen to be talking to and under what circumstances. I may say to a group of fellow activists that I hate gay men because of their greater willingness to attend parties than to engage in political activity; to a group of gay men that I risk losing my fag card because I have changed major parts on my car's engine; and during a debate with an "ex-gay" person that I am as definitively gay as they come. To some, I am queer because I am gay. To others, I am queer because of the way that I go about being gay. To myself, I am queer because of my love/hate relationship with the identity category "gay."

All so much postmodern navel gazing, no doubt.

Yet some sort of fundamental change is afoot. Queer theory does in fact indicate the emergence of new forms of thought, or at least new ways of working with existing categories and concepts. It operates at the conjunction of particular strands in feminist and lesbian/gay intellectual and political work, on one hand, and particular strands of Continental philosophy, on the other hand. This genealogy of queer theory is not an exhaustive account of all that has occurred under the rubric of "queer theory" in the last, say, ten years or so. It is, rather, an attempt to trace out certain of the major outlines of queer theoretical thought, to provide some intellectual and historical context—to trace out and, I hope, illuminate some major points.

Michael Warner began the Introduction to the collection *Fear of a Queer Planet* with the question "What do queers want?"[12] He never answered his own question; even one who read carefully all of the contributions to his volume would not come away with any clear sense of what the answer might be. Anyone who expects from a book definitive, clear-cut exposition of answers to such questions should probably abort the present mission now. If queer theorists have anything in common, it might be that they consistently celebrate the unformed, inchoate, provisional character of the field, and they look with suspicion on the possibility that, after a tumultuous, boisterous, and unfocused adolescence, queer theory will settle into the adulthood of traditional disciplinarity, with a clearly defined field of inquiry, a journal or two, and a few doctoral programs at the more advanced universities.

Queer theory begins with a suspicion: that the predominant modes of intellectual and political activity in western culture during the late twentieth century do not serve the needs and interests of queers and that perhaps they cannot be made to do so. Queer theory is oppositional. But queer theorists have not arrived at a scheme for what should replace existing modes. Instead, they seem to agree that the present project should consist primarily of elaborating the problems with existing intellectual and political modes, especially by studying how those modes function, while leaving as open as possible the question of what should replace them.

Note the conjunction of intellectual and political activity. Agreeing with the French philosopher Michel Foucault, queer theorists would generally argue that power and knowledge, far from being distinct, mutually antagonistic realms in modern western culture, in fact operate very much in tandem. One might even suggest that power and knowledge serve as the mutually constituting conditions of operation for each other. The conditions of possibility for queer theory probably arose somewhere between the publication of two of Foucault's major works: *The Order of Things: An Archaeology of the Human Sciences* in 1966 and *Discipline and Punish: The Birth of the Prison* in 1975.[13] We should immediately insist, however, that here Foucault's texts serve primarily as markers—the role of his thought in enabling queer theory, while important, should not be overestimated.

No, Foucault should stand, at least for purposes of introduction, as an indicator. In *The Order of Things* he argued for the existence of three epistemes since the Middle Ages: the Renaissance, from roughly 1500 to 1650; the classical era, from 1650 to the end of the eighteenth century; and the modern period, since the turn of the nineteenth century. The signal feature of the modern period, in Foucault's reading, was the emergence of man as the subject and object of knowledge, the central organizing feature around which the human sciences were elaborated. A nominalist, Foucault understood by "man" a conceptual framework that provided the pretheoretical ground on which such disciplines as psychology, sociology, and literary criticism could develop. Each of the three epistemes that he described had a distinct conceptual organization. An "episteme" thus designates a period in which a certain ordering of knowledge, a certain "historical a priori,"[14] holds sway, guiding inquiry by providing characteristic questions and modes of analysis while remaining largely opaque to those who operate within it.

On Foucault's view, the modern episteme of man looked set to disappear, folding into something different that he could not specify. For purposes of queer theory, we may understand "man" more literally than

Foucault did—as a concept with highly specific characteristics of sexual and gender identity. Inquiry since 1800 has not only revolved around "man" as the central organizing concept; it has also reflected the assumptions and perspectives of men—typically heterosexual and white, of course. "Queer" indicates a failure to fit not only categories of sexual identity but also categories of gender identity. The conditions of possibility for queer theory involve not only resistance to prevailing definitions of sexual identity but—equally and antecedently—resistance to prevailing definitions of gender identity as well.

Seems to be about definition

Contesting Identity

And it is a particular form of resistance. For nearly two hundred years, from roughly 1789 to 1980, members of excluded groups could protest their exclusion from the rights and responsibilities of U.S. politics only by demanding inclusion. Such demands typically took the form of arguments that those in the excluded group possessed the characteristics that allowed white men to govern themselves—that they were fully persons. The exclusion, and therefore the objection, rested on claims about identity. Poor men, slaves, women, and sodomites, according to the protest, were identical to rich white men—at least for purposes of government. Beginning around 1980, at first feminist theorists and then queer theorists with increased gusto began to question this whole mode of organization—the very assumption that a claim to universal identity should serve as the grounding assumption from which political thought and action begins.

During the nineteenth century, women's rights activists in the United States began with the observation that few men as individuals, and certainly neither institutions nor society as a whole, lived up to their stated equation between a universal human identity and legal or political status—"We hold these truths to be self-evident, that all men are created equal, that they are endowed by their Creator with certain inalienable rights." Either "men" was not a synonym for "human" and women had no reason to expect equal rights and treatment or "men" was a synonym for "human" and therefore universal, but the men who claimed to believe that sentiment would honor it only in the breach. Elizabeth Cady Stanton knew that whatever qualities in "man" made them all equal she possessed in like measure. She believed that the Declaration of Independence contained an unheeded universal injunction, and she sought to resolve the confusion with her revision—"all men and women are created equal."[15] As long as men failed to recognize the legitimacy of this revision, the women's rights movement would represent all women's demands for inclusion—"woman" clearly constituted an entirely reliable, unfractured category for women's rights activists. Until the 1970s, no one seriously disputed the assumption that a single feminist movement or set of priorities could represent all women as a class. As late as 1983, in introducing the twentieth-anniversary edition of *The Feminine Mystique*, Betty Friedan wrote as if the feminists in a resurgent movement of the 1960s had unproblematically represented all women.[16]

To arrive at such an understanding of second-wave feminism, Friedan had to ignore a vast array of significant fractures that had emerged among feminists, and among women generally, in the interim. This is not to say that second-wave feminism was a unified movement even in its beginnings. Friedan became a leading figure in the liberal, reformist wing of the movement, but many women became feminists during the 1960s because of their frustrations with the unreflecting, and unrepentant, sexism of supposedly radical men in the New Left and antiwar movements. Some of the first radical feminists worked to extend the radical, usually Marxian, analysis of oppression based on race and, above all, class, to include gender. The problem in the New Left and the antiwar movements, on this view, was a fairly simple failure to recognize that gender oppression constituted a political, rather than merely a personal, issue—or, as the famous feminist phrase has it, the personal is political. But even that useful phrase left open for radical feminists the question: Was the primary problem class oppression under capitalism or gender oppression under patriarchy? Different answers to this question caused significant splits among feminists during the late 1960s and early 1970s.[17]

Such relatively arcane debates may seem insignificant in retrospect—certainly not sufficient to justify questioning the intellectual and political purchase of "woman" as a category. The same period saw what appeared to be a major triumph of unity for the liberal wing of the women's movement: Congress passed the Equal Rights Amendment (ERA), sending it to the states for ratification in 1972. Alice Paul and activists in the National Women's Party had introduced the ERA in Congress for the first time in 1921, immediately after the ratification of the Woman Suffrage Amendment. For fifty-one years, however, advocates for working-class women had opposed the ERA for fear that it would eliminate hard-won labor protections that applied only to women. With the new protective legislation of Lyndon Johnson's Great Society, the labor-oriented political leaders who had long opposed the ERA could join with the business and professional women who had long favored it, resulting in the requisite two-thirds-majority win in Congress.

But, especially after the 1973 *Roe v. Wade* decision, in which the Supreme Court struck down most state laws prohibiting abortion, the drive to ratify the ERA met a new, unexpected form of opposition in highly motivated, well organized antifeminist women who opposed legal abortion, lesbian/gay civil rights, and feminism, all of which they associated with the ERA.[18] Still, even the conservative opponents of the amendment did not all agree in their reasons for opposing it. Traditionalist conservative women saw it as a threat to their roles as wives and mothers—in the absence of legal sex discrimination, states would no longer be able to require husbands to support their wives.[19] In queer theoretical terms borrowed from Foucault, they were subjects in the dual sense: "subject to someone else by control and dependence, and tied to his [*sic*] own identity by a conscience or self-knowledge."[20] They were subjects in both these senses, and they engaged in political activity with the express purpose of perpetuating that subjectivity. Libertarian women, by contrast, saw the ERA as yet another illegitimate expansion of federal power.[21] The ultimate failure of the ERA to win ratification demonstrated that, whatever biological or anatomical endowments they might share, not all women agreed on major political, social, and economic issues. Identity does not determine politics.

Throughout all of these debates among women's rights activists and feminists, as through all aspects of U.S. culture and politics, ran the issue of race. During the nineteenth and first half of the twentieth centuries, black women created organizations that paralleled segregated white women's groups, or they created entirely distinct organizations dedicated to their unique needs. While many white feminists of the second wave found their inspiration for feminist activism in the African American civil rights movement, relations between white and black women around issues of gender discrimination and oppression remained strained.[22] Black women scholars such as bell hooks have argued forcefully that the feminist movement, as privileged white women defined it, ignored black women's problems. According to hooks, "Specific problems and dilemmas of leisure class white housewives were real concerns that merited consideration and change but they were not the pressing political concerns of masses of women. Masses of women were concerned about economic survival, ethnic and racial discrimination, etc."[23] This criticism points to the cracks of race and class in the supposed monolith of women's solidarity as grounded in a common gender identity.

But whatever their failings in terms of practice, white feminists of the second wave at least acknowledged in principle that racial discrimination was bad and that black women faced a double oppression on the basis of race and gender. Differences of sexuality proved more complicated. Lesbians might constitute a "lavender menace" that would undermine the women's movement, according to Friedan in her role as a founder of the National Organization for Women (NOW). Or they might seem like the most feminist of feminists, according to such lesbian feminist groups as the Furies or the Radicalesbians. Activists who originally called themselves "radical feminists" paid relatively little attention to the issue of lesbians, arguing that the question of sexual practice distracted from the real goal of women's liberation.[24] Black lesbian feminists noted the double bind of facing homophobia from black heterosexuals and racism from white lesbian feminists.[25]

Lesbian feminists, in turn, had their suspicions about older lesbians, who often modeled their relationships on heterosexual marriages, with one butch partner and one femme partner. They also battled sexism from their supposed allies, gay men, as much as from their alleged oppressors, nongay men.[26] In the politics of the 1960s and 1970s, "homosexuality" proved more reliable as a category that marked difference, and acceptable discrimination, from the outside than as a rallying point for lesbians and gay men who opposed discrimination. Early on, lesbian/gay civil rights activists actually made the category itself a target. Near the end of the civil rights revolution, after African Americans had achieved their major legislative gains and feminists were reaching their apogee of radical organizing gay liberation burst on the scenes with the Stonewall Riots of June 1969. A long-standing problem for African Americans and women was posed more obviously and acutely for "homosexuals" and became an immediate target for gay liberationist activists—authoritative individuals and their institutions defined "homosexuality" as necessarily pathological. Lesbian/gay activists protested the American Psychiatric Association's (APA) categorization of "homosexuality" as a mental illness. Using the tactics of civil rights protest, lesbian/gay activists persuaded the APA to drop "homosexuality" as a diagnosis from its official nosology, the *Diagnostic and Statistical Manual of Disorders (DSM)*.[27]

This focus on the APA and the *DSM* exemplified the new issues that organizing around gender and sexuality added to the traditional concerns of civil rights activists. Women and sexual minorities had long faced a barrage of "expert" information about their bodies and identities that depended for its coherence on ignorance and distortion of their actual experiences.[28] The prevailing definitions of "woman" and "homosexual" precisely excluded those who fit the category from producing reliable knowledge about themselves. Physicians and psychologists, all presumably "heterosexual men," knew more about "women" and "homosexuals" on the basis of their abstract, institutionally authoritative theorizing than "women" and "homosexuals" could possibly know on the basis of their own experiences.[29] Although the epistemology, like the politics, of the late eighteenth century ostensibly rested on an analysis of a universal human identity, subdivisions of race, gender, and sexual practice served to exclude many—perhaps most—individuals from the universal category "human."

During the 1970s, then, only straight, white men could claim the security of a universal identity category. Lesbians, whether feminist or not; feminists, whether lesbian or not; "homosexuals," whether female or male; and any of the above even more so if they were black shared only their lack of equal access to the rights and responsibilities, or "privileges and immunities," that citizens of the United States supposedly took for granted. For many scholars and activists, the restricted access to privileges and immunities that straight, white men enjoyed began to look less like a failure than an endemic feature of the system. Rather than continue to pursue Stanton's strategy of playing by the rules, adding to the list of those who are created equal, some feminist, lesbian, and gay scholars and activists chose to examine the rules and question the assumptions about universal identity that lay behind them.

Queer theory coalesced out of the growing sense among some feminists and sexual minorities that their access to equal rights and treatment would depend not on working out the glitches in an otherwise workable system but on rethinking from the ground up categories of persons and the distributions of power among them. Actually living up to the universal claims of liberalism—that all men are created equal—would have made quite a mess of things. In practice, almost no one whose opinion mattered really intended to free the slaves or allow women to vote. Fortunately, science offered a way out: Political equality and scientific method justified one another, and both depended on the capacity for reason—the ability to think systematically and dispassionately about the world, to assess problems and go about solving them, to formulate and test hypotheses. Those whose admission to the charmed circle of universal identity would cause untold practical problems also lacked the requisite capacity for reason: Their exclusion became legitimate. That virtually all of the political and scientific leaders who disparaged the reasoning abilities of women, blacks, and sodomites happened to be presumptively heterosexual, white men made no difference—those leaders drew their conclusions from the universal, incontestable laws of reason.[30] A very neat system indeed.

In response, some black, feminist, lesbian, and gay scholars put the methods of the human sciences to the service of elaborating positive accounts of their experiences and identities. Intellectually and politically, they responded rationally within the logic of the system by producing, according to the existing rules of inquiry, a truth of themselves different from the prejudicial stereotypes that justified discrimination against them. This practice rested on the presumption that the use of the human sciences to bring the experiences of gender and sexual identities fully into consciousness, into discourse, would have the effect of delegitimizing discrimination. The problem with identity categories, on this view, lay in the erroneous content that ill-informed experts had supplied rather than in the categories themselves or in the organization of knowledge that enables or requires such categories.

The work of queer theorists, by contrast, tends toward the following suspicion: If our rights depend on our common identity as humans, then we all have to look alike, act alike, be alike in order to have rights. Of course, this is not how the system is supposed to work, but the experiences of women and minorities in the United States indicate that it does, in fact, work this way. This is not to suggest a total absence of change, even improvement, in the existing system.[31] Rather, it is to suggest that the model of free, rational individuals forming political institutions that guarantee our liberty may not be a terribly accurate way of thinking about how we govern ourselves on a daily basis.

Contesting Liberalism

Paradoxically, queer theory both depends on and critiques the liberalism of the twentieth-century United States.[32] If we wish to adduce rules of method, we might suggest that queer theorists suspect that we live in a paradoxical world and that attention to the history and function of paradoxes, as opposed to denunciation of them as failures of logic or reason, is a highly productive enterprise, both intellectually and politically. We should also insist on the point that critique does not necessarily entail wholesale dismissal or a refusal to acknowledge that the present framework has features that may remain desirable in future frameworks. Precisely because "liberalism" is so amorphous and labile, it captures a wide array of political, economic, social, and cultural beliefs and practices that make up the milieu in which queer theorists learned to think and began to write. No individual, queer or otherwise, can simply erase that context from her or his mind the moment flaws appear in its operation. Neither would queer theorists deprecate important features of political liberalism from which they benefit, especially the principled commitment to free inquiry and expression or to discrimination solely on the basis of merit—even as they point out the numerous ways in which even, perhaps especially, the most strenuous defenders of those principles seem hell-bent on honoring them only in the breach.

Lesbian, gay, bisexual, and transgender activists have taken up the tactics of civil rights protest on their own behalf. This is preeminently a post–World War II phenomenon. Unlike the African American and feminist movements of the 1950s and 1960s, queer protest had no clear antecedent in the United States during the nineteenth century. By their mere existence, lesbian, gay, bisexual, and transgender civil rights activists changed the meaning of "civil rights," even as they modeled their movement, morally and tactically, on earlier movements and solicited support from such African American civil rights leaders as Coretta Scott King, Jesse Jackson, and John Lewis.[33]

But why did the black inhabitants of U.S. inner cities riot in the summer of 1965, as if in response to President Johnson's signing of the Voting Rights Act of that year? Why did the enormous personal sacrifice and heroic achievement of so many leaders and protestors seem to avail so little for the average African American? The standard explanation, of course, points to the benefits, but also the limitations, of the Civil Rights Act of 1964 and the Voting Rights Act of 1965—formal equality in political and legal matters but not in economic matters. This led to the expression of continued frustration with U.S. liberalism among those who had never much benefited from it.

Even if we accept this explanation, however, another puzzling phenomenon remains. Throughout the 1960s, those who expressed significant discontent included not only the most deprived citizens of the United States but also many of its most privileged. Whether in the Port Huron Statement of the Students for a Democratic Society, Friedan's *Feminine Mystique*, or the counterculture of the hippies, people who seemed to have everything that U.S. abundance could offer felt alienation, depression, and the need to engage in political protest or to abandon politics in favor of cultural resistance. Similarly, after the exhausting 1970s—which saw important advances in lesbian/gay civil rights but also the development of significant backlash leading to the Republican electoral victories of the 1980s—feminist, lesbian, and gay activists and intellectuals, even in some cases those who had benefited from the policy changes of the 1960s, remained dissatisfied with the culture and politics of twentieth-century U.S. liberalism. In every case, the connections among profound dissatisfaction, individual identity, and the institutions of politics and government were central yet far from clear.

In his archaeological studies, Foucault professed no ability to explain historical causation. This element of archaeology persists in Foucault's genealogies—his more politically oriented studies of the 1970s, *Discipline and Punish* and Volume 1 of *The History of Sexuality*. At one level, this looks like an absurd claim; all of Foucault's major works contain numerous causal statements. They do not, however, contain attempts to explain causally the major shifts from one period or episteme to another. That persons in a particular period began to incarcerate the mad and study mental illness or develop the practices that would become clinical medicine, there was no doubt. But to explain, in some final sense, why they did so—Foucault refused to attempt such explanations. On this radically empiricist, radically historicist view, it is possible to describe the intentions of individuals and small groups insofar as they left evidence of those intentions, but all efforts at historical explanation at a high level of generality—the nation, the society, the era or epoch—involved appeals to external explanatory frameworks that no evidence would support. Such frameworks precede and shape, rather than emerge out of, historical research.

Similarly, it seems quite unlikely that we will ever arrive at a definitive explanation at the macro level for why, in the years after World War

II and apparently at the height of its success, U.S. liberalism began to fall apart. I offer this very brief overview of civil rights protest as part of an introduction to queer theory, not because I think it somehow definitively explains why queer theorists think what they think but because it gives some idea of the context out of which they thought. And perhaps the central feature of that context is the failure of policy change in the realm of government to deliver fully on the promise of this nation's founding documents. We may all be created equal, but something in our culture clearly gives many, perhaps most, of us the message that we should abandon all hope of ever achieving true equality of opportunity or treatment. This is not to disparage the important policy changes that have taken place; the Fourteenth and Fifteenth Amendments, *Brown v. Board of Education*, the 1964 and 1965 Civil Rights Acts—all have had an enormous impact on the politics and society of the United States.

Nor is the queer theoretical point that these important changes pertain to race first, to gender second, and to sexuality hardly at all. Queer theorists hold no sour grapes for having arrived at the end of the civil rights revolution. Instead, they wonder how to organize an effective politics among groups of individuals who, even when they see themselves as oppressed, seem little motivated to challenge that oppression. They wonder how meanings and practices of identity circulate in our culture such that perceptions of entitlement and abjection along lines of race, gender, sexuality, class, and so on become the very horizons of individual self-perception for most persons, demonstrably playing a much more important role than any stirring statements of principle in determining the willingness of those individuals to participate in political processes, including protest.

Contesting Truth

For Foucault, the difficulty stemmed from the organization of knowledge in the episteme of "man." In the mid-1960s, at roughly the same time that feminists began their second wave, just before the emergence of gay liberation, Foucault began to question the self-evident unity of "man" as the subject and object of knowledge, as the conceptual ground from which inquiry begins in modern, western culture. Foucault and certain other scholars who raised such questions at the time are commonly called "poststructuralists," a term that requires much more careful specification in order to become useful than it usually receives. The term "poststruc-turalism" contains a very simple statement of chronology: It comes after "structuralism." Foucault invested considerable rhetorical energy in insist-ing that he did not practice "structuralist" modes of analysis.[34] He had to insist that he was not a structuralist because many observers insisted that he was.

One can legitimately read Foucault's first famous book, *The Order of Things*, as, among other things, a polemic against phenomenology.[35] In both *The Order of Things* and his next book, *The Archaeology of Knowl-edge*, Foucault challenged the primacy of the knowing subject as the guarantor of knowledge.[36] He described "epistemes" in which "dis-courses" served as the source for the rules that knowing subjects used in specifying the objects of their inquiries and in making true statements about those objects. "Truth," on this view, results neither from some cor-respondence between statements and the world that those statements purportedly refer to nor from the universal validity of the method of inquiry and the logical principles on which that method is based. Instead, "truth" is exclusively a function of the application of discursive rules, which the knowing subject remains at least partially unaware of even as she or he applies them. The most basic rules for the production of truth constitute the horizon of our identities in such a manner that we cannot recognize these rules, much less critique or otherwise account for them. Even in the absence of any explicit references to structuralist methods or principles in Foucault's work, his arguments looked structuralist to many. His claim that "thought silently thinks," embedded in an exami-nation of "discourse," in some respects bears considerable resemblance to the structures of binary oppositions—good/bad, raw/cooked—that, according to structuralists, govern human understanding.[37]

But, as Jacques Derrida pointed out, by the late 1960s structuralism no longer seemed compelling. The recognition of ethnocentrism raised doubts about the capacity of European observers to account so fully for the knowledge structures of other cultures. French anthropologist Claude Lévi-Strauss originated structuralist analysis with his readings of myths in "primitive" cultures. But the very argument in favor of knowledge as dependent on structures of meaning, combined with polit-ical resistance to colonialism in third world nations, undermined the self-representations of European scholars as knowing subjects who could describe fully the meanings of another culture in structural terms. This political/intellectual move paralleled the similar doubts about identity and its intellectual and political implications that feminists (and civil rights activists, and the New Left, and the counterculture, and newly militant gay liberationists) had begun to raise in the United States.

For Derrida, "This moment is not first and foremost a moment of philosophical or scientific discourse[;] it is also a moment which is political, economic, technical, and so forth. One can say in total assurance that there is nothing fortuitous about the fact that the critique of ethnocentrism—the very condition of ethnology—should be systematically and historically contemporaneous with the destruction of the history of metaphysics. Both belong to a single and same era."[38] The history of philosophy and ideas, which had long functioned interdependently with assumptions about the identity of "man," does not operate independently of other types of history. Political and economic events help constitute the conditions of possibility for a given body of thought, and those events, including doubts about the claims to intellectual and political neutrality of western thinkers, had brought to an end the historical circumstances in which "man" as the ground of knowledge had appeared self-evident.

With his descriptions of past epistemes in *The Order of Things*, Foucault created a problem for himself similar to the undoing of ethnology. If knowing subjects cannot specify fully the discursive rules of the episteme in which they live, how could Foucault describe the modern episteme of "man," which presumably governed Foucault's own intellectual training? He could escape this dilemma via the historical character of his analysis: Epistemes change, and although Foucault claimed not to know why they changed, he believed that his archaeological method allowed him to describe the discursive rules of one episteme from the perspective of a subsequent episteme. This approach allowed Foucault to understand the philosophy and science of the European classical age better than phenomenologists did. It did so because Foucault refused to demand of the classical age why Galileo and René Descartes had failed to ask certain questions or solve certain problems that seemed, to phenomenologists, essential to the elaboration of a theory of truth and central to the thought of both the classical and the modern ages. Instead, he made the historical argument that the discursive rules of the classical age, the organization of knowledge, made certain questions central but other questions impossible.[39] Rather than present himself as a philosopher who would solve the problem of providing knowledge with certain ground in universal principles, Foucault played the role of the archaeologist who can specify the discursive rules that enabled and limited thought in another age but who remains equally enabled and limited by current discursive rules.

Foucault was not a phenomenologist. But by defining his inquiry as "archaeology," Foucault introduced a historical element that also distinguished him from structuralists. Structuralist accounts of culture raised questions about the significance of historical change by explaining culture in terms of binary oppositions that seemed to possess a certain timeless endurance. Structures of meaning—especially insofar as they ultimately rested on some self-evident central term, such as the immediate experience of a deity, or some other first principle—constituted the fundamental ground of experience against which historical changes pale into insignificance. But in Derrida's formulation, the structurality of structure had become a question as well.[40] According to Foucault's account in *The Order of Things*, rather than resting on some self-evident, immediate experience, the structures themselves changed over time. They exhibit a historical logic of their own, one that could not be reduced to any more fundamental level of observation or analysis, whether economy, politics, or some other. By posing a fundamental challenge to both phenomenology and structuralism, Foucault, Derrida, and other "poststructuralist" philosophers seemed to undermine the most basic foundations of the western organization of knowledge. The practice of categorizing such philosophers with a term that serves only to place them in chronological relation to a preceding body of thought reflects the absence of any new orthodoxy or single explanatory principle that would provide at once coherence among the work of several thinkers and a more conventionally descriptive name. Group identity is not a priority for a set of philosophers who may have in common only that they doubt the usefulness of the phenomenological and structuralist poles as epistemological frameworks or of epistemological frameworks *tout court* insofar as the point of such frameworks is to provide a certain ground for knowledge. Poststructuralism is queer.

Foucault elaborated new procedures for inquiry—"archaeology" and, later, "genealogy"—because he found existing procedures inadequate. With these new procedures, Foucault effectively abandoned the philosophical quest to provide some certain grounds for knowledge claims, some ultimate basis for "truth." He argued that, far from resting on any ultimate or certain ground, truth claims are the products of historically variable discursive regimes that determine rules for inquiry. This philosophical move away from philosophy constituted the elaboration of a "language of difference," in which concern for difference displaced the traditional philosophical concern for identity.[41] We must understand "identity" in two senses here: The identity of the scholar as knowing subject at once confirms and is confirmed by truth as conceptual identity, or a generalized principle of congruence between description and reality as governed by the abstraction of total self-identity, or logic—the law of the excluded middle. "Truth" depends on the identity of "man" and vice versa. The "language of difference" that Foucault, Derrida, and other scholars began to use fundamentally changed the terms of the debate. The language of difference operates at the threshold of two epistemes, leaving open the question of the direction in which this new inquiry will lead. Thought silently thinks. Foucault did not know what he was doing. Whatever it was, it fit neatly neither philosophy nor history conventionally defined.

Foucault as poststructuralist insisted on the immanence of the scholar, her or his embeddedness within culture and history. His break with the traditions of modern philosophy came above all else with his abandonment of the attempt to ground knowledge in some sort of transcendent principles. The poststructuralist challenge to both phenomenology—the transcendent subject as knower—and structuralism—transhistorical structures of meaning as the ground of knowledge and subjectivity—has left all subjects, philosophers included, with no platform on which to rest the claim that scholars can poke their heads above the flux of history in order to gain a transcendent, or, more modestly, even a transhistorical, vantage point. The object of freeing thought from what it silently thinks depends on historical inquiry because we have no other avenue from which to approach the cultural determination of what and how we think. Abandoning an idealist conception of human identity renders the line between philosophy and history far less clear—hence the historical character of Foucault's major philosophical works.

But this historical inquiry looks peculiar because it begins with assumptions that, in some cases, differ radically from those of most historians and because it allows scholars to study as historical phenomena aspects of identity—gender, sexuality, who knows what else—that once seemed biologically fixed and therefore immutable. This book is a genealogy, rather than a history, of queer theory because the historical character of both genealogy as mode of inquiry and queer theory as genealogical inquiry into gender and sexual identities raises pressing questions about the character of historical inquiry traditionally defined, especially insofar as historians understand their craft as a scientific pursuit of knowledge about the past.

According to its proponents, structuralism was a science, and as such it would confer upon social scientists—sociologists, economists, historians—the same certainty of knowledge that other scientists enjoyed. In 1958 Lévi-Strauss claimed that "structural linguistics will certainly play the same renovating role with respect to the social sciences that nuclear physics, for example, has played for the physical sciences."[42] But, as Derrida pointed out, that certainty of knowledge rested on the certain identity of Eurocentrism. Structuralism offered certainty. Poststructuralism brought only uncertainty.

Contesting History

The hope for certainty dies hard. Many scholars, including a significant number of historians, saw considerable danger in Foucault's historicization of knowledge. They recognized, often only implicitly, that the standard conception of historical inquiry as a social science rests on the hope that someone, someday, will vindicate some set of transhistorical, if not transcendent, principles for inquiry. They insisted that scholarly inquiry, including historical inquiry, proceeds according to some objectively verifiable principles of reason, even if no one has yet managed to offer such verification in a compelling manner. Yet both the fragmentation of identity along lines of gender and sexuality and the fragmentation of truth at the hands of poststructuralist philosophers bode ill for any project that would vindicate universal or objective principles of reason and thus the discipline of history traditionally defined.

Here we face the vexed question of something commonly called "postmodernism." I had rather eschew the term altogether here if only because debates on the topic have long since degenerated into gross oversimplifications and persistent reliance on straw opponents by those who believe that they see in "postmodernism" a fundamental threat to all that they hold intellectually and politically dear. In what was perhaps a quintessentially "postmodern" observation, however, Foucault noted repeatedly that the historical density of language itself contributes to the determination of the character of discourse. Given that many observers will read "Foucault" and immediately think "postmodern," it behooves me to address the issue. I believe it is relevant exclusively as a historical question in two senses: First, something snapped in the years immediately after World War II, perhaps as a direct result of the war itself, although we will probably never know for sure; second, the breach of the postwar period carries significant implications for the organization of knowledge, especially for historians, but we historians seem very much at odds among ourselves in trying to decide what it all means.

In short, an epistemic break seems to have occurred, as Foucault believed. That debates over "postmodernism" indicate a fundamental rupture in scholarly conceptualizations is illustrated by the difficulty of even specifying what the debate is about. I begin by stipulating that, in my view, the most coherent and compelling statement about "postmodernism" as an issue for knowledge comes from Jean-François Lyotard in *The Postmodern Condition: A Report on Knowledge*.[43] In doing so, I do not wish to suggest that I necessarily see Foucault's work as a clear exemplification of the postmodern condition that Lyotard described. Whether Foucault is or is not an exemplar of "postmodernism" is not an interesting question for present purposes. Foucault's work prompts us to look skeptically at such totalizing generalizations as "modernism" and "postmodernism."[44] Instead, Lyotard's account of narrative and scientific strategies for legitimating knowledge, and the exhaustion of the legitimating power of long-standing metanarratives, describes well the difficulty that historians and other social scientists face in the late twentieth century. That difficulty and the epistemic break of which it is a function turn on conceptions of individual identity as Foucault addressed them in much of his work.

No better indicator of historians' self-consciousness about their discipline and their anxiety about its epistemological underpinnings could exist than the 1994 survey by the Organization of American Historians (OAH). Writing about the results of that survey, historian Kenneth Cmiel noted that most historians liked the diversity of their profession but hated the fragmentation.[45]

As Cmiel's article title, "History against Itself," suggests, the problem is one of identity. Many historians professed a genuine ethical commitment to the inclusion of as many different stories as possible in their understandings of the past. They acknowledged the legitimacy of charges from African Americans, feminists, and others that politically and intellectually indefensible practices of exclusion had distorted our understanding of the past. They demonstrated that acknowledgment in part by working diligently to include the stories of African Americans and women in their understanding and teaching of the past and to make race and gender central categories for historical understanding. However, they remained committed to the idea that the practices of exclusion that prompted the complaints represented a failure to abide by otherwise valid principles of inquiry. The rules for professional historians, and the identity of "professional historian," should in principle remain available to all, with discrimination solely on the basis of intellectual ability rather than race, gender, sexuality, or anything else. Adding race, gender, and sexuality would change our substantive understanding of the past but not the procedures that we use to investigate that past. Cmiel quoted one survey respondent as identifying "multicultural approaches if put into a unifying framework" as the best aspect of the discipline in its current state. At its worst, however, "multiculturalism is in danger of Balkanizing both U.S. history and politics."[46]

The perception of impending balkanization must have stemmed, at least in part, from the growing realization that including African Americans, women, and openly lesbian/gay persons in the faculty and adding race, gender, and sexuality to the study of the past seemed to entail a profound threat to any "unifying framework," and therefore to any consistent set of procedures for inquiry, that might provide the discipline with intellectual coherence. The fragmentation of the discipline resulted from the proliferation of historians, all bringing different combinations of topical, methodical, and theoretical commitments to their work. From the perspective of women and minority scholars, the problem was this: Who would impose the unifying framework that legitimates the knowledge claims of the discipline? According to epistemology, the framework rests on some sort of necessity: We inquire according to these principles because these principles reflect accurately the way the world works; therefore, these principles will guide us to the truth.

Yet women and minorities who demanded equal access on the basis of universal identity and demonstrated ability faced persistent and increasingly subtle resistance from many of the men who controlled political and intellectual institutions.[47] Some such women and minorities began to suspect that the moral and epistemological justifications for existing practices and institutions depended more on differences in access to power than on rational or ethical necessity. They also suspected that the resistance of some scholars to evidence and argument challenging their basic assumptions about gender and sexuality belied their self-understanding as rational, autonomous subjects. Even those who would defend universal epistemological principles began to speak in terms of "unifying frameworks" and other such optional, or arbitrary, legitimizing strategies. When they began to argue on behalf of chosen structures or frameworks, they implicitly, and perhaps inadvertently, conceded the point that we have no necessary structures on which to ground knowledge. In suggesting that modern structures of knowledge had recently begun to exhibit a remarkable fragility, Foucault offered more description than prescription.[48] By insisting that philosophy and other modes of inquiry change according to political, economic, and social events, Derrida and Foucault only described the world around them in the late 1960s and anticipated the uncertainty of and contests about thought that would persist for at least another thirty years.

The defense of alleged objectivity and universals proceeded apace, however, even as such defenses took on an increasingly desperate tone. The arguments among historians tended to take the form of claims for the "scientific" status of the discipline, which status its advocates grounded in claims about the character of human identity. Joyce Appleby, Lynn Hunt, and Margaret Jacob found themselves in the quandary of having benefited from the effort to include women and minorities among histories and historians even as they deplored the balkanization of truth that resulted. They insisted that historical inquiry must retain some epistemological grounding in "science." Yet their argument rested not on a rigorous philosophical explication of how history is a form of scientific knowledge but on a breathtakingly reductive account of something called "postmodernism" and warnings of the dire consequences that would result from the abandonment of scientific objectivity.[49] Ironically, their model of "scientific, objective" history as underwriting the moral claims of oppressed minorities to greater freedom and participation in U.S. democracy illustrates precisely Lyotard's account in *The Postmodern Condition* of science as legitimate insofar as it facilitates the drive toward freedom of the unified social subject.[50] In defining the episteme of man, Foucault offered Auguste Comte and Karl Marx as the positivist and eschatological poles of discourse about man as "empirico-transcendental doublet," as the conceptual core of knowledge that will claim self-justification through the empirical truth of the claims that it makes about reality and the eschatological or transcendental truth of claims that anticipate the ultimate outcome of history.[51]

Where the defense of scientific history takes the eschatological form in Appleby, Hunt, and Jacob's work, it takes the positivist form in

Murray Murphey's *Philosophical Foundations of Historical Knowledge*. Murphey argues in effect that all humans share some "hard wired" set of cognitive capacities, the universality of which guarantees the translatability of language, and therefore of thought, across cultures and over time.[52] Murphey takes an emphatically positivist position, in Foucault's sense and in Lyotard's sense, by eschewing any claim to a "first philosophy"; the justification of scientific knowledge, for Murphey, is entirely an internal matter that scientists settle with the empirical truth of their claims about reality.[53] He then stresses the empirical claims of those scientists—mostly cognitive psychologists—that supposedly demonstrate the existence of specieswide concepts, such as causation and the solidity of objects, in infants. Such empirical results ostensibly demonstrate the universality of certain grounding concepts on which all languages rest. Murphey's argument depends crucially, however, on an unevidenced leap from infancy back into the womb—what cognitive psychologists can demonstrate in infants must, for Murphey, indicate "hard wired cognitive processes" common to all human fetuses. He thus assumes the very continuity of human identity across time that his empirical evidence is supposed to prove.[54]

Unfortunately for Murphey, both philosophical and neurological research demonstrate that, not only the concepts, but the very anatomy of cognition continue to develop in children well after birth.[55] Furthermore, while researchers can assign primary functions to certain regions of the brain, they also find that brains can adapt to noncatastrophic damage by, in effect, rewiring themselves and locating functions outside the usual regions.[56] Whatever neuroanatomical characteristics all human beings share at birth exist at much too rudimentary a level to support Murphey's claims to be specieswide, "hard wired" concepts present from before birth. In other words, the very science that Murphey hopes will provide a biologically based species identity for all humans as the ground for historical inquiry actually demonstrates the crucial role that history—each individual's unique experience of the world—plays in constituting identity, not merely at the level of personality, preference, or other psychological characteristics but at the neural level as well.

Murphey's primary target was not "postmodernism," but Willard van Orman Quine's thesis about the indeterminacy of translation. Archaeologically, however, he shares space with Appleby, Hunt, and Jacob insofar as they see in "postmodernism" a threatening insistence on the indeterminacy of representation stemming from human dependence on language as the irreducible medium of discourse. The solution for both stems from linking science as the epistemological foundation for historical inquiry to the character of human identity. Appleby, Hunt, and Jacob made the political argument that abandoning science as the foundation for history entailed the loss of a morally desirable commitment to political and social progress. The logic of history is eschatological. Murphey made the epistemological argument that the science of perception and cognition revealed the universal characteristics of human identity, which in turn guaranteed the validity of historical inquiry. The logic of history is positivistic.

Whether he is "postmodern" or not, Foucault claimed an important link between human identity—"man"—and history. In that respect he, too, shared archaeological space with Appleby, Hunt, Jacob, and Murphey. He differed with them, however, in insisting that history shapes identity—or, as he put it, "subjectivity." Some future scholar may wish to adduce an empirical test by which we could adjudicate between the Foucaultian and the eschatological/positivist models of identity and history. Such an empirical test would depend on more than the evidence of neuroanatomical research, which is not designed to address the question and is indicative, but not dispositive, in this context. As a matter of intellectual discourse, however, Foucault's archaeology accounts for the failure of intellectual engagement across the epistemic divide in a way that Appleby, Hunt, Jacob, and Murphey's efforts to shore up the edifice of "scientific" history cannot. Foucault's local, historicist account of history explains more than do Appleby, Hunt, Jacob, and Murphey's universalizing, scientific accounts. Foucault's archaeology also accounts better for the tendency of a growing number of scholars—historians, but literary critics and philosophers as well—to take up a similarly historicized understanding of identity, in some cases, as we shall see, without prior knowledge of Foucault's work.

Contesting Subjectivity

Foucault's "postmodern" philosophy and the queer theory that draws on it depend on and therefore privilege history. They begin with an understanding of all aspects of human identity, but especially gender and sexuality, as historically variable. That claiming the historical variability of human identity threatens so fundamentally the self-understandings of many historians is a phenomenon worthy of scrutiny, but not here. Rather, I would close this introduction by performing some of the more traditional work that one expects from an introduction.

The summer 1991 issue of *differences: A Journal of Feminist Cultural Studies* bears the title "Queer Theory: Lesbian and Gay Sexualities." Introducing that issue, feminist film theorist Teresa de Lauretis invoked the term "queer" as a means for enabling and describing certain political and discursive conjunctions without relying on the assumptions of a settled definition or identity.[57] Under the threat of AIDS and political backlash, lesbians and gay men have developed alliances, and they share the status of emergent cultural or subcultural forms distinct from, but still in some ways encompassed by, more easily recognizable forms. Yet in Lauretis's reading, the common formulation "lesbian and gay" threatened to elide the specific histories and identities that lesbians have long claimed. Such elision, in turn, reflects the continuing historical weight of a language that takes the male form as definitive and the female form as variant, if recognized as worthy of a separate term at all. It occurred despite the intention of many authors, in using "lesbian and gay," to mark the specificity of lesbian experience by modifying the more general "gay" and abandoning the older "homosexual." The categories carry a historical weight all their own, the resulting density of which perpetuates invisibility, particular authors' intentions to the contrary notwithstanding.

Another problem that "lesbian and gay" presented for Lauretis stemmed from the artificiality and inadequacy of perpetually adding on linguistic markers the farther one got from the white, middle-class, heterosexual center of the culture. One might be not only gay but black, not only lesbian but Chicana. One might be not only a black lesbian but working class and past age sixty. With the formulation "[sexuality marker] + [race/ethnicity marker] + [class marker] + [age marker]," one began to reach the point of diminishing practical and theoretical returns, despite the political and intellectual imperative to include all comers in a movement by and for the culturally and politically marginal. One also ran the risk of implying that identity and its constituent markers function as a sort of formula—given the correct inputs, the mathematicians of sexual alterity could compute you.

But the historical logic of queerness is too complicated for computation, and it has moved very quickly since 1991. Writing in 1996, Brett Beemyn and Mickey Eliason echoed Lauretis by pointing to *The Les-*

bian and Gay Studies Reader of 1993 as an indicator of both the advances and limitations of lesbian and gay studies. They wished to insist on the importance of including bisexual and transgender persons in any discussion of queerness. Beemyn and Eliason thus included Ki Namaste's essay "'Tragic Misreadings': Queer Theory's Erasure of Transgender Subjectivity" in their collection *Queer Studies: A Lesbian, Gay, Bisexual, and Transgender Anthology*.[58] Namaste cataloged various ways in which gay bars and pride celebrations, but also noted queer theorists Butler and Sedgwick, invoked drag for their own entertainment and theory even as they failed to consider the subjectivities—or in some cases accept the presence of—transgender persons.[59] Once examined, the coherence of "heterosexual/homosexual" as an exhaustive account of naturally occurring combinations of gender and sexuality soon fell apart.

But this is an observation not only of how the categories work from the outside but also of the negotiations involved among those who supposedly fit the categories. How do we understand the categories of gender and sexuality themselves, or the interactions between them, in light of recent disputes over the language of the Employment Nondiscrimination Act (ENDA)? ENDA would prohibit employment discrimination on the basis of sexual orientation. Transgender activists have consistently protested the bill's failure to include gender identity among the protected categories. One of their strategies has been to identify the number of lesbians and gay men for whom employment discrimination takes the form of complaints about their gender expression—lesbians who are too butch, gay men who are too femme. According to this argument, ENDA without protections for gender identity or expression would be no protection at all even for many of the lesbians and gay men whom the bill supposedly benefits.[60] Our assumptions about the meaning of "sexual orientation" and "gender" may blind us to the ways in which these categories actually function on a daily basis.

Queer theorists strive to work through this historical, illogical logic of sexual and gender identity as it informs the lives of specific lesbians, gay men, bisexuals, and transgender persons, all or any of whom may come in varying skin tones, ages, national or regional origins, and class backgrounds, all of which variations variously impact their experiences of their queerness. This working through of the specifics of variously overlapping, disjunctive, cooperative, clashing identity categories has drawn from and led back to significant questions about the concept of identity itself. The logic of identity looks increasingly peculiar—increasingly queer—under the lens of queer theory. On one hand, "identity" seems to connote a certain uniqueness—each individual human supposedly possesses an identity entirely particular to her or him, one that no other human shares. On the other hand, such unique identity depends necessarily on certain basic similarities or commonalities in order to become recognizable to others. The truly unique human would be unrecognizable as human. "Identity" in the sense of uniqueness implies that each human is a category unto her- or himself. Yet the peculiar requirements of identity politics in the late twentieth century increasingly point up the ways in which categories of identity fragment those supposedly unique individuals and significantly determine the options open to any given one of them.

So identity is queer, and in two senses: Unique human identities depend on repetition and commonalities, and logic as identity (A, not A) emerges from difference. Queer theory is political in its insistence that the unqueer reading of identity—the perpetuation of the idea that individuals somehow "naturally" fit into purely empirical identity categories—serves to distribute power among persons. Further, the persons who benefit from this distribution of power remain committed to their unqueer reading of identity as much or more because of the power benefits as because of any rational or logical force behind that reading. Genealogy—a historicized reading of categories that begins with a refusal to accept the "naturalness" or inevitability of those categories—involves the effort to find the choices, accidents, and circumstances that brought particular categories into use as means for dividing up persons into types. One vastly oversimplified but still useful way to understand queer theory begins with the proposition that many persons do not fit the available categories and that such failure of fit reflects a problem not with the persons but with the categories.

Queer theorists often read identity as a sort of language, or discourse. To some critics, such focus on language reflects a certain superficiality among queer theorists, a refusal to recognize that which is "real" or "material" in the lives of oppressed people. Such criticism, often more simplistic than the work it aims at, overlooks the basic point that language itself is real and material, and it overlooks the important ways in which identity functions like a language. From a finite array of elements, manipulated according to a finite set of rules, both produce an infinite, yet infinitely intelligible, array of outcomes. The intelligibility of each depends on the accumulation of meaning through repetition. Identity categories and nouns convey meaning according to a structure of binary oppositions, with one term of any pair valued more highly than the other. For this argument, queer theorists commonly rely on that other French philosopher, the one who focused attention on binaries to begin with: Derrida and his derridean deconstruction. Finally, while identity results from individuals' interactions with the "real" world, we have access to that world only through language.

The political problem becomes clear if we compare identity categories to nouns. Nouns refer to unique objects in the world, whether persons or trees, but they require a measure of generality in order to perform their function. Any noun necessarily subsumes certain unique features of an object within its generalizing capacity to refer. Absent such subsumption, a noun uttered by one person would remain unintelligible to another. Further, that referential subsumption acquires its ability to convey meaning only as a result of convention and over time; meaning depends on culture and history. Returning to our examples of violence, anyone who would persist in asserting the allegedly apolitical, immaterial implications of linguistically oriented queer theory must explain how issues of definition and representation failed to play a significant role in the attacks on James Byrd, Matthew Shepard, Billy Jack Gaither, and Barry Winchell, to name only the most famous recent examples. The meanings that attach to the nouns "nigger" and "faggot," the process of attaching those meanings to specific persons, and the process of circulating those meanings through the culture such that they had at least sufficient authority to motivate some individuals to attack specific other individuals, will not admit of thoroughgoing analysis within a conceptual framework that begins with a sharp distinction between the linguistic, on one hand, and the material and political, on the other.

Queer theorists typically wish to investigate the historical and cultural underpinnings of nouns such as "woman," "homosexual," "gay," and "lesbian" in order to examine what sorts of generalizations and assumptions enable the referential functions, and determine the meanings, of those terms. From a political perspective, it may not matter terribly that we ignore many unique aspects of any given tree when we refer to it as "tree." It may matter terribly, however, that we ignore unique aspects of women and queers by referring to them as "woman," "homosexual," "transgender," and so on. And it may matter terribly that some among us would insist on forcing the persons to fit particular definitions of the categories and/or that neither the categories nor the persons who fit them should exist at all.

The practice of assigning persons to categories, while it depends on relations of authority, power, and force operating in specific institutions, also depends on the logic and justification that the categories themselves provide. Queer theorists examine the meanings that attach to pairs of categories: man/woman, heterosexual/homosexual, white/black, young/old, rich/poor. Rather than accept a naturalized ontology according to which such terms simply reflect existing distinctions in the world among persons, queer theorists insist that persons do not divide so neatly into binary categories. "Queer" became useful for the theory and politics of sexual minorities during the late 1980s and 1990s not only because it is easier to say than "lesbian/gay/bisexual/transgender" but also because the proliferation of different groups who demand inclusion in the movement demonstrates the intellectual and moral bankruptcy of binary identity categories. What is the opposite of transgender? Heterosexual? Does a preoperative male-to-female transgender person date women or men in order to be heterosexual? Does s/he then switch after surgery? What if this person is married? What if this person is a priest? Insofar as we stuff each other into binary categories anyway, the process is historical and political; we cannot understand these categories apart from their past and their change over time.

This problem becomes even more complicated, and integral to queer theory, when the person in question fits more than one devalued category. Lauretis and Butler, also writing in *differences*, both made the point that they wished to prevent the subsumption of characteristically lesbian experience within the terms of "homosexuality" or "lesbian and gay studies."[61] In the case of "lesbian and gay studies," as Lauretis and Butler both pointed out, the potential remained for the elision of lesbian lives despite the invocation of the term "lesbian" as part of various authors' deliberate efforts not to perform such elision. Similarly, Namaste wished to resist the subsumption of specifically transgender subjectivity into lesbian/gay identity via queer theory. Differences of sexuality were necessary for the elaboration of queer theory, but differences of gender were equally necessary. The originators of queer theory are all feminist scholars, and their concerns dealt not only with sexuality but also with the intersections of sexuality, gender, and other identity categories that have long served as the basis for foreclosing, rather than pursuing, understanding of the lives of marginal persons.

The problem for queer theorists stems not merely from empirically unsound, yet authoritative, mischaracterizations of the lives and experiences of women, lesbians, and gay men; it also stems from the resilience of historically constituted practices and meanings as they inform the very language that we use to describe, much less combat, the problem. "Queer" has the virtue of offering, in the context of academic inquiry into gender identity and sexual identity, a relatively novel term that connotes etymologically a crossing of boundaries but that refers to nothing in particular, thus leaving the question of its denotations open to contest and revision.[62]

1

Foucault Didn't Know What He Was Doing, and Neither Do I

Our civilization has developed the most complex system of knowledge, the most sophisticated structures of power: what has this kind of knowledge, this type of power made of us? In what way are those fundamental experiences of madness, suffering, death, crime, desire, individuality connected, even if we are not aware of it, with knowledge and power? I am sure I'll never get the answer; but that does not mean that we don't have to ask the question.

—Michel Foucault

So what was Foucault up to? For queer theorists, sexuality provides the most obvious point of entry into Foucault's work. But Foucault wrote much more than *The History of Sexuality*. And even though he repeatedly changed both his mind and the direction of his writing, all while refusing the comforts of an ostensibly consistent, uniform identity, still his study of sexuality forms part of his larger work. At the same time, I make no claim here to offer the definitive account of that work. Any such claim would demonstrate ignorance of Foucault's own expectations and opinions about his ideas. He emphatically rejected any role as a prescriptive intellectual, one who has figured out the truth and will now instruct the rest of us on how to act according to it. Instead, he hoped to provide the sort of analyses that others would put to use in their own, unpredictable ways. My account of Foucault's work emphasizes the points that have proven most useful to queer theorists.

Certainly both Foucault and queer theorists were concerned with issues of truth. But they understood truth in a decidedly different manner from the philosophical tradition in which Foucault was trained. Not that Foucault saw himself as escaping that tradition. He specified Friedrich Nietzsche most famously but also Martin Heidegger as significant influences on his own thinking. It is worth noting, however, that both Nietzsche and Heidegger took as a major theme in their thought the desuetude—not to say bankruptcy—of that tradition as they found it. Foucault usually did not express his differences with the traditions of western philosophy quite so baldly. Instead, he chose unusual topics for his investigations and unusual methods for studying those topics.[1]

Foucault once identified two areas of inquiry as central to his work: the mechanisms for separating truth from falsity and the mechanisms by which individuals governed themselves and each other using the truths that they so derived. His concern for truth and the government of individual identity was not unique among French philosophers after World War II. To paraphrase another major figure of the period, on Foucault's view, one is not born a man. It is instructive to compare Simone de Beauvoir's major work, *The Second Sex*, which appeared nearly twenty years before *The Order of Things*. It is especially striking to read Beauvoir's introduction in light of feminist debates of the 1980s and queer theoretical readings of Foucault's work: "Are there women, really? . . . One wonders if women still exist, if they will always exist, whether or not it is desirable that they should, what place they occupy in this world, what their place should be. . . . It would appear, then, that every female human being is not necessarily a woman: to be so considered she must share in that mysterious and threatened reality known as femininity."[2] There is no indication that Foucault read Beauvoir, certainly not that he took her observations on the cultural basis for the identity "woman" as a jumping-off point for his idea about the historical specificity of "man."

Rather, this parallel suggests two points. Archaeologically, it confirms the suspicion that the period around World War II was crucial for the elaboration of suspicions about naturalized accounts of human identity in terms of nature or biology. It also indicates what we might call the epistemological privilege of those who view binaries of identity from the bottom. One characteristic of disciplinary power as Foucault critiqued it is its ability to provide justification or ignorance to those who exercise that power—authorities typically refuse to acknowledge their own participation in domination because they possess some rational explanation for the power that they wield. On Foucault's view, intellectuals should not try to tell others what to do or how to think; instead, they should provide the critical armature for resistance by denaturalizing exercises of disciplinary power. But the "specific intellectual" must direct her or his critique at institutions, practices, and discourses that she or he has intimate, personal knowledge of. From this perspective, it only makes sense that both Beauvoir and Foucault would bring critical perspectives to axes of power difference that they knew personally—gender and sexuality, respectively—and that they would approach the philosophical traditions of their culture from odd angles.

Here we confront the problem of biography. The canons of intellectual history dictate that I provide some account, however brief, of Foucault's life in order to explain, or help explain, his ideas. That this chapter contains precious little biographical information about Foucault reflects no belief on my part that the historical circumstances of his life are irrelevant to understanding his work. Quite the contrary—perhaps the most consistent theme in Foucault's work, the point that appears over and over, is that historical circumstance plays a huge role in determining who we are, what we think, and how we recognize ourselves. Even so, I give little biographical information about Foucault in this chapter precisely because such information, in the present context, is far too important. Biographical information about Foucault has just the sort of discursive density that he himself described—it serves far too readily as the means by which one can easily "explain" his intellectual work. The goal of queer theory is to investigate the historical circumstances by which "sexuality"—especially the charge of "homosexuality"—can automatically render subjects the somewhat pitiable victims of a determinism that "heterosexual" subjects supposedly remain free of. That at least some purveyors of specularizing biography as destiny would deploy sexuality against Foucault's life and work in just this way is clear, leaving little room for biographical discussion of Foucault that does not risk falling prey to the very phenomenon that I resist here.[3]

We can safely make the following biographical observation: Foucault's concern with issues of power, especially with how knowledge under the sign of "rationalism" enables the exercise of certain forms of power, began in earnest only after the student uprisings in France and elsewhere in May 1968. However, the claims of the students and other radicals—especially those who insisted on sexual repression as the central abuse of power in modern western societies—as well as the hyper-theoretical analyses that the students pursued in keeping with the Marxism of the moment struck Foucault as somehow missing the point. Like many scholars in this period, Foucault saw knowledge, especially scientific knowledge, as a significant source of domination. But his account of that conjunction of power and knowledge differed fundamentally from those of other scholars during the period.

Power and Knowledge

The self-described "Nietzschean Marxist" of 1950, Foucault went on to suspect that the process of scientific investigation constituted the subjectivity of the scientist as much as it did the objectivity of the object under study. Making the point with respect to *Madness and Civilization*,[4] Foucault stated that "to the construction of the object madness, there corresponded a rational subject who 'knew' about madness and who understood it."[5] Absent any external claims to reason, the rationalities of sciences, on Foucault's view, looked like an internal matter of elaborating rules for the production of true statements about objects of inquiry. He stated, "What most struck me in Nietzsche is that for him the rationality of a science, a practice, or a discourse isn't measured by the truth that it is in a position to produce. Rather, truth itself has a share in the history of discourse, and in some ways has an internal effect on a discourse, or on a practice."[6] This Nietzschean approach to science, with its emphasis on the internal rationality of discursive practices, reflected Foucault's frustration with the uniform commitment to a philosophy of the knowing subject, whether in Hegelian, phenomenological, or Marxian/existentialist terms, in the years immediately after World War II.

But how did Foucault get from a Nietzschean approach to science to the history of sexuality? Via what I have come to call practices of order. We might pose the central question this way: Why do we as a culture devote so much time and energy to knowledge about sex? This knowledge about sex certainly involves repression, simple and absolute prohibitions on certain acts and statements. But Foucault insisted that

such repression formed only part of a larger system in which we operate under a generalized injunction to tell, to confess, to speak of sex as
the truth of ourselves. Such speech, in order to be effective, must clearly
follow certain carefully elaborated rules, but only some of those rules
take the form of repression or prohibition.[7] "Sex," Foucault once said,
"is boring."[8] He originally planned six volumes under the rubric of the
history of sexuality, but sexuality itself was not the key issue.

Rather, sexuality looked to Foucault like the central term in what,
near the end of his life, he called "techniques of the self." He also spoke
of sexuality in terms of "government," broadly understood to mean not
only the state and politics but also government of the self and of the
household and the relationships among those levels.[9] Sexuality provided the key element by which administrators in the emerging nation-
states of early modern Europe could link the most personal, intimate
practices of an individual or a family to the most general concerns for
the productivity of the entire population. It formed a crucial part of the
practices of order.

In a certain sense, Foucault's genealogical project was quite simple.
He wished to demonstrate how we use institutions and practices to
impose order on our society by imposing order on ourselves through the
device of individual identity. Note at the outset that Foucault did not
consider the imposition of order on a society as bad per se. Late in life
he stated, "My point is not that everything is bad, but that everything is
dangerous which is not exactly the same thing as bad. If everything is
dangerous, then we always have something to do. So my position leads
not to apathy but to a hyper- and pessimistic activism."[10] The practices
of order work good or ill depending on numerous circumstances.

Foucault had to defend himself against the charge of inculcating apathy because his account of the practices of order offended against key
assumptions of modern philosophy and political theory. In a passage
from his first book, *Histoire de la folie*, that does not appear in the English translation, he contrasted Descartes's analysis of madness to that of
Michel de Montaigne. He argued that, for Montaigne, madness always
haunted reason as an ineradicable possibility; in Foucault's gloss, for
Montaigne, "One is never sure that he is not dreaming, never certain
of not being a fool."[11] Something—Foucault would not claim to specify what—intervened between the time of Montaigne's writings and
Descartes's writings such that, for Descartes, "reason" definitionally
excluded the possibility of unreason. A given person might be mad, but

such madness specifically and emphatically removed that individual from the province of reason, leaving persons susceptible to madness but reason itself always pure. Although Foucault did not use the term until later, this difference between Montaigne and Descartes looks like an epistemic break—a fundamental change in the constitution of a conceptual object, a change that we can recognize and describe as intertwined with other types of changes but that we cannot reliably "explain" in the sense of providing a definitive causal account of it.

Foucault returned to a canonical figure in modern western philosophy and examined his work. He did so not to decide on its "truth" or "falsity" but, instead, to examine as a historical question the relationship between ideas and administration, between conceptions of individual identity and the practices of order, including the state as well as other forms of government. His major works do not take the form of philosophical texts conventionally defined; instead, they take the form of historical works, precisely because, for Foucault, Descartes's firm distinction between reason and unreason, between madness and civilization, looked not like the elaboration of eternal principles of logic, reason, or identity but like a historically specific elaboration of a particular organization of knowledge and relationships of power. Foucault made no claim to repudiate or refute Descartes's claims. But in taking this approach to a philosophical question, he rejected a basic assumption that had defined much of modern philosophy since Descartes: that something called "reason" fundamentally informs human identity transhistorically and that the philosopher's job is to elucidate those principles of reason and their connection to human identity, such that humans may increase the extent to which they abide by those principles.

Perhaps the most interesting and important feature of this move remains implicit. By examining Descartes's account of reason and madness as he did, Foucault completely refused the constitutive duality in which reason reflects some abstract principle or ideal—Reason as guaranteed by God—according to which truth and freedom come at the expense of, or in opposition to, the material, embodied aspects of human existence. Foucault did not argue against Cartesian dualism; he treated it as an interesting historical phenomenon that no longer seems applicable. For Foucault, questions of politics and ethics become not a matter of installing obedience to God or Reason over unruly will; they become a matter of specific practices by which relatively powerful authorities, operating through specific institutions and justifying their actions according to specific discourses, install obedience in relatively powerless subjects.

In the interim between the first volume of *The History of Sexuality* and the two subsequent volumes, Foucault provided a sort of summation of his work to date. Particular experiences, such as madness, physical illness, crime, and sexuality, become the objects of particular types of knowledge, such as psychiatry, medicine, criminology, and sexology. Authorities operating through institutions elaborate these fields of knowledge and apply them to specific individuals with the expectation of producing certain types of subjects and certain types of knowledge about those subjects. Foucault saw himself as examining the relationship between forms of knowledge and exercises of power.[12] For queer theorists, of course, the most interesting of these conjunctions of experience, knowledge, and power revolved around sexuality and gender.

In other words, for Foucault "experience" is not an originary, irreducible level of conceptualization or analysis for understanding and explaining human identity or history.[13] Rather, experience is the thing to explain: How do we transmit the meanings and preferences of our culture via various institutions and practices such that the vast majority of individuals in a given society understand in largely similar terms not only what happens to them in their own lives but also how the world works at a broader level? Foucault rejected any notion of human nature, preferring to emphasize instead the cultural and historical determinations of experience and identity. One immediate implication of this position is the rejection of any conception of subjects as self-identical wholes. This point, explicit in the genealogical studies of the 1970s, became apparent to observers who read *The Order of Things* beginning in 1966.

In a certain sense, *The Order of Things* continues the historicization of Descartes's account of identity that Foucault began in *Histoire de la folie*. Although subsequent philosophers raised significant doubts about the specifics of Descartes's account, only during the first half of the twentieth century did they begin to abandon his basic project of grounding individual identity in some originary guarantee beyond the vicissitudes of historical change. As Appleby, Hunt, Jacob, and Murphey demonstrate, outside of academic philosophy this project still looks viable to many people. But Foucault, like many twentieth-century philosophers, concluded that the project of explaining human identity as a phenomenon foundationally immune to historical variation no longer made sense. *The Order of Things* links Foucault's historicization of individual identity with a historicization of "the human sciences"—psychology, sociology, ethnology—or the study of that identity via its constitutive limits of death, desire, and subjection to law.

With *Discipline and Punish* and *The History of Sexuality*, Foucault shifted his emphasis from the epistemological question of how "historical a priori" constitute the basic assumptions and practices of the human sciences to the question of how the human sciences serve the political needs of enabling and justifying exercises of disciplinary power. In doing so, he shared with a number of continental philosophers of the post-World War II period concern for the ethical and political implications of accepting rationality on the scientific model as the standard for all truth. By insisting on the epistemological independence of the human sciences from the hard sciences, Foucault contributed to the drive to reopen a field for ethical discourse distinct from the epistemological tyranny of scientific rationality. But insofar as the Cartesian dispensation continues to govern thought on the topic, the idea that ethics might operate independently of science struck many people as dangerous.

Consequently, well before *The History of Sexuality*, Foucault had to answer criticisms that his historical approach to questions of knowledge precluded any effective political resistance or "progressive politics." Many observers saw in *The Order of Things* the implicit claim that humans and their reasoning capacity had far less control over the practices and institutions with which they lived than one might hope if one harbored expectations of significantly improving those practices and institutions or scrapping them and starting over. Certainly, neither thought nor language under Foucault's description in *The Order of Things* was a fully transparent, manipulable tool for the ever more precise representation of reality. Rather, both possess a density and specificity all their own that plays a determining role in how subjects perceive the world and what they can say about it. Foucault begins by recounting a Chinese taxonomy, the elements and organization of which are sufficiently strange to produce his observation of "the stark impossibility of thinking *that*."[14] Similarly, the human sciences and the practices of order have a logic all their own, a logic that Foucault studied in his genealogies. Humans are as much subject to historical determination at the level of thought, at the level of reason, and at the level of practice as at any other level.

But this is not the historical determination of a teleology in the manner of Georg W. F. Hegel or Karl Marx. Rather, Foucault's archaeologies and genealogies demonstrate the fully internal character of historical change. Critics see in Foucault's work the end of politics, especially the end of resistance, because for them the politics of resistance depend on what Foucault called "the inexhaustible presence of a Logos, the sovereignty of a pure subject, the deep teleology of a primeval destination."[15] The beginning point for such politics is the determination of the truth that rational subjects must work toward in keeping with the ends of history—the external eschaton toward which social process should lead. For Foucault, political resistance depends instead on the study of specific practices, the practices of order by which we govern ourselves on a daily basis. He claimed that he was "trying to define how, to what extent, at what level discourses, particularly scientific discourses, can be objects of a political practice, and in what system of dependence they can exist in relation to it."[16] The presumption of unfolding rationality places scientific discourses, and the practices that subtend them, at a remove from politics, while Foucault's archaeologies and genealogies analyze them in terms of political—which is to say human—practice, even as they destroy the self-flattering presumption that reason is universal and that we, as rational individuals, can bend our institutions and practices to its demands.

Genealogy abandons telos. It "rejects the metahistorical deployment of ideal significations and indefinite teleologies."[17] Foucault as genealogist inverted the telescope of political theory. Rather than stare off into the stars, elaborating a theory of what a just or good or rational society ought to look like, he turned the lens back on the peculiar institutions with which we impose order on ourselves below the level of state and society. He demonstrated that humans and their identities are highly malleable objects of ongoing processes. Those processes—or practices—are, for Foucault, arbitrary in the sense that the practices of prisons, or of sexuality, obey no transcendent or transhistorical laws; in no way do they reflect the operation of some unified subjectivity, a deeper, teleological force of history, or the operation of any sort of natural law. At the very least, one who would understand those practices fully must begin by refusing the comforts of such explanatory or justificatory schemes. Also, any assessment of those practices must remain resolutely local, attached to the individuals and institutions who participate in them.

The practices of order are heavily overdetermined, however—far from arbitrary—in the sense that humans elaborate and deploy those practices to numerous ends and in numerous ways, from the largest, most complex, carefully defined institutions to the most casual, offhanded statements in daily conversation. One of the chief virtues of Foucault's genealogies stems from his recognition that no single entity or group—the state, the bourgeoisie, the patriarchy, what have you—exercises unilateral control over this process, directing the practices of order to suit its own needs in every instance. He also insisted that the elaboration and deployment of any practice is necessarily an uncertain business, always already fragmented with the possibility for gross or incremental failures because of error, competition, resistance, or internal fracture. Certainly, some individuals and groups have more control over and benefit more from these practices than others, and such disparities of power will probably prove useful in choosing which practices merit genealogical investigation.

Indeed, Foucault may have gone a bit overboard in his insistence on the fluidity of power relations within existing practices. Or we should understand his claims as a suspicion that will prevent us from universalizing any specific instance of oppression but that should not prevent us from recognizing patterns of oppression where we have compelling evidence for them. Foucault wrote nothing about race. But one would not expect him to, since he developed his ideas in France, where race does not carry the central importance that it does in the United States. Still, genealogies of racial practices of order in the United States will probably prove a rich field of investigation for many years to come. More readily chargeable as shortcomings in Foucault's genealogies are his failures to deal effectively with either gender or class. Especially in the case of sexuality, it seems quite striking at times how manifestly significant are gender and class to the elaboration of these practices and how thoroughly Foucault failed to include them as axes of analysis. Again, we may not find surprising his apparent inability to recognize the ramifications of gender for practices of order. He grew up, received his primary intellectual training, and began his scholarly career before feminists in western Europe and the United States had begun to demonstrate clearly the centrality of gender as a category for intellectual, social, and political practice and the pervasiveness and effectiveness of gendered practices of order. As we will see, some feminist scholars writing after the second wave have clarified the importance of gender for any genealogical understanding of order.

Class is a bit more puzzling. Like many French intellectuals of his generation, Foucault knew his Marx, and he joined the French Communist Party (FCP). Although he remained involved in various sorts of radical politics for the rest of his life, however, Foucault became disillusioned with the FCP and its willingness to parrot the Soviet party line during Stalin's reign of terror. We might attribute the absence of significant discussion of class in *The History of Sexuality* to Foucault's desire to challenge as thoroughly as possible received understandings of the subject. *The History of Sexuality* exemplifies Foucault's desire, common in his major works, to begin a specific inquiry by upsetting the reader's expectations. Where sexuality was the topic, this approach would have resulted not only from Foucault's intellectual suspicion that received understandings in some ways concealed more than they revealed but also from his political suspicion that the dominance of Marxian class analysis among political activists and observers, and the dominance of theories centered on the knowing subject among philosophers, in post–World War II France served more to preclude than to enable perspicacious inquiry into the character of power and domination.

But Foucault also insisted on the impossibility of "explaining" sexuality as a function of some other, ostensibly more fundamental, phenomenon. Here his position paralleled that of second-wave feminists, especially those who insisted, against the men in the New Left, that gender discrimination demanded analysis as a political problem. Certainly, sexuality as a set of practices and meanings that structure the power differentials in interactions among individuals often operates in conjunction with other sets of practices and meanings, such as those that we call "class," "race," and "gender." But sexuality may also provide the basis for challenging or disrupting the operation of class, race, and gender. Regardless, none of these axes of power reduces to, or is dependent on, the others. Sexuality merited genealogical study on its own because it has the capacity to organize the exercise of power independently of other identity characteristics and because it fundamentally informs subjectivity before subjects become conscious participants in politics.

The History of Sexuality

Although, in terms of topic, *The History of Sexuality* offers the most obvious exploration of practices of order for queer theorists, *Discipline and Punish* is the most fully developed of Foucault's genealogies. Queer theorists are more likely to attend to *Discipline and Punish* than to the last two volumes of *The History of Sexuality*, in which Foucault moved away from the sort of genealogical analysis that has proven most useful to them. In *Discipline and Punish* he described the disciplinary techniques that, beginning in the late eighteenth century, proliferated with the growing number of prisons, schools, armies, hospitals, and factories that required the close coordination of numerous individuals.[18]

In previous exercises of power, subjects attracted the sovereign's attention only when they violated his laws. Foucault offered the famous example of the French regicide's execution in 1757. The king's power rested in his ability to require that the body of one who threatened his life bear the public imprint of royal authority. The executioner did not simply kill the regicide but slowly tortured him to death in public. Disciplinary power, by contrast, characterizes institutions where the subjects remain under constant supervision. Authorities divide the time of inmates, students, soldiers, and workers, demanding of them constant repetition of tasks and minute attention to regulations in order to guarantee their productivity. In prisons, schools, hospitals, factories, and barracks, authoritative individuals exercise power by supervising minutely the practices of their subjects and requiring their precise conformity to standards of conduct. Such institutions may frequently serve the interests of the state, but they do not reflect directly or seamlessly the interests of the hegemonic political classes.

In the case of sexuality, disciplinary power operates more fluidly among a variety of institutions, even outside of specific institutions. Part 4 of *The History of Sexuality*, the longest section of the book, bears the title "The Deployment of Sexuality." This phrase suggests at least two ideas: that sexuality entered the world at a specific time and that it did so as a result of deliberation. With these claims, *The History of Sexuality* exemplifies Foucaultian genealogy. A purported biological universal, the sexuality that lies at the core of every human subject looked to Foucault like a major apparatus in the technology of disciplinary power, a central set of concepts and practices that allowed authorities to constitute political preferences as necessary moral responses to unruly human nature. Thus, Foucault made sexuality the object of historical investigation. Its history reflects no rational or progressive development. The deployment of sexuality involves instead the gradual expansion of certain practices on the basis of local needs and strategies.

According to Foucault, with increasing agricultural production and a declining threat of plague during the seventeenth and eighteenth centuries, government officials in western Europe began to perceive populations as resources. These resources demanded a measure of care from officials who would use them in the service of the state. Already this sounds like a conspiracy theory. But the deliberation that Foucault found behind the deployment of sexuality reflected not a grand design or the unilateral control of some group over the social whole. Rather, it reflected the proliferation of specific practices geared toward specific goals and creating specific knowledges. The political changes of the emerging nation-states provided one of many elements through which the deployment of sexuality became useful and effective.

In *The History of Sexuality*, Foucault asserted rather enigmatically that "power relations are both intentional and nonsubjective." He also stated that "power comes from below."[19] Foucault wished to begin an empirical investigation at the level of the specific practices by which individuals exercised power over one another. He wished to pursue this project without relying on a totalizing theoretical framework, such as Marxian class analysis or liberal theories of law and right, that, in his view, either imposed upon such exercises of power a global coherence and rationale that they lack or distracted attention from exercises of power at the microlevel of specific institutions, practices, and relationships. The individuals who exercise power in specific institutions do so intentionally on the basis of local strategies, or designs for producing specific effects. These local strategies and institutions may accumulate into larger patterns and serve larger interests. But to posit a single social group, such as the bourgeoisie or the patriarchy, that unilaterally wields power over others through these mechanisms entails the presumption of either a univocally willing collectivity—a unified social subject—or a unifying historical telos that does not exist.[20]

To begin to appreciate Foucault's understanding of "power," we must avoid the temptation to ontologize it, to make of it a thing. It is a matter of relationships, of interactions among individuals, and very few relationships are entirely devoid of power differentials. The disciplinary practices and institutions of our culture provide us with myriad expectations about the conduct of our relationships, expectations that usually make any given interaction go more smoothly, especially with strangers. But these expectations may also enable and perpetuate domination. Near the end of his life, Foucault spoke about friendship as a possible sort of relationship imbued with relatively few of the practices of order that characterize other sorts of relationships. He saw in gay life the possibility for exploring such new types of friendships. The focus of such friendships would not be sex, nor would the goal be quasi-marital monogamy. This notion of friendship depends on a call to the invention of new forms of life and identity, not the discovery of a putatively precultural authenticity. And the opportunity exists for lesbians and gay men, not because of some inherent characteristic in "homosexuality" but because of the necessarily oppositional character of lesbian/gay identity at this historical moment with respect to this particular culture.[21]

Foucault's genealogy of the deployment of sexuality depended above all else on the specific practice of confession. A major moment in the genealogy of sexuality comes with the observation that various medical authorities, including psychoanalysts, adapted the Catholic practice of confession to purposes largely unrelated to its origins in the church. These various confessional practices shared the effect of inciting in their subjects a constant reflection on their every erotic thought, impulse, or action. Authoritative investigators, whether parents or physicians, could thus inculcate in their subjects the expectation that the subjects possessed a unique identity centered on their sexuality, which identity they could discern and maintain coherently only through constant self-review and regulation.[22] Foucault gave the specific example of examinations by the physician Charcot, at a Paris hospital known as the Salpêtrière.[23] Within the discourse of sexuality, Charcot and his fellow physicians examined their patients' sexual thoughts and actions in order to discover the truths of their beings. At the other extreme from individual confessions, beginning in the eighteenth century authorities used information about demographics and public health to manage the population.

There are two important points to note here. First, practices precede their justifications. The practice of confession existed long before anyone justified it as the means to elicit the truth of sexuality from individual subjects. Similarly, in *Madness and Civilization* and *The Birth of the Clinic*,[24] Foucault demonstrated that the practices of treating mental illness and the practices of clinical medicine preceded the conceptual changes that would eventually serve to justify them. The genealogist looks for discontinuities and refuses the unifying framework of rational subjectivity as the basis for historical inquiry; scholarly practice, or method, becomes an ad hoc affair for which the attempt to elaborate a theoretical justification would undermine the very point of the exercise. The principled justifications for a given practice or set of practices are often irrelevant for understanding the specific historical events that brought those practices about.

Foucault referred explicitly to Nietzsche in elaborating his definition of genealogy. *On the Genealogy of Morals* provides a useful statement of this point. "The 'purpose of law,'" according to Nietzsche, "is absolutely the last thing to employ in the history of the origin of law.... The cause of the origin of a thing and its eventual utility, its actual employment and place in a system of purposes, lie worlds apart; whatever exists, having somehow come into being, is again and again reinterpreted to new ends, taken over, transformed, and redirected by some power superior to it."[25] Power is nonsubjective in the sense that, for Foucault, there is no point in trying to understand the deployment of disciplinary power in general, or sexuality specifically, as the function of a guiding intent or rationality that designs a practice to achieve a particular end. Rather, existing practices get adapted to local needs. As these practices prove their utility, more individuals in more institutions adopt them, at which point someone provides a retrospective justification. Practices precede their justifications, and justifications typically serve, among other things, to distract our attention from the fundamentally arbitrary character of the order that governs our lives.

The second important point is that the practice of confession installs a particular form of power relations. In confession, both truth and, in a certain sense, power emerge from the subject who confesses. But truth and power depend on the presence of an authoritative auditor who demands the confession and who validates its truth through interpretation. While confession inherently reveals the truth of the confessing subject insofar as it reveals what was hidden, still the truth of confession also depends on interpretation according to expert knowledge. Even if the explicit standard for truth involves some appeal to the subject's "true" or "authentic" self or identity, the process of producing that truth remains incomplete until the authority has conferred an imprimatur based on generalized principles of knowledge that necessarily precede the information that the subject offers. No matter what the subject says, the authority knows the truth when she or he sees it. Confession provides the point of intersection between the individual case and the theoretical elaboration of experts.

Sexuality provided a conceptual and practical grid on which administrators, investigators, and other observers at disparate locations and with disparate short-term goals could coordinate to some extent both the disciplining of individuals and the regulation of populations. Sexuality provided the justification for the practices of creating subjects and managing populations that early modern administrators cultivated. These disciplines and regulations did not serve to repress a set of biological drives. Rather, authorities incited the very desires that they claimed only to repress. They pursued such incitements not cynically, to dupe subjects, but ingenuously, with the belief that they would discover the truth of their subjects. Foucault offered two meanings for the term "subject": "subject to someone else by control and dependence, and tied to his own identity by a conscience or self-knowledge."[26] The relationship between the two lies in the role that the "someone else" plays in tying the subject to her or his identity. Teachers, wardens, supervisors, physicians all work to implant in the subject an awareness of her or his own identity by demanding the subject's constant observance of the institution's standards or through meticulous observation of the subject's deviations from those standards. At the end of *The History of Sexuality*, Foucault noted an interesting reversal that occurred during the early modern period. Where once a distinct identity had been the privilege of the powerful, who had dynasties and coats of arms and stories extolling their great deeds, in the modern realm of disciplinary power, authorities keep the most detailed records on the identities of the deviant and powerless. Prisoners and patients become case histories and files full of identifying information.[27]

Sexuality as Discursive Power

Such exercises of power, for Foucault, are not only disciplinary but also discursive. Foucault elaborated his understanding of "discourse" most fully in *The Archaeology of Knowledge*[28] and used the term frequently in *The History of Sexuality*. He meant by it a set of rules for the constitution of conceptual objects and the production of statements about those objects. Objects of inquiry do not await discovery independently of the discourses within which one produces knowledge about them. Nor do scholars come naturally equipped with universal principles of reason that will guide them to the truth. Discourses constitute both the objects and the subjects of inquiry. Discourses in the deployment of sexuality produced "sex" as an object of knowledge. Foucault argued that "the notion of 'sex' made it possible to group together, in an artificial unity, anatomical elements, biological functions, conducts, sensations, and pleasures, and it enabled one to make use of this fictitious unity as a causal principle, an omnipresent meaning, a secret to be discovered everywhere."[29] The disciplinary power of institutions and the artificial unity of sexuality have in common that both serve to produce and perpetuate individual identity.

The terms "discourse" and "discursive power" have become common among many scholars who work off of Foucault and other poststructuralists. An excessive emphasis on discourse itself, however, diverts attention from other aspects of the deployment of sexuality.[30] Foucault also developed the idea of the *dispositif* as a heuristic device for understanding relationships of power at the local level; this term receives far less attention from scholars in the United States, perhaps because no obvious English equivalent exists. Hubert Dreyfus and Paul Rabinow translate it as "grid of intelligibility." Translating Gilles Deleuze's discussion of the term, Timothy Armstrong gives "apparatus."[31] Given its usefulness as a concept, it seems plausible to use the French term.

With *dispositif*, Foucault described the congeries of discourses, practices, institutions, architectures, among other things, that variously intertwine and overlap in the constitution of an object of inquiry. A *dispositif* contrasts to the "ideal significations" that Foucault referred to in "Nietzsche, Genealogy, History." "Prison" as an abstract term could govern inquiry by creating an identity the specific content of which would provide ample opportunity for scholarly debate. That identity would also have an origin that historians could discover. One could argue endlessly about whether a given institution at the margins of the definition really constituted a "prison" or something else. For the genealogist, the prison, a building with a highly specific design and construction, constitutes a major element in a *dispositif* that includes discourses of law and right, discourses of punishment and moral guidance, and practices of subjectification in which prisoners become both the objects of knowledge and, ideally, proper sorts of moral subjects. A *dispositif* is much more fluid, open at its margins, than is an ideal signification. The point of Foucault's genealogy of the prison was not to write a progressive story about institutions that belong to the category denominated "prisons."[32] The elements in any *dispositif* will change over time. Some elements may have incarceration as the primary goal or function of their designers, while others will relate to imprisonment only tangentially. The elaboration of a *dispositif* will come in response to some pressing need but may produce consequences that its originators did not intend.[33] Again, Foucault understands power as intentional and nonsubjective. Actors with specific objectives will elaborate a *dispositif* to meet those objectives, but their success will necessarily remain partial.

Within the *dispositif* of the prison, officials produce knowledge about prisoners. For Foucault, the exercise of power and the production of knowledge intertwine inextricably. He argued that we should dispense with the idea that one must choose between having power and having knowledge; rather, he insisted, knowledge production always depends on, and in turn influences, relationships of power.[34] The exercise of disciplinary power produces knowledge about the subjects of its exercise; that knowledge then provides the basis for improved and expanded techniques of discipline. This process, on Foucault's view, produced subjects, rather than simply acting on existing identities.

Some critics worry that if the project of specifying the foundational ground of identity beyond historical change has become, as Foucault suggests, otiose, then we have no way of explaining resistance to domination. If power constitutes subjects, then how do subjects resist?[35] First and foremost, it is worth pointing out that many subjects do not resist. If the capacity for resistance is a universal characteristic of human identity, operating outside relations of power, then why do disparities of power along axes of race, class, gender, sexuality, age, you name it persist?[36] Women alone, certainly women combined with men who suffer discrimination or domination on the basis of their racial or sexual minority status, constitute a numerical majority of the population. Why not just rise up and take over? Either we really are the moral and physical incompetents of misogynist, racist, and homophobic imaginings or the discourses that produce and justify those imaginings have their effects in constituting our subjectivity in a manner that we cannot completely control. Most potentially revolutionary subjects also experience divided loyalties; their ostensibly shared experience of discrimination is not necessarily sufficient to ensure that a white gay man and a black nongay man will cooperate effectively in political matters. Resistance along one axis of power may coexist with attachment to the status quo along another axis.

For Foucault, in any relationship where power operates, the possibility for resistance occurs as well. He described resistance in terms of "reverse discourses," with "homosexuality" serving as the exemplar:

> There is no question that the appearance in nineteenth-century psychiatry, jurisprudence, and literature of a whole series of discourses on the species and subspecies of homosexuality, inversion, pederasty, and "psychic hermaphrodism" made possible a strong advance of social controls into this area of "perversity"; but it also made possible the formation of a "reverse" discourse; homosexuality began to speak in its own behalf, to demand that its legitimacy or "naturality" be acknowledged, often in the same vocabulary, using the same categories by which it was medically disqualified.[37]

The protocols for "scientific" descriptions of "homosexuals" provided the opportunity for "homosexuals" to adopt a group identity and respond on their own behalf.[38]

This process exemplifies the intentional and nonsubjective character of discursive power. Psychiatrists once believed—some still do—that they could cure "homosexuality." In order to effect such intent, however, they must rely on the discursive regularities of the episteme, which they cannot control unilaterally. Certainly the psychiatrist usually has an enormous advantage over the patient, if only because the psychiatrist can usually command the cooperation of family, friends, and perhaps the state. The substrate on which the specific relationship of power operates tilts heavily in favor of authority. But criteria for mental illness imply criteria for mental health, which "homosexuals" can, and have, invoked against the claims of psychiatry. At the same time, the contest between advocates of a pathological conception of gay identity and opponents of that conception does not reduce simply to a matter of empirical research conducted according to established protocols. During the 1950s, psychologist Evelyn Hooker demonstrated that trained mental health professionals using standard psychological tests cannot reliably distinguish gay from nongay men.[39] Such research, if reproduced, would seem to provide the definitive scientific proof to decide if gay identity necessarily indicates psychopathology. That no researcher has yet bothered to replicate Hooker's experiments indicates that political debates about lesbian/gay civil rights revolve around issues of conceptualization that precede, and inform, empirical research.

"Homosexuals" cannot simply create or find a space outside of the operation of the discursive power that enables psychiatrists to label them as such. If they could, then they could also thereby cease to bear the identity "homosexual." But those "homosexuals" who evade the identity category do so through disavowal—staying in the closet, refusing to signify that aspect of their identities—not through resistance to the meanings of the category. In Foucault's account, no aspect of the "homosexual's" being, physical, mental, emotional, or historical, escapes the taint of the diagnosis.[40] No space from which to base resistance remains within the person but outside the "homosexual." She or he must articulate resistance within the terms of the identity, because the identity itself, or the definition of it, provides the supposed justification for oppression. For any given minority group, the logic of resistance will depend on the specific historical circumstances and terms of the practices from which its members suffer. The relevance to oppositional minority groups of political strategies defined in terms of universal principles of reason is not clear. On Foucault's view, such universal principles, rather than promote resistance, simply install their own form of discipline.

The Archaeological Context

Foucault was certainly not unique among post–World War II philosophers in his concern for the implications of accepting "reason" or "rationality" as both epistemological and moral standard. Reading archaeologically, one can place him in relationship to several other post–World War II European thinkers to suggest that they shared certain concerns while recognizing that they may have approached those concerns from different angles and may perhaps have disagreed with one another vigorously. To reiterate, Beauvoir's questions about the relationship between females and femininity seem to anticipate Foucault's ideas about subjectivity, even though there is no indication that Beauvoir's work had a direct impact on Foucault. Similarly, Foucault recognized important similarities between his concerns and those of the Frankfurt School, even as he expressed reservations about the specifics of its members' approaches.

At the beginning of *The History of Sexuality*, Foucault critiqued the idea of liberation as resulting from resistance to sexual oppression. Clearly, one of his targets in that critique was Herbert Marcuse's *Eros and Civilization*,[41] the most thoroughgoing effort by a member of the Frankfurt School to integrate Marxism and Freudian psychoanalysis. From Foucault's perspective, Marcuse's approach suffered from the same problems as did most other accounts of sexual repression: It relied on an ideal of a true or natural or authentic self that law oppressed through external restrictions on instincts. On Foucault's view, authorities produce bodies, souls, and sexualities with their normalizing practices of order. A focus on an authentic self as the site of a naturalized sexuality and power in the form of law missed the most important aspects of modern, disciplinary power.

Foucault, then, did not share Marcuse's optimism about the possibilities of liberation through sexual freedom. Neither, however, did he share the depth of pessimism that Marcuse's colleagues Max Horkheimer and Theodor Adorno displayed in their masterwork, *Dialectic of Enlightenment*. For Horkheimer and Adorno, instrumental reason under the dispensation of the Enlightenment had so thoroughly colonized thought that no escape from barbarism seemed likely. Although so pessimistic a conclusion might seem specific to exiled German intellectuals during World War II, and Horkheimer and Adorno certainly insisted on the historical specificity of thought, they reiterated their doubts about the future in the preface to the 1972 edition of their book: "The development toward total integration recognized in this book is interrupted, but not abrogated. It threatens to advance beyond dictatorships and wars."[42]

Foucault attributed to members of the Frankfurt School the specification of important problems that he continued to work on. He shared with them the concern that the Enlightenment project, broadly conceived as "attaining freedom through the exercise of reason," had become dangerous—not as dangerous for Foucault, however, as for Horkheimer and Adorno. Foucault's hyperactive pessimism, predicated on the belief that everything is not bad but dangerous, turned on his conception of subjectivity. His own account of the difference between his position and that of the Frankfurt School is key:

> Schematically one can affirm that the conception of the "subject" that was adopted by the Frankfurt School was quite traditional, was of a philosophical character. Then, it was noticeably impregnated with humanism of a Marxist type. That also explains the particular articulation of the latter with certain Freudian concepts, in the relationship between alienation and repression, between "liberation," disalienation, and the end of exploitation. I'm convinced that given these premises, the Frankfurt School cannot by any means admit that the problem is not to recover our "lost" identity, to free our imprisoned nature, our deepest truth; but instead, the problem is to move toward something radically Other. The center, then, seems still to be found in Marx's phrase: man produces man. It's all in how you look at it. For me, what must be produced is not man identical to himself, exactly as nature would have designed him or according to his essence; on the contrary, we must produce something that doesn't yet exist and about which we cannot know how and what it will be.[43]

A Nietzschean Marxist differs from Hegelian Marxists in rejecting the assumption of a continuous, self-identical subjectivity, whether at the level of individuals or at the level of History. The Marxist humanism of the twentieth century had substituted a naturalized, liberated individual, free to express her or his true self, for the proletariat as the ideal subject driving historical development.

But in whatever form, the continuous, self-identical subject as the motor of history gave rise to utopia/dystopia by positing a system that contains within itself the seed of its ultimate, perfect elaboration. By refusing any original or eschatological principle, Foucault returned the debate about power to the realm of interaction—and therefore probable conflict—among humans. We have no need to worry, as Horkheimer and Adorno did, that the unfolding Reason of the Enlightenment will realize its project of total domination because the principles of reason vary in their application and impact according to historical circumstances. On the other hand, neither should we hope that the unfolding Reason of the Enlightenment will solve all of our problems for us.

If the intellectual poles of the 1950s, before the advent of poststructuralism, consisted of structuralism and phenomenology or hermeneutics, then the move toward poststructuralism now forms the pole opposite those philosophers who retain some attachment to a notion of subjectivity as Foucault critiqued it. Whether this is a dialectical move or not I will not venture to guess. But it does seem that Foucault's principle rival in this battle would reconcile the structuralist and phenomenological poles of the previous argument by describing the ultimate realization of Enlightenment as a matter of formulating the rational principles of language such that they will serve as the transparent medium for expressions of individual subjectivity. This, of course, is the project of Jürgen Habermas, who has criticized Foucault, Derrida, and other poststructuralists ferociously for their supposed abandonment of the Enlightenment project.

It is useful to rehearse briefly the differences between Foucault and Habermas in this context, because they reveal how thoroughly Foucault has changed the terms of the debate.[44] Habermas's central idea is his theory of communicative rationality.[45] Rather than suspect, with Horkheimer, Adorno, and Foucault, that reason itself has become the problem, Habermas insists that it remains the solution, but with a very important modification. On Habermas's view, the pessimists err in their conception of reason. They focus on its instrumental uses, the drive in western culture since the scientific revolution to use reason as a means of governing relationships between persons and things such that persons can manipulate and control things. Habermas chooses to emphasize communicative uses of reason, those whose primary goal is not to exercise control over a thing, but to achieve understanding and assent among a group of persons—not relationships between persons and things, but relationships between persons and persons. The ultimate goal is to establish communicative, rather than instrumental, reason as the basis for adjudicating political differences.

In 1981 Habermas published a rumination on the theme of "Modernity versus Postmodernity," in which he described Foucault and Derrida as "Young Conservatives" because of their "irreconcilable anti-modernism."[46] Foucault responded obliquely to this charge in his essay "What Is Enlightenment?" which appeared in 1984, the year of his death.[47] Although the essay contains only one reference to Habermas, in a list of other philosophers who exemplified modern philosophy's preoccupation with the titular question, it clearly serves, among other things, as Foucault's account of the differences that he perceived between his work and that of Habermas. Foucault took as his theme a brief essay by Immanuel Kant that had appeared with the same title two hundred years before. Habermas objected to Foucault's effort to define his work in terms of Kantian Enlightenment: "How can Foucault's self-understanding as a thinker in the tradition of the Enlightenment be compatible with his unmistakable critique of precisely this form of knowledge, which is that of modernity?"[48] For Habermas the rationalist, Foucault could not have it both ways: He must either define himself in terms of a tradition or critique it.

Foucault defined Enlightenment in terms of a "philosophical ethos." The first element of that ethos entailed rejecting the "blackmail of the Enlightenment."[49] He refused to accept the dichotomy of choosing for or against the Enlightenment, because insofar as the name indicated a specifiable philosophical and cultural tradition, that tradition had fundamentally shaped Foucault's thought, his most basic understanding of the world. But the core principle of the modernity that brought about the possibility of Enlightenment, on Foucault's view, was the question of our relationship to the present:

> We must try to proceed with the analysis of ourselves as beings who are historically determined, to a certain extent, by the Enlightenment. Such an analysis implies a series of historical inquiries that are as precise as possible; and these inquiries will not be oriented retrospectively toward the "essential kernel of rationality" that can be found in the Enlightenment and that would have to be preserved in any event; they will be oriented toward the "contemporary limits of the necessary," that is, toward what is not or is no longer indispensable for the constitution of ourselves as autonomous subjects.[50]

Where Habermas saw the potential for freedom in the unfolding of Reason toward the achievement of communicative rationality, Foucault saw it in the historicization of what seems necessary about our identities.

There is an interesting sense in which Foucault and Habermas are not that far apart. Both emphasize relationships among individuals rather than the individuals themselves. We might transpose Foucault's work on disciplinary power into Habermas's idiom by suggesting that disciplinary power exemplifies humans' use of instrumental reason against one another. Install communicative rationality as the guiding principle of a society, and *Discipline and Punish* disappears. On the other hand, near the end of *The Theory of Communicative Action*, Habermas wrote that "two questions must be answered: (i) whether a reason that has objectively split up into its moments can still preserve its unity; and (ii) how expert cultures can be mediated with everyday practice."[51] Foucault answered the first question negatively in *The Order of Things*, in effect arguing that there was never "a reason" to split up in the first place, much less one that might retain some endangered unity—or, similarly, that the conception of philosophy in terms of a quest for unified reason was the product of a specific historical a priori, which is now in the process of falling away, making the question moot at best and otiose at worst.

Ultimately, the dialectic of Enlightenment has produced in Habermas the unification of liberalism and Marxism. While Habermas routinely refers to the ills of capitalism and invokes a tradition of sociology running back to Marx, his historical eschaton is the nonrevolutionary realization of a conflict-free society in which organic individuals reconcile the differences among themselves, and among their communities, through communicative action, through nonstrategic communication designed to gain assent from free, rational individuals. Habermas insisted that his scheme depends on no foundations, but in the end it becomes very difficult to understand where exactly the reason that guarantees the efficacy of communicative action resides. If it is neither an origin, informing the identity of humans as a species, nor a telos toward which History unfolds according to its own logic, then it lacks the force of inevitability, at which point we must ask how it will come about. Perhaps Habermas, having discovered the theory of communicative action, will teach it to the rest of the world. But this simply returns him to the same problematic: If the world refuses to listen, does Habermas abandon the project or attempt to coerce the assent of others?[52]

Foucault identified the central concern while stating, on one hand, the differences between his archaeological and genealogical studies and, on the other, an older notion of critique:

> Criticism is no longer going to be practiced in the search for formal structures with universal value, but rather as a historical investigation into the events that have led us to constitute ourselves and recognize ourselves as sub-

jects of what we are doing, thinking, saying. . . . This means that the histori-cal ontology of ourselves must turn away from all projects that claim to be global or radical. In fact we know from experience that the claim to escape from the system of contemporary reality so as to produce the overall programs of another society, of another way of thinking, another culture, another vision of the world, has led only to the return of the most dangerous traditions.[53]

Perhaps Habermas is correct to describe Foucault's rejection of the global and radical as "conservative," but I rather think such a description reveals only the poverty of political vocabulary in a conceptual world where there are only two options—either commitment to progress under the Enlightenment as Habermas defines it or conservatism.

The issue comes back to the discursive constitution of subjects according to epistemic regularities. Foucault could not choose for or against the Enlightenment, because that set of ideas informed the cul-ture in which he grew up. But the recognition of such historical deter-mination of thought does not preclude critique and resistance. Rather, it enjoins us to pursue empirical, local, historical critiques of the spe-cific *dispositifs*—the practices, discourses, architectures of the institu-tions in which we live daily—as the means of discerning the contingent and historical within what we perceive as natural and inevitable.

Although Foucault gave a name to this process, it is probably a mis-take to identify him as the originator, in the traditional sense, of genealogical inquiry and resistance. His work is a particular crystal-lization of ideas and suspicions that have become increasingly common during the post–World War II era. Neither Habermas nor Foucault was unique in posing Habermas's second query: "how expert cultures can be mediated with everyday practice." However, the answers to that question that *Discipline and Punish* and *The History of Sexuality* offer are unique and potentially very useful. Foucault's notion of the insurrection of subordinated knowledges provides a useful bridge from the set of questions that motivated him, among many other thinkers of the period, to queer theorists.

Foucault described this insurrection in the process of defining "genealogy." Genealogies are "anti-sciences," but, in order to forestall at least some of the more reductive critics, we must clarify imediately the sense in which Foucault used that term: "We are concerned . . . with the insurrection of knowledges that are opposed primarily not to the contents, methods or concepts of a science, but to the effects of the cen-tralizing powers which are linked to the institution and functioning of an organized scientific discourse within a society such as ours."[54] The claim to the status of "science" confers power on those who succeed in their claim. Foucault offered Marxism and psychoanalysis as examples of this phenomenon—striving to exercise power by claiming to pursue a scientific form of inquiry.

In addition, Foucault described two different types of knowledge as participating in this insurrection: accumulated erudition from the past that the drive for internally consistent, systematized knowledge had overridden; and the "disqualified" knowledge of specific subjects whose knowledge claims lacked the requisite level of theoretical elaboration. The emerging stories of lesbian/gay studies and the theoretical reflections of queer theorists fit these descriptions. According to the scientific explanations of the 1950s and 1960s, to ask after the stories of "homosexuals" as anything other than a compilation of case studies for psychological purposes would have been a waste of time; such stories possessed no other edifying value. By 1990, building on the work of empirical recovery that had begun during the 1970s with scholars who acquired a politicized perspective on sexuality and gender, queer theorists would start to question the conceptual framework that enabled and justified the effects of power around claims to science as applied to "deviant"—nonmale, nonheterosexual—identities.

2

I Am the Very Model of the Modern Homosexual

Gay Male Historians and the History of Sexuality

If by "episteme" we understand a period in which a particular set of questions or mode of conceptualization prevails, then we may find that a new episteme governing issues of sexuality emerged during the mid-1970s. Queer theory did not materialize full-fledged in 1975. However, as debates among gay male historians over the "social construction" of sexual identity categories indicate, evidence can mean very different things to different people—all equally competent—depending on the conceptual frameworks that they bring. At first the issue primarily concerned the history of sexual identity categories. Gay male historians debating the "social construction" of sexuality paid relatively little attention to Michel Foucault's arguments about the end of the episteme of man. The implications of a new episteme do not become clear instantaneously, even if hunches about what sorts of questions to ask and evidence to consider come in flashes of inspiration. Jonathan Ned Katz, a pioneering gay historian, has written that "contrary to ivory tower supposition, work on the social construction of sex did not begin with Michel Foucault."[1] For some U.S. scholars, Foucault's presence on their intellectual horizons may have annoyed more than edified. Regardless, Foucault was not a "social constructionist."

Katz's statement reveals an ironic consequence of the implication of knowledge in power. Foucault acquired an unearned reputation as the originator of "work on the social construction of sex" because *The History of Sexuality* had the effect of helping to legitimize the historical study of sex.[2] No doubt his status as a major French philosopher contributed to his legitimating role. But Foucault's history of sexuality became the original exemplar of social constructionist accounts more because of U.S. historians' reading of it than because of any effort on Foucault's part. During the 1980s, debate raged among historians of sexuality over "social construction" versus "essentialism" although no scholar ever described himself as essentialist. Essentialism probably best described the position of activists who argued that claims to lesbian/gay civil rights depended on the assertion of a minority identity.[3] Among gay male historians, the debate between social constructionists and essentialists took the form of disputes about whether men who had sex with other men, predominantly or exclusively, before the creation of the category "homosexual" still fit that category.

That this debate occurred primarily in terms of disputes over the meaning of historical evidence reflected the participants' focus on the substantive claims of *The History of Sexuality* rather than on its novel approach to understanding the historian's task. The debate itself, however, indicates the archaeological change in conceptualizations of sexuality underway in the period from roughly 1975 to 1990. Gay male historians who participated in the social constructionist debates often seemed to argue past one another, indicating that they brought fundamentally different conceptualizations to the evidence that they argued about. Regardless, the compilation of historical data about variations in sexual identities in the past produced a genealogical effect, thoroughly undermining the presumption that sexual identity categories inhere in human bodies—that compilation contributed to the insurrection of subordinated knowledges.

Historicizing "Homosexuality"

This is not to say that all such historians saw themselves as genealogists or protoqueer theorists. In the late 1970s and the 1980s, gay male historians in the United States usually operated from a fairly traditional leftist perspective. They wrote gay history in order to provide the basis for a critique of existing, excessively restrictive sexual identity categories by demonstrating that those categories had varied over time; if sexual identity categories had changed in the past, one could change them again. Their project looked very similar to that which Foucault critiqued at the beginning of *The History of Sexuality*. He questioned the value of liberatory political programs in which the participants hoped to achieve freedom by finding their "true" sexual natures.[4] Gay male historians who refrained from recommending a search for one's true sexual identity still appealed to some notion of authenticity, or a larger array of options in sexual identities, that would serve as the basis for liberation.

Foucault did not originate social constructionist work in the history of sexuality. Women's historian Carroll Smith-Rosenberg shares that honor with Katz and with British scholar Jeffrey Weeks. In 1976, just seven years after the Stonewall Riots that marked the beginning of the militant lesbian/gay civil rights movement, Katz published the first major U.S. work in lesbian/gay history, the massive *Gay American History: Lesbians and Gay Men in the USA. A Documentary History*.[5] In the introduction to this remarkable book, Katz called for a thoroughly historicized conception of "homosexuality" to replace the ahistorical, psychological definition that predominated then. He also noted that, before the advent of the psychological model, most who defined same-sex eroticism characterized it as sinful. He did not make the distinction, crucial to Foucault's analysis, between the sin as an act that anyone might commit and a psychologized personality type peculiar to specific individuals.[6]

As Katz himself claimed, he had a specific vision about the possibilities for future research in lesbian/gay history in the United States. His description of his work revealed a strong sense that he had pioneered in a very important area and that he carried an enormous responsibility to his readers and to lesbians and gay men generally.[7] He attended carefully to changes in the burgeoning field of lesbian/gay history when he published a second collection of documents, *Gay/Lesbian Almanac: A New Documentary* in 1983.[8]

In introducing that work, Katz explored the question of terminology at some length. He wished to correct his own earlier use of the term "homosexual" in *Gay American History*, where he used the word indifferently to refer to the entire 400-year period of the book. He had since concluded that he could only use the term "homosexual" correctly when referring to the period since its invention in 1869.[9] In explaining his focus on terminology, Katz offered a justification that sounded vaguely poststructuralist. "I have stressed words and concepts here," he wrote, "because they intervene between us and our perception of the specific historical qualities of past relations, feelings, acts, persons, and societies."[10] We must attend to the historical specificity of words because they do not simply reflect "reality" transparently; on the contrary, they have a profound impact on how we perceive and think.

But Katz made this observation on the limits of representation in the service of a liberatory political program that revolved around desires and pleasures. The historicization of sexual identities would serve to eradicate the influence of professionals, not only physicians and lawyers and priests but also historians, in specifying "normal" or "natural" sexual practices. Here Katz used his position outside the academy as the ground for a radical statement of the possibilities of self-determination. Ironically, he used the stereotype of the ivory tower as a foil to arrive at a position that in many ways looks much like Foucault's.[11]

The difference remains important. For Katz, the accumulation of documentary evidence that demonstrated the historical variety of sexual practices and identities would serve the project of liberation. "If the 'lesbian,' 'gay,' 'homosexual,' and 'heterosexual' are not given biologically, but constructed historically," he argued, "we can together work to reconstruct ourselves and our society in radically new, more satisfying forms. Viewed historically, 'lesbian' and 'gay,' 'homosexual' and 'heterosexual,' are ways of loving which we together make, and can struggle to remake, according to our changing needs."[12] Katz's goals were radical. He demonstrated concern about the differences of power in relationships between lesbian and gay persons and authoritative persons who defined lesbian/gay identity. He wished to allow ordinary individuals much greater leeway—complete freedom?—to define their sexual identities.

Here lies the difference between the social science version of the history of sexuality and Foucault's genealogy. Katz wrote about the history of sexuality in order to bring to light the true experiences of sexual minorities from the past. For Katz, this project promised to allow for a more just social organization on the basis of better information about sexual minorities. For Foucault, by contrast, better information about sexual minorities may serve the purpose of tying individuals yet more closely to their sexed subjectivities. Foucault called for the creation of something entirely new rather than a return to an allegedly authentic sexual self. But for Foucault the issue remained undecidable a priori. No one can predict fully the political effects of a given inquiry, especially an inquiry as new and untested as Katz's. The specifics of historical inquiry might serve to challenge the domination of the generalizing social sciences.

Weeks seemed to agree with Katz, even though he adopted an explicitly Foucaultian analysis. Like Katz, Weeks historicized sexual identity only to end up with a program for liberation that rested on sexual self-definition. He did not see himself in such terms. His first book, *Coming Out: Homosexual Politics in Britain from the Nineteenth Century to the Present*, he described as, among other things, a critique of the sexual liberalism that had characterized most of the reform efforts he described. For Weeks, a radically historicized conceptualization of sexual identity disproved the assumption that gender characteristics inhere in biologically sexed bodies. It also cast doubt on the possibility for any purely rational agreement about what those sexed bodies should or should not do with one another and in what combinations. According to the sexual liberalism that he criticized, reasonable people should be able to discern precisely the proper social roles for persons with a given genital configuration. Once they have made that determination, little room for argument remains.[13] Whether we get there via revolutionary politics or via empirical research, the goal is to find the truth of sex that will allow us all to be free.

By criticizing this model, Weeks seemed to pursue a project that was very similar to Foucault's. However, Weeks's own recollection of how he came to think of sexual identities as historically specific offers some clues about his differences with Foucault. Like Katz, Weeks found work on the social construction of sexual identities before he learned of *The History of Sexuality*. On the historical contingency of identities generally, he mentioned specifically E. P. Thompson's *The Making of the English Working Class*,[14] the famous study of class-conscious identities. On "homosexual" identities specifically, he cited the article "The Homosexual Role," which sociologist Mary McIntosh published in 1968. In a manner that seemed to anticipate Foucault's approach, McIntosh argued that "homosexuality" is not an identity but a social role that permits authority figures to distinguish sharply between acceptable and unacceptable behavior and to prevent the latter by stigmatizing it.[15] In this early work, Weeks's background as a socialist and sociologist showed in his concern for "material needs as defined by those who control society" as the motivating factors behind the perpetuation of ideologies, including the ideology of a psychopathological "homosexual" identity.[16]

By the time Weeks wrote *Sexuality and Its Discontents*, which was published in 1985, he had considerably revised his views. He noted in the preface to the second edition of *Coming Out* that he wrote that book before *The History of Sexuality* appeared in English. Weeks made this point about chronology precisely to refute the "myth . . . that the 'social constructionist' approach to homosexuality results from the work of Foucault."[17] The similarities in the accounts of Weeks and Foucault stemmed from their coincident movement in the same direction, not from Weeks's following Foucault. The relationship among the writings of Weeks, Katz, and Foucault suggested epistemic change, the intellectual manifestation and perpetuation of social, political, and economic changes that produced similar results at disparate locations for disparate scholars. Revising his earlier view of sexuality as a function of capitalist social relations, Weeks had come to see it as "the product of a host of autonomous and interacting traditions and social prejudices: religious, moral, economic, familial, medical, juridical."[18]

Weeks's analysis raises the major question: What does it mean to historicize identity? What does such a conceptual move accomplish? For Foucault, arguing for the historical specificity of sexual identity entailed arguing for the historical specificity of all individual identity and directing attention to the processes by which we produce identities. Only by incessantly searching for the truth of our selves in sex do we develop any notion of a stable identity in the first place. Weeks, by contrast, accepted that identity as a necessary element of rational teleology; only individuals who bring autonomous rationality to the study of history and sexuality will contribute to the advance toward human liberation.

Weeks predicted the demise of sexuality. At the end of *Sexuality and Its Discontents*, he wrote that "the majestic edifice of 'sexuality' was constructed in a long history, by many hands, and refracted through many minds. Its 'laws,' norms and proscriptions still organise and control the lives of millions of people. But its unquestioned reign is approaching an end."[19] The end of sexuality. Utopian indeed, as Weeks recognized. Utopias, of course, imply visions of the better future that will supplant the flawed present. For Weeks, that better future was one that rested on a "radical pluralist approach" of appreciating the diversity of sexual desires and ways of life.[20] This was not just sloppy, feel-good liberalism that ignored power differentials within relationships. Rather, "a radical sexual politics affirms a freedom to be able to choose between" sexual desires, ways of life, and relationships.[21]

But Weeks's utopia merely reinscribed sexuality as the source of truth, rather than bringing about the demise of sexuality. The range of possibilities may be larger, but in Weeks's analysis the presumption remained that in his utopian future we would continue to organize our major life choices around matters of sex. The difference between Weeks's utopia and the specification of perversities that sexologists produced at the end of the nineteenth century lay merely in the number of sexual identities available. According to Weeks, "Identity is not a destiny but a choice."[22] He considered this choice profoundly, and quite narrowly, conditioned by antecedent events in the history of sexuality, to be sure, but a choice all the same. Thanks to the increasing self-consciousness of intellectual and political critiques of sexuality, "we have the opportunity to construct an alternative vision based on a realistic hope for the end of sexual domination and subordination, for new sexual and social relations, for new, and genuine, opportunities for pleasure and choice. We have the chance to regain control of our bodies, to recognise their potentialities to the full, to take ourselves beyond the boundaries of sexuality as we know it."[23] The same autonomous, self-willing individuals would choose sexual identities in the future, but they would choose more freely from among a wider range of options. They would do so on the basis of "control of our bodies," the same goal that Foucault specified as the problem rather than the solution. And apparently there is no possibility that individuals in Weeks's utopia still will not find a suitable choice, even among a much broader array of options.

The history and politics of sexuality occasioned, for Foucault, the opportunity, or the requirement, to reexamine precisely these sorts of assumptions about the relationship between individuals, or "bodies" as Foucault might have put it, and the social order.[24] Weeks offered "the vision of a freer, unalienated sexual world . . . as an antidote and alternative to the meretriciousness, restrictions, and oppressions of the present."[25] But the "meretriciousness, restrictions, and oppressions of the present" rested precisely on the incitement to confess the truth of sex, which will make us inhabitants of modern consumer culture happy, beautiful, rich, and sexually fulfilled. Surely the coincidence of incitements to "freedom of choice" in sexual identities and consumer products should give us pause. We must neither conflate sexuality and consumer capitalism nor reduce one to dependence on the other. We should, however, notice the archaeological congruence in the analysis of individual subjectivities that both rely on. For Weeks and Katz, historical evidence of variation in sexual identity categories proves that we have some control over sexuality, giving us hope in our struggle toward liberation, the specifics of which are obvious. For Foucault, that same evidence offers the opportunity to crawl inside the system, maybe gum it up, maybe disassemble some part of it, with consequences that will remain largely unknown until they emerge.

The Social Constructionist Debate

Work on the social construction of sex, then, did not begin with Foucault. But as Katz himself demonstrated, the name if not the ideas had attained such widespread currency by the early 1980s that anyone who wrote on the topic of sexual matters in history had to mention Foucault, if only to dismiss, appropriate, or modify his ideas. The significant difference between Foucault and gay male historians in the United States was their understanding of the question that they wanted to answer. Throughout the 1980s, two themes predominated in much work on the history of sexuality in the United States: One was the debate over essentialist versus social constructionist accounts of sexual identity; the other was the search for the beginnings of modern gay (male) identity. These two questions were closely related: Those who believed that "homosexual," lesbian, or gay male identities reflect biological factors that manifest themselves in the gender of sexual object choice, "essentialists" in the terms of this debate, would see no point in searching for the historical origins of identities that presumably have existed as long as our species has. The almost complete triumph of the social constructionist position, in turn, would contribute crucially to the conditions of possibility for queer theory, which assumes the radical historical variability of sexual identity categories.

Foucault did not take the essentialist position. Neither, however, did he take the social constructionist position, if by that we mean the attempt to explain some discrete, persistent phenomenon whose historical origins we can, in principle, discover. For Foucault, sexuality was inescapably intertwined with power and knowledge; he studied the history of sexuality not to understand better the discreet phenomenon called "sexuality" as it persisted but changed through time. He studied the history of sexuality not to understand sexuality itself but to understand the various operations of institutions and discourses in which authoritative individuals used examinations and specifications of sexual thoughts and practices to control their subjects (including themselves). This distinction is crucial to an understanding of *The History of Sexuality* as a genealogy. The confessional discourses of sexuality depend on constant reflection and examination, because the identities that they produce remain always uncertain, dependent on the continued relationship of surveillance between the authority and the subject. Identities are relational, not ontological. Historians who viewed sexuality as a social construction with some common element persisting through time made of it an ideal signification, a teleologically driven reification, just as much as those who viewed sexuality as a biological essence did.

The enormous merit of gay male historians' work notwithstanding, they dulled the edge of their political critiques when they overlooked Foucault's analysis of subjectivity. The argument that sexual identities vary historically was novel in an intellectual and political context where most people assumed that these identities emerge naturally and inevitably from biological drives. But those who argued for the historical variation of sexual identities did not challenge the basic social structures and representational schemes that produced "naturalized" sexual identities in the first place. The autonomous, rational subject who would choose from a broader array of sexual identities in Katz' and Weeks' accounts, however carefully we allow, à la Marx, for the historical specificity of her or his choices, was still the subject of the "ideal significations and indefinite teleologies" that Foucault hoped to eschew. From this perspective, the classical liberalism that Weeks criticized shares teleological metanarratives with romantic and Marxist critiques that Weeks and Katz endorsed. This metanarrative of progress based on the perpetually improving self-awareness of autonomous subjects underwrote these social constructionists' search for the origins of "homosexual" or gay male identity.

The distinction between social constructionist work in the history of sexuality and Foucaultian genealogy appears in John D'Emilio's work. *Sexual Politics, Sexual Communities: The Making of a Homosexual Minority in the United States, 1940–1970*, D'Emilio's major study of lesbian/gay history, explored the beginning of self-conscious political identity among lesbians and gay men in the years immediately preceding the Stonewall Riots of 1969, which mark the start of the modern lesbian/gay rights movement. For the period that D'Emilio covered in his book, however, the concept of a separate "homosexual" identity was already well established. As D'Emilio described, the activists in the 1950s faced the question of what position they would take with respect to that identity and how they would go about changing it.[26]

D'Emilio dealt more directly with the question of the possibilities for the emergence of modern lesbian/gay identities in his 1983 article "Capitalism and Gay Identity." Dissatisfied with the accounts of "homosexual" identity that Weeks and Foucault had offered, D'Emilio "wanted to be able to ground social construction theory, which posited that gay identity was historically specific rather than universal, in concrete social processes."[27] He described the possibility for lesbian/gay identities as a function of the separation of subsistence from family relationships, a separation that resulted from the spread of mass commodity production. Some people have always had primary or exclusive attraction to others of the same gender. But since roughly 1800, the opportunities have increased steadily for individuals, usually male, to earn their living, and thus to develop their sense of personal identity, by participating in wage labor apart from a family unit organized around a potentially reproductive couple. Thus, the shift of commodity production outside the home and the consequent spread of wage labor, usually in urban areas, enabled the formation of gay and lesbian identities.

On one level D'Emilio's account served as a useful corrective to Foucault's excesses. Writing as he did in a context in which Marxism had a far greater hold on intellectual imaginations than it has ever had in the United States, Foucault found considerable urgency in the project of explaining why class was not the ultimate and originary form of oppression and why all power did not flow outward from the bourgeoisie. Thus, he explicitly developed his analysis of sexuality as the primary device in an exercise of power that roughly coincided with the spread of commercial production and exchange as the dominant economic system in Western Europe but that merchants and factory owners first applied to themselves in their soul-searching religions and their medicalized conception of the potential sexual practices within their own families.[28]

Foucault showed that sexuality does not constitute a set of ideas and practices that result from, and therefore depend on, capitalist modes of production. D'Emilio, however, showed that Foucault provided precious little sense of how the institutional and discursive practices that he outlined actually functioned in specific societies and in the lives of specific individuals. In his various explorations of the social history of sexuality in the United States, D'Emilio elaborated more specifically how particular individuals operated within the confines of particular social and economic structures. This specificity has considerable value. But D'Emilio ran the risk of losing the radical edge of Foucault's critique. *The History of Sexuality* is not primarily about the rise of "homosexual" identities but about the truth of sex as a ruse of power. D'Emilio missed one of Foucault's main points: that all sexual identities, not just "homosexual" ones, vary historically.

Thus, D'Emilio described as "heterosexual" the families that individuals who experienced same-sex desire lived in before "homosexual" identities became possible.[29] But historicizing "homosexual" identities without also historicizing "heterosexual" identities, thus leaving unchallenged the supposedly transhistorical "naturalness" of "heterosexuality," lost much of the value in historicizing sexuality in the first place. Subjects accept the search for their truth in sex precisely because of the presumption, much trumpeted by priests and physicians, that "heterosexuality" is "natural," a word that means many different things, but always means "transhistorical." Unexamined, "heterosexuality" functions as ideal signification, as a purportedly universal category beyond the contingencies of history.

Katz solved this problem in 1995 with the publication of *The Invention of Heterosexuality*. Even at that late date, Katz expected that his thesis of the recent provenance of "heterosexuality"—roughly coincident with the invention of "homosexuality"—would strike many readers as absurd. But Katz's inquiry into the historical deployment of heterosexuality allowed him to investigate the political investments that supported the concept. Again showing his willingness to keep up with the times, Katz offered a very queer theoretical observation in his introduction: "The intimidating notion that heterosexuality refers to everything differently sexed and gendered and eroticized is, it turns out, one of the conceptual dodges that keeps heterosexuality from becoming the focus of sustained, critical analysis. You can't analyze everything."[30] But if you start with the suspicion that it is historically variable and that it has its own, specific history, rather than serving primarily as an adjunct to the history, say, of capitalism, then you can analyze the invention of heterosexuality.

The continuing problems with Marxist approaches to the history of sexuality became clearer in an early contribution to social construction theory, Robert A. Padgug's 1979 article "Sexual Matters: On Conceptualizing Sexuality in History."[31] Padgug pointed out the telling isomorphism between sexuality and the "private" sphere of human life: Sexuality serves to demarcate those elements—home, family, emotion, erotic practice—that are supposedly distinct from the "public" realm of law, work, and politics. He also noted that Marxists often fail to recognize the artificiality of this distinction; insofar as they rely on the base/superstructure distinction, they even tend to reproduce it.[32] Consequently, the few socialists, whether Marxist or otherwise, who have dealt effectively with sexual/private matters have also been feminists (and usually women).[33]

In order to develop a specifically Marxist analysis of sexuality, Padgug needed a way to overcome this public/private distinction. Here one might think that it would be useful to consider Foucault's analysis of middle-class families, which he described as the primary locus of a sexuality that agents of such public institutions as churches, hospitals, and schools incite and govern.[34] But Padgug seemed to regard *The History of Sexuality* as just that, a historical description that could offer little in the way of analytic purchase on this problem. Foucault insisted that Marxism could no more explain all forms of oppression or the effects of all social relations than any other totalizing theory. Ironically, much of the analysis of social relations that Padgug derived from Marx and Marxists to understand sexuality looked much like what Foucault said about power. Padgug consistently refused to reify sexual categories, insisting instead that "sexuality is relational," that categories serve to determine the boundaries of possible behaviors for individuals who may either acquiesce in or resist those boundaries.[35]

The best Padgug could muster, however, was a brief consideration and dismissal of Freud as the source of a possible reconciliation of the public and private. He may have been right that some psychology is necessary to account fully for the intersection of publicly determined sexual categories (or class, gender, or racial categories) and individual consciousness. One of the most perplexing aspects of prejudicial stereotypes is their capacity to invade even, or especially, the subjectivities of those individuals who are the butt of them. To assume that psychology can mean only psychoanalysis, however, seems enormously limiting.

Foucault pointed to a potential place to look for a psychological theory: The incitement to confess the truth of sex serves as a point of contact between publicly determined sexual categories and individual consciousness. The efficacy of prejudicial categories in inhabiting the consciousness of those who suffer by them puzzles anyone operating with the assumption that subjects can bring their own constitutive limits to consciousness. It puzzles the genealogist less because Foucault argued that authoritative individuals who operate in powerful institutions produce, rather than merely influence, subjectivity. They provide hegemonic interpretations of minority identities as constitutive features of the minority's own subjectivity. But in Padgug's article, Marx, Freud, and Foucault remained analytically distinct, each with one piece of the puzzle yet lacking the bigger picture that would allow subsequent scholars to fit those pieces together.

Whatever its limitations, Padgug's article became an important, early manifestation of the argument in favor of the social construction of sexuality. He had made the enormously useful point that sexuality requires some explicit conceptualization as a topic for historical inquiry. Throughout the 1980s, debate raged among historians of sexuality over the question of whether sexual identities are transhistorical, "essential" categories that inhere in human beings and have remained largely the same in every culture or "social constructions," products of specific social relations that vary widely from culture to culture. Although historians working in virtually every period of Western history joined the debate to some extent, its most interesting partisans studied ancient societies, in part because the cultures of ancient Greece and Rome, on which our own culture supposedly rests, provide ample evidence for a casual acceptance of same-sex eroticism and in part because John Boswell, the only scholar of any repute who espoused something like the essentialist position, happened to display towering erudition in classical as well as medieval texts.

This debate had a profound impact on lesbian/gay studies in the United States. *Hidden from History: Reclaiming the Gay and Lesbian Past*, the first anthology of lesbian/gay history, appeared in 1989. Under the heading "The Ancient World," John Boswell's, Robert Padgug's, and David Halperin's statements about essentialism versus social constructionism formed the opening section of the book. In 1990, Sedgwick felt compelled to address the subject in *Epistemology of the Closet*. In 1992, Duggan's article "Making It Perfectly Queer" in the *Socialist Review* explicitly advocated a constructionist approach to lesbian/gay theory.[36]

Halperin offered the most careful elaboration of the theory that ancient Greeks lacked discrete sexual identity categories such as ours, and he did so in explicitly Foucaultian terms. Halperin argued that, if by "sexuality" we mean "the key to unlocking the deepest mysteries of

the human personality," in a very Foucaultian formulation, Athenian citizens (males by definition) had no concept of sexuality.[37] Rather, they
regarded differences in sexual tastes as no more important an aspect of
an individual's character than differences in tastes for types of food.
The important identity category for Athenian citizens was political status. A citizen could take as his sexual partner anyone, regardless of gender, who was not a citizen—that is, who occupied a lower position on
the status hierarchy—as long as the citizen performed the role of the
penetrator rather than the penetrated. This organization of erotic practice in terms of political distinctions, Halperin noted, was common in
ancient Mediterranean societies. [38]

Thus, we may suspect that Boswell missed something important in
his defense of the perpetual "homosexual." He described an ancient Ara-
bic psychology text that included the gender of sexual object choice in
a list of psychologically distinctive human characteristics. Here, surely,
his evidence showed the existence of a recognizably modern sense of
"sexuality," according to Halperin's definition, but in the medieval world.
However, when Boswell contended in a footnote that "Qusta, in fact,
believed that homosexuality was often inherited, as did ar-Razi and other
Muslim scientific writers," his argument fell apart. He insisted that
"treating 'passive sexual behavior' (i.e., the reception of semen in anal
intercourse) in men as a hereditary condition ... in which the role of
insertor with either men or women is thought 'normal,' but the position
of the 'insertee' is regarded as bizarre or even pathological ... should
be taken as a *special aspect of Muslim sexual taxonomy rather than as indicative of attitudes toward 'homosexuality.'*"[39] But Halperin's framework gave
a more parsimonious explanation: The passive role in anal intercourse
gained its significance not from a Muslim sexual taxonomy but from a
Muslim status taxonomy. If the passive male in this instance violated a
hierarchy that included, among other things, sexual acts, then one need
posit no "special aspect of Muslim sexual taxonomy" to explain the psychological categories. Boswell saw this as a special aspect of a sexual taxonomy because he assumed that any reference to sexual acts could have
meaning only within the realm known as "sexuality."

Note also that Boswell conflated "homosexuality" with the role of
insertee in the Muslim version, whereas according to modern psychological theory one is "homosexual" if one has sex with someone of the
same gender, regardless of who penetrates whom or even in the absence
of penetration. Further, the category "homosexual" encompasses both

men and women, with gender of sexual object choice as the distinguishing characteristic. Boswell's own description of the evidence indicates that medieval Muslim categories did not apply equally to women and men; in any taxonomy for which "the reception of semen" offers a definitive distinction, "homosexual" relations between women, in contrast to the modern regime of sexuality, would remain irrelevant.

But on close reading, the actual area of disagreement between Boswell and Halperin nearly disappeared altogether. Both agreed that people in the ancient Mediterranean recognized among themselves differences in sexual tastes and that those people attached very little significance to such differences. Halperin likened the attitude of Athenian citizens toward tastes in sex to attitudes of modern individuals toward tastes in food: something that one might notice about another person, but not terribly revealing about that person's character.[40] Boswell likened "homosexual" persons to Jewish or black persons in that, in his view, they demonstrably have existed throughout human history; the variable was the degree to which those particularities of identity stood out as the basis for opprobrium and invidious discrimination in different societies.[41]

An important difference remained, however. Boswell and Halperin clearly had vastly different views on the role that language plays in human culture. Boswell assimilated the constructionist debate to the debate between realists and nominalists; realists see language as describing actual distinctions that people perceive in the real world, whereas nominalists see language as reflecting arbitrary distinctions that humans impose on an otherwise undifferentiated world. Halperin, in contrast, took the view that "concepts in the human sciences . . . do not merely describe reality but, at least partly, constitute it."[42]

"The human sciences" here meant not only the "cultural histor[y] of antiquity," which Halperin and Boswell pursued, and the other academic disciplines but also psychology and sexology.[43] Halperin argued that, when nineteenth-century psychologists defined the term "homosexuality," they had the capacity, on the basis of that definition, to influence their patients' lives in profound and often unpleasant (not to say violent) ways. Boswell did not deny the point, but he apparently did deny that the power to "treat" in any way depended on the power to define. For Boswell, whether one is a realist or a nominalist is a question solely of referentiality: Words either refer to real distinctions or they do not, but in themselves words are basically inert.

Thus, Boswell supported his argument about the universal applicability of the term "homosexual" by comparing the constructionist debate to a hypothetical debate over the meaning of the words "blue" and "red." He did so to evade problems of lexical confusion in a debate that is "paralyzed by words."[44] This position presents the difficulty of explaining why the term "homosexual" usually entails such dire political consequences in our culture, whereas the terms "blue" and "red" do not. One difficulty that historians have in debating the issue, Boswell argued, is that "there is still no essential agreement in the scientific community about the nature of human sexuality. Whether humans are 'homosexual' or 'heterosexual' or 'bisexual' by birth, by training, by choice, or at all is still an open question."[45] Boswell's scheme could not encompass the one possibility that Foucault offered: Scientists will never discover the truth of sexuality because their definition of what they seek results, not from any rigorous empirical investigation of a "real" world, but from political disputes over acceptable behavior and attempts to inculcate such behavior while restricting its opposite. Boswell's faith in science, in a Foucaultian view, was badly misplaced.

Clearly, however, Boswell occupied a useful position in this debate in that his defense of the perpetual "homosexual" showed how fine the distinctions could be and what large areas of overlap remained among the disputants. All agreed on the political significance of the debate. Boswell held fast to his position primarily because he believed that, in the absence of gay people in the past, gay people in the present would suffer under the political liability of having no history.[46] And Boswell demonstrated brilliantly the political utility of well-documented claims on behalf of the perpetual "homosexual" from so august an institutional location as Yale University. His first book on the subject, *Christianity, Social Tolerance, and Homosexuality*, won the 1981 American Book Award for History. In this work, he presented the argument that the intense loathing of same-sex eroticism that has supposedly characterized western Christianity since its inception actually dates only to the late twelfth century and has no sound basis in biblical morality.[47] In 1994 Boswell published *Same-Sex Unions in Premodern Europe*, in which he described a ritual that the eastern church used to bless same-sex unions; the book served as a rhetorical smart bomb, exploding in the wall that closes off representations of same-sex eroticism from circulation in our culture.[48] The spectacle of interested parties herniating themselves in hopes of repairing the damage will no doubt continue to prove amusing.[49] Perpetual homosexual or no, such work from so highly respected a scholar serves to reveal the political investments in scholarly refusals to recognize same-sex eroticism.

But Boswell was mistaken to think that the perpetual homosexual must underwrite all gay-affirmative historical work. He pursued the traditional liberal project of promoting formal equality for lesbians and gay men. Lesbian and gay activists will not likely abandon that project soon, not least because to do so would be foolish. And in pursuing liberal politics, progressive metanarratives accounting for the development of identities as ideal signifiers remain crucial.

Just How Modern Are These "Homosexuals"?

Many scholars put Foucault's poststructuralist account of sexuality to the service of political programs that eschew certain liberal assumptions but not assumptions about subjectivity and epistemology. They tried to engage Foucault's argument by dating more precisely the emergence of a recognizably "modern" sexuality or, usually, a gay male identity sometime before the late nineteenth century, when the "homosexual" was supposedly born. But like scientific attempts to find the seat of sexuality in individual bodies, historical efforts to find the genesis of "sexuality" or "homosexual" identities in the past suffered from the irreducible indeterminacy of the object of investigation.

The primary source of definitional indeterminacy involved the question of which historical actors were responsible for creating identity categories. Sedgwick detected confusion in the defining characteristics of modern "homosexual" identity when she compared Foucault's account to Halperin's.[50] Foucault described the distinctive characteristic of "homosexual" men as "a certain way of inverting the masculine and feminine in oneself." Halperin described "the 'straight-acting and -appearing gay male,' a man distinct from other men in absolutely no other respect besides that of his sexuality."[51] Two scholars who claimed to agree on the recent emergence of the "modern homosexual" defined that "modern homosexual" in diametrically opposite terms: as the apotheosis of gender confusion in Foucault's terms but as the apotheosis of gender certainty in Halperin's.

Constructionist examinations of sexual identity in English persistently referred to the emergence during the late seventeenth and early eighteenth centuries in England of "molly houses," or semipublic places where men could meet for socializing and sex.[52] This posed an apparent problem for Foucault's, Weeks's, and Halperin's insistence on the late nineteenth century as the period when "homosexual" as an identity category first appeared. In *Homosexuality in Renaissance England*, Alan Bray explored this question at some length. Although he agreed broadly with Weeks, Bray doubted the importance of medical discourse as the source for the definition of "homosexual" identity.[53]

Bray argued that, through most of the seventeenth century, men frequently had sodomitical sex with one another but did not conceive of themselves as "sodomites" according to the definition of their culture. In a society characterized by late marriage and a high incidence of unrelated workers sharing beds in their employers' households, anal intercourse became a common method of sexual outlet for many men. The associations with the term "sodomite" were so profoundly foreign and negative (Papists were usually sodomites, according to popular wisdom of the day) that only during periods of upheaval or when specific instances threatened public order did acts of sodomy attract official attention. Until roughly 1700, actual acts of sodomy had no particular significance in the larger culture, whatever the symbolic uses of attributing a weakness for it to Catholics; thus, sodomy reflected nothing about the nature of the individual who committed it.[54]

Around 1700, however, a specific subculture and identity category appeared in London. Bray offered an intriguing interpretation according to which the new attentiveness to specific acts of sodomy that gave rise to an identity category, an association between the act and the individual's character, reflected the philosophical shift toward empiricism and emphasis on particularity in all things that characterized the late seventeenth and early eighteenth centuries. This explanation necessarily remained somewhat vague; Bray made no claim to find a direct relationship between philosophy and conceptions of sexual practice and identity.[55] Because much of Bray's evidence came from trials and reports of the Societies for the Reformation of Manners and from literature, we know about the mollies and their houses more from public authorities and publicly significant representations than from the mollies themselves.

And here, it seems, lay the source of the confusion that Sedgwick pointed to. Foucault and Halperin could offer descriptions of "homosexual" identity that opposed each other on a central point because they were describing different phenomena. In the late nineteenth century, physicians began to formulate a psychological definition of "sexual perversion" linked to identity that included a significant element of gen-der inversion. As historian George Chauncey has shown, however, the element of gender inversion disappeared from later accounts, even if the assumption of gender confusion remains firmly embedded in popular stereotypes of lesbians and gay men. The "straight-acting and -appear-ing gay male" of Halperin's description, by contrast, came from the personal advertisements common in the gay male culture of the late twentieth century. Sedgwick also noted that Foucault and many of the historians who work from his ideas have tended to present a linear development of changing sexual identities.[56] In this view, the sin model, in which sodomy was an act that anyone might succumb to, held sway until the rise of sexology in the late nineteenth century. Then the psy-chological model of "homosexual" persons whose sexual object choice reveals the "nature" of their characters attained widespread currency.

This account looked suspect on numerous grounds. Bray concluded from his research on renaissance England that "there is no linear his-tory of homosexuality to be written at all."[57] Sedgwick found that this account resulted in a monolithic conception of a modern gay identity that was by no means as uniform as the developmental narrative would suggest. Also, she disputed the presumption of Foucault's narrative that the medical category had completely superseded the sin model. Clearly, such is not the case in the United States. Sedgwick correctly pointed out that anti–lesbian/gay sentiment and action in the United States often manifest themselves most potently precisely where the sin model and the psychology model interact.[58] The history of "homosexuality" does not move in a straight line. Competing conceptualizations over-lap and interact, often in unpredictable ways.

Even though he described the historical shift from sinner to psy-chopath in linear terms, Foucault's own description of genealogy and the operation of discursive power made such narratives untenable. He argued that discourses are not monolithic. Discourses also produce their own resistance.[59] In *The History of Sexuality*, the substantive claims that Foucault made about the emergence of a "homosexual" identity actu-ally contradicted his genealogical analysis of power. Again, Sedgwick correctly called Foucault's substantive claim "an act of polemical bravado," but many historians have taken him too literally on "the birth of the homosexual as a species."[60]

Foucault's account in *The History of Sexuality* lacked any concrete exploration into how these different frameworks for understanding sexual acts operated in the lives of specific individuals. Building on D'Emilio's work, Chauncey began to fill in this lacuna for the United States, in much the same way that Bray did for renaissance England. In his article "From Sexual Inversion to Homosexuality: The Changing Medical Conceptualization of Female 'Deviance,'" Chauncey examined medical texts published between 1880 and 1930 to determine how physicians during the period thought of sexual deviance. According to his periodization, physicians during the last third of the nineteenth century commonly used the term "inversion," which described a general reversal of "normal" gender characteristics, including sexual object choice. Around the turn of the century, however, physicians increasingly focused on sexual object choice, to the exclusion of other gender markers, as the primary evidence of perversion. With this new focus, they used the term "homosexuality" instead of "inversion."[61] For the United States, at least, Foucault's account of the medical definition of "homosexuality" proved inaccurate on this point.

Chauncey avoided Foucault's substantive error by performing a genealogical analysis. Foucault assumed that the term "homosexuality" had retained a large measure of definitional stability from the moment of its invention, with physicians and sexologists merely perfecting their understanding of the phenomenon. Perhaps his commitment to nominalism and the presumption of discontinuity failed him in the excitement of discovering a new species. Chauncey attended more closely to the play of contingency as physicians worked to define their object of research. He thus avoided writing about "homosexuality" as an ideal signification within a linear story.

In more recent work, Chauncey offered further correctives to Foucault's scheme. In the massive *Gay New York*, he demonstrated that the medicalized conception of sexual identity did not achieve general currency among New Yorkers until World War II. Chauncey wrote that his study "confirms several of Michel Foucault's most speculative and brilliant insights," but "it modifies the periodization based on those insights by giving equal weight to working-class culture. Most significantly, it shows that the 'modern homosexual,' whose preeminence is usually thought to have been established in the nineteenth century, did not dominate Western urban industrial culture until well into the twentieth century, at least in one of the world capitals of that culture."[62] *The History of Sexuality* proved most useful for the overview it gave and the approach it suggested rather than for the details it contained about the characteristics and chronology of specific sexual identities. As Chauncey demonstrated, and as Foucault speculated, those details vary enormously depending on class, geography, probably race, and certainly gender.

Foucault, then, got the central point right: The "science" of sex, directed at the search for the "truth" of the individual, is much more a political than a positivist enterprise. In "From Sexual Inversion to Homosexuality," Chauncey attributed physicians' effusion of concern for unusual sexual and gender behavior in the last third of the nineteenth century to larger historical and political trends, including the growing visibility of gay male subcultures and anxiety about rapidly changing gender roles.[63] He gave concrete evidence for Foucault's claim that sexuality serves as a means of importing political, which is to say ethical, standards into the ostensibly value-neutral language of "science" and as a means of using science to enforce political preferences.

Foucault's substantive statements about sexual identities carry their greatest force in the context of his larger claims about power and knowledge. Methods of inquiry cannot operate independently of that which one inquires about. Social scientists assume that their inquiries will serve the goal of human self-understanding. The more we know about sexual minorities in the past, the greater our present choices. But for Foucault, the social scientific investigation of the meaning of human experience constitutes more the imposition of meaning through authoritatively generalized accounts of identity than it constitutes the discovery of authentic meaning in experience. Perhaps exhibiting an epistemic shift in miniature, the constructionist versus essentialist debate eventually petered out without definitive resolution, although the constructionist position currently holds sway among most scholars in the social sciences and humanities. Resolved or not, however, the constructionist versus essentialist debate helped to clear necessary conceptual room for the emergence of queer theory, which began by assuming the historical variability and political determination of sexual identity categories.

Gender Difference
Feminist Scholars on the Truth of Gender and Sexuality

he history of sexuality was a topic in the very first article of the very first issue of the very first volume of the new journal, *Signs: Journal of Women in Culture and Society*. Although they tend to be less defensive about the point, feminist scholars have just as strong a claim—if not stronger—as gay male scholars to a significant interest in the historical variability of sexual identity categories before the publication of *The History of Sexuality*.[1] Carroll Smith-Rosenberg's ground-breaking 1975 article, "The Female World of Love and Ritual: Relations Between Women in Nineteenth-Century America,"[2] offered fascinating historical evidence supporting her conclusion that twentieth-century historians could not simply read their own categories backward into the past without doing injustice to the lives of women in the past.

The debates of feminist scholars proved broader than those of gay male historians in at least three respects. First and foremost, feminists rarely considered sexuality without also considering gender, which was for them the primary category for analysis. Second, while considerable discussion revolved around the utility of Foucault's work for feminists, this was only part of a larger discussion about the implications of poststructuralist philosophy, sometimes characterized as "postmodernism," for feminism. Finally, feminist scholars discussed the implications of historical variability in identity categories across a much wider range of disciplines and political positions than did gay male scholars. As Joan Wallach Scott has explained, feminist historians created an interesting quandary for themselves: They pointed to significant women in the past to buttress women's claims to equality in the present but demonstrated in the process the enormous variability of women's lives. Doing so raised significant questions about the viability of the universal identity category "woman."[3] Doubts about "woman" as a category in conjunction with doubts about "homosexual" as a category would combine to enable queer theory.

Feminist uses of Foucault may serve as an entrée into the larger debates of the 1980s, when feminist philosophers and literary critics increasingly found Foucault's work useful for their theoretical tasks. In 1988 an edited volume of feminist writings about Foucault appeared. The collection, *Feminism and Foucault: Reflections on Resistance*, exemplified the wide-ranging, thoughtfully skeptical, politically savvy approach that scholars from various disciplines brought to the question. In the opening lines of the book, editors Irene Diamond and Lee Quinby explicitly refused to claim any new orthodoxy: "The essays here are notable for challenging tendencies toward either feminist or Foucaultian orthodoxy precisely because of the new views of empowerment and resistance gained with the two approaches."[4]

Rather than orthodoxy, feminists began to articulate a set of queries. In some instances they posed common feminist questions about society and invoked Foucault as part of their efforts to find answers. In other instances, they turned the questions on Foucault's work, challenging what they saw as omissions or mistakes. For scholars who investigated the connection between sexuality and gender, Foucault's willingness to explore sexuality with little mention of gender seemed problematic. Yet his analysis of sexuality as a function of power resonated with both the personal experiences and theoretical positions of a growing number of feminists. Those who wanted to adapt his analysis of power, however, had to respond to critics who charged that he offered a totalizing account in which agency and resistance proved impossible.

By 1990 the basic lines of argument for and against feminists' use of Foucault had solidified. Critics repeated the charges that Foucault ignored gender, and he made resistance seem impossible because he called into question both the idea of individual identity as rational and autonomous, and the existence of universal moral standards. Proponents spent less time defending Foucault's work against such charges and more time developing their own accounts of how we deploy gender and sexuality. In the process, proponents advanced novel arguments about the character of gender, sexuality, and identity that would prove crucial to the elaboration of queer theory.

Historicizing Sexuality

When feminist scholars began to learn of Foucault's work, they already had ample reason to attend to historians who wrote about matters sexual. Smith-Rosenberg's "The Female World of Love and Ritual" had a huge impact among feminist scholars. Writing on female friendships, Smith-Rosenberg described the letters and diaries of respectable, middle-class white women of the nineteenth century. In those letters and diaries she found surprisingly unselfconscious expressions of the women's intense love for one another.[5] The unavoidable question became, Were these women lesbians? Smith-Rosenberg answered the question by dismissing it. She argued that lesbian identity, and concomitant speculation about possible genital contact that modern definitions of lesbian identity raised in historians' minds, had no relevance in the emotional and social realm of nineteenth-century women. She also noted that modern scholars' assumption of some probable connection between intense emotional involvement and sexual practice resulted more from post-Freudian psychological theories than from any historical evidence about these women's lives. For Smith-Rosenberg, because the friendships of nineteenth-century women constituted more a social than a psychosexual phenomenon, they were not likely to contain any sexual truth of the sort that twentieth-century historians would expect to find.[6] On the basis of her own empirical evidence and without having read *The History of Sexuality*, she came to a conclusion remarkably similar to Foucault's: At least among educated white women in the nineteenth century, "sexuality" had once not existed in the world.

The importance of female friendships became a leitmotif of early women's history, offering highly provocative questions about women's identity and lesbian identity. Smith-Rosenberg's article became essential reading for feminist scholars. Meanwhile Blanch Wiesen Cook, writing about intense friendships and support networks among well-known reformers and activists around the turn of the twentieth century, pointed to an opposite difficulty for post-Freudian scholars who would examine women's lives in the nineteenth and early twentieth centuries. Cook argued that prevailing psychological definitions of "lesbian," the psychological truth of lesbian identity, carried such a resounding freight of negative connotations that chivalrous historians had refused to see evidence of sexual contact among the women they wrote about. According to Cook, historians writing about such women as Jane Addams, Crystal Eastman, and Jeanette Marks apparently believed that they would diminish their subjects' reputations by describing them as lesbians, even if compelling evidence existed for their involvement in lesbian relationships.[7] For Cook, on the subject of lesbians, psychological truth impeded the search for historical truth. It made little sense to assume that close women friends always had sex. Cook pointed out, however, that genteel attempts to explain away all women's relationships as asexual, on the assumption that nice ladies whose accomplishments we respect must not have done that, offered no improvement.

The reason for such attitudes toward lesbians proved easy enough to find according to Lillian Faderman. She demonstrated that sexologists of the late nineteenth century had "morbidified" intense love relationships between women, attributing to those relationships a varying array of pathologies and had minimized the importance of the affection that women felt for one another.[8] Faderman's 1978 article "The Morbidification of Love between Women" appeared the same year as the English translation of *The History of Sexuality*. Thus, in treating of the historical specificity of sexuality, Foucault addressed a topic that had already sparked considerable interest among feminist scholars in the United States.

From the vantage point of 1980, feminist historians and literary critics typically read *The History of Sexuality* as a work of history, in isolation from Foucault's other work. Feminist scholars such as Smith-Rosenberg, Cook, and Faderman had already begun to write accounts of the history of sexuality that resembled Foucault's, however, and they linked questions of sexuality inextricably to questions of gender and of power. Consequently, they recognized quickly that Foucault had made claims about far more than the historicity of sexual identities. They began to look past the title of *The History of Sexuality*, and notice that much of the volume deals not with sex and sexuality but with the political history of late medieval and early modern Europe. They read among Foucault's other texts as well to see if these might prove useful in analyzing the functioning of gender hierarchies. Among their first tasks feminists identified the ways in which Foucault's analysis of power reflected his failure to appreciate women's consistently lesser access to power. Even so, some feminist theorists recognized that they could use Foucault's ideas to sharpen their critiques of Western epistemologies and schemes of representation just as feminist historians had used these ideas to improve their understanding of how social structures and institutions function.

The editors of *Signs* demonstrated the significance for feminists of debates about gender and sexuality by publishing two special issues on sex and sexuality in 1980. Introducing the first of their special issues, the editors entered the feminist sexuality debates by expressing the hope that debates among feminists about questions of sexuality would move beyond a simplistic polarization. For some women, one's status as a feminist depended on opposition to certain sexual practices, especially those involving pornography and sadomasochism or other types of role playing. These "anti-porn" feminists argued that all such sexual practices resulted from and perpetuated gender hierarchies that feminists, by definition, must resist. Sexual libertarian feminists responded that pornography and sadomasochism put to the use of women's pleasure, especially in lesbian relationships, subverted rather than perpetuating the gender hierarchies from which they sprang. The editors of *Signs* hoped to move the debate forward by insisting on the complexity of relationships between women's sexual practices and gender hierarchies in the surrounding culture. They wished to challenge the pole of "one, normative pattern" versus the pole of "an atomistic sexual expressiveness."[9]

The editors' hope proved misplaced, however. In 1982 a women's anti-porn group picketed and leafleted a conference of feminists at Barnard College to protest the alleged antifeminist opinions of the sexual libertarians among the conference's organizers and participants.[10] Feminists argued among themselves, with one group persuading Barnard College authorities to restrict circulation of their opponents' written and pictorial representations of sex. Members of each group described the others as antifeminist. Protesters denounced conference participants by name for allegedly antifeminist sexual practices.

At the Barnard College conference, sexual libertarian anthropologist Gayle Rubin delivered a paper entitled "Thinking Sex: Notes for a Radical Theory of the Politics of Sexuality."[11] Although not explicitly addressed to the controversy surrounding the conference, the paper dealt with many of the same issues of sexual politics. In this intellectual tour de force, Rubin compared modern conflicts over sexuality to conflicts over religion in previous periods. Although sexuality and politics remain always intertwined, the level of overt contest surrounding sexuality varies. Rubin offered her essay as an attempt to produce "elements of a descriptive and conceptual framework for thinking about sex and its politics."[12]

Rubin listed characteristics that any given sexual activity might display. In each case, she expressed the characteristic as a binarism in which one term (heterosexual, married, monogamous) carried social sanction while the other (homosexual, unmarried, promiscuous) bore opprobrium. She then pointed out the functional similarities between these sexual hierarchies and those based on race, ethnicity, and religion. An important similarity lay in the attribution of illness or other incompetence to individuals whose practices fell on the lower half of the binary. Such a representational move, the insistence that proscribed behavior reflected some incompetence in those who so behaved, justified their exclusion from a polity defined as the province of individuals with fully integrated personalities and an unfettered capacity for reason.[13]

While working on "Thinking Sex," Rubin did not realize the extent of Foucault's impact on the fundamental reconceptualization of sexuality that she also contributed substantially to. This reconceptualization offered a "more discursive model" of sexuality in contrast to the structuralist emphasis on binarisms.[14] In "Thinking Sex," Rubin had only begun this transition. She continued to refer to binarisms of sexual activity, but she grouped several binaries together within a larger social and political context. She cited *The History of Sexuality* as an example of "constructivist" accounts of sexuality similar to those of gay historians Jeffrey Weeks and Jonathan Ned Katz.[15] Although Rubin mentioned none of Foucault's earlier works, her account of the distinction between reason and incompetence in sexual matters resembles markedly Foucault's account of distinctions based on insanity in *Madness and Civilization*.[16]

This shift from a binary to a discursive model of sexuality might serve as an example of epistemic change. Two scholars, in some ways very different and working in different nations, responded in similar ways to similar political and intellectual changes. The similarities in Rubin's and Foucault's analyses of sexuality resulted from no transcendent perspective or historical telos drawing them toward a new truth. They resulted from the broad parallels in the historical backgrounds from which they worked on issues of sexuality.

Foucault wrote *The History of Sexuality* in the guise of the magisterially removed scholar who describes distant events. Rubin wrote "Thinking Sex" as a direct participant in current political battles over representations of sex. Her tone conveyed her sense of outrage and anxiety over the consequences of attributing enormous significance to sexual practices. But in many ways her conclusions closely resembled Foucault's. She "argued for theoretical as well as sexual pluralism" because she thought that, just as Marxism could not fully explain gender hierarchies, so feminism, whether Catharine MacKinnon's radical or any other variety, could not fully explain hierarchies of sexual practice and identity.[17] She agreed with Foucault's suspicion that no single theory or set of theories could explain all forms of oppression. Those at the Barnard College conference who hoped to censor the participants subsumed sexual issues entirely within feminism. They arrogated the capacity to determine unilaterally the impact of any sexual act on gender relationships and the right to judge anyone whose sexual activity they disapproved of. Rubin and other feminist sex radicals, such as Pat Califia, saw a separate realm of oppression based on sexual practice; that realm related in important ways to, but still differed significantly from, gender oppression. Insofar as activists who claimed a privileged analysis of gender oppression proved willing to oppress other women on the basis of differences in sexual practice, the activities of the anti-porn feminists seemed to confirm this assessment.

Two years after the Barnard College conference, Diamond and Quinby examined the feminist sexuality debates from a Foucaultian perspective. They found especially suspect the call from both sides of the debate for "control over one's body," with its component of control over sexuality. For Diamond and Quinby, the desire to control reflected a fantasy of scientific control over culture that no one could achieve and that would not serve feminists' interests if anyone could achieve it.[18] They cited *The History of Sexuality* and *Power/Knowledge*,[19] Colin Gordon's collection of Foucault's essays and interviews, in support of their contention that feminists must resist the impulse to seek the key to liberation from gender hierarchies in a "natural," unfettered sexuality and the consequent effort to define sexual practices as necessarily feminist or antifeminist.

By taking this position, Diamond and Quinby contributed to an emerging debate over the proper goals of feminist scholarship and activism. Some feminists defended an older model of equality with men according to the terms of garden-variety liberalism. Others had begun to suspect that arguments from natural or Constitutional rights and legal changes would not achieve feminist ends because the practices of gender hierarchies operated as a constitutive element of—thought silently thinking within—every gendered subject. In this view, gender oppression appeared to be a deeply engrained aspect of thought, or of the conceptual background that enabled thought, the episteme in Foucault's sense. Rights claims and legal changes might help, and probably would not hurt, but the changes necessary to extirpate gender oppression would involve a much more fundamental transformation of the culture.

For Diamond and Quinby, feminists must attend to the "technologies of sex" not only in the particular debate at hand but also in general. Because of historical necessity, feminists remain implicated in the processes through which we attach political significance to sexual practices.[20] From Diamond and Quinby's Foucaultian perspective, feminists on both sides of the sexuality debates mistook the issue. "Thus we see," they wrote, "that the specification of sexual diversity is part of the deployment of sexuality. To claim, therefore, that lesbianism—or any sexual identity—is in itself a challenge to prevailing power relations is to accept the terms of the enterprise one seeks to defeat."[21] The problem for feminists stemmed not from having a minority sexual identity or from participating in characteristically "masculinist" or "antifeminist" sexual practices. It stemmed from accepting the idea that sexual practice revealed the truth of identity and thus the key to women's liberation from gender hierarchies. In Diamond and Quinby's view, sexuality as the source of truth results from, and therefore necessarily remains implicated in, power relations. They wanted to change the terms of the debate altogether, so that feminists would investigate not whether the use of pornography or sadomasochism necessarily had antifeminist effects but how such practices came to achieve their enormous importance and particular significance in the first place.

But the remaining difference between Rubin's and Foucault's positions points to a major issue that feminists had to resolve before adopting Foucault's analysis. Foucault wanted to remove issues of sexual practice and identity from the realm of public administration. He called not only for the repeal of all legislation criminalizing specific sex acts but also for an end to the practice of organizing political movements around sexual identities and issues. Like most feminists, Rubin would agree broadly, although with significant exceptions, with Foucault's point about sex crimes. She wrote approvingly, however, of political movements organized on the basis of sexual minority status.

This difference raised problems for Diamond and Quinby's analysis. After mentioning both abortion and lesbian sexual practice as examples of how the emphasis on sexual issues can cloud the investigation of gender difference, they felt compelled to state their opposition to laws restricting either practice.[22] The attempt to resist the conjunction of sexuality with the truth of individual identity in the long run may have unwanted consequences in the short run insofar as institutional practices, especially in the form of statist repression, would not disappear instantly just because all feminists suddenly became Foucaultians. In the present political context, organizations based on minority sexual identities offered the only effective means for protesting laws that criminalize sex.

Feminist uses of Foucault thus pointed to the central dilemma of identity politics. We claim to distribute rights on the basis of our universal identity as humans. In practice, groups with minority identities suffer exclusion from this universality. Only by organizing on the basis of the minority identity that justifies their exclusion can individuals effectively protest that exclusion. The only options are to remain silent and suffer discrimination or to speak against discrimination, thereby tying oneself more firmly to the minority identity. Feminists increasingly realized that their situation constituted a logical impossibility: Work within existing political institutions served only to reinforce the assumptions of a culture that remained at best thoroughly gendered, at worst thoroughly masculinist; work directed at changing cultural assumptions might leave women open to the most drastic public policy fantasies of the antifeminist imagination. Foucault argued for the historical specificity of the ostensibly universal identity categories that ground our politics, but these categories retain their centrality to our political practice regardless. The practices of liberalism exceed their justifications. Queer theorists and activists would try to resolve this dilemma by critiquing the rules of the debate and by elaborating the possibility of political alliances and actions that did not depend on the antecedent specification of an identity common to all potential activists.

Discussing the intersection between feminists and Foucault in 1982, Biddy Martin offered a similar analysis of the quandary that identity politics creates.[23] People who live in a political culture that predicates rights and political legitimacy on one's status as an autonomous, responsible individual build oppositional political programs around the deconstruction of the subject only at their peril. As a theoretical critique, it may make sense to argue that the use of the identity categories "woman" or "lesbian" serves only to reinforce the very ideological and political structures that gave rise to sexism and lesbophobia in the first place. As a matter of daily resistances and practical strategies, this theoretical critique serves only to point out more clearly the terms on which everyone must negotiate power differentials: One who surrenders personal identity also surrenders all claims to resistance, even to meaningful existence within the political realm.

Critics commonly level against poststructuralist accounts of identity, including Foucault's, the charge of precluding the possibility for resistance. If authorities and institutions in a culture characterized by masculinist assumptions constitute subjects to perceive themselves as rational, autonomous individuals, then it turns out that the concepts of agency and resistance take part in, rather than subverting, those discourses and practices. Whence will change come in such a system? This observation posed an acute dilemma for feminists: Historically the identity category "woman" had manifestly failed to provide an adequate basis for uniting disparate individual women; however, the philosophical critique of identity that might offer a theoretical guidepost to the route out of the historical impasse seemed to suggest instead that all such efforts would come to naught.

British scholar Lois McNay rehearsed this argument in 1992. In her book *Foucault and Feminism*, she took the unusual tack of suggesting that, in the second and third volumes of his history of sexuality, Foucault returned to an "Enlightenment" conception of individuals as "self-determining agents."[24] In these works she found a reassertion of selfhood as the source of agency that serves as the basis for individual resistance to oppressive practices. McNay's argument relied on a simplistic conjunction of agency, resistance, and autonomy. She complained about Foucault's description of "docile bodies," claiming that he had betrayed his own theoretical point about the labile, indeterminate character of power with studies of institutions that appeared monolithic in their imposition of power. According to McNay, Foucault's description of female bodies as thoroughly imbued with sexuality made it impossible to understand how women could ever "act creatively and autonomously in other areas."[25]

Feminist philosopher Sandra Lee Bartky had already explored this question in an essay in Diamond and Quinby's *Feminism and Foucault*, published in 1988.[26] Bartky noted that Foucault wrote as if the practices and institutions of the deployment of sexuality had largely the same impact on male and female bodies. Focusing on standards of personal appearance, including issues of weight and body size, Bartky and another contributor to the volume, Susan Bordo, who concentrated more specifically on the problem of anorexia, demonstrated that women often act autonomously—they govern themselves according to the dictates of a disciplinary power that operates even below the institutional level. Women whose bodily dimensions violate the standards of our culture exemplify the operation of disciplinary power outside of schools, prisons, hospitals, or factories, even though specific instances of disciplinary power may well take place within the physical confines of such institutions. Thus, as Bartky stated, "women regarded as overweight ... report that they are regularly admonished to diet, sometimes by people they scarcely know."[27] The psychiatrist or prison warden who exercises disiplinary power over patient or inmate must have some training and command some specific body of knowledge in order to legitimize his or her normalizing practices. But anyone and everyone knows a fat woman when they see one, and anyone and everyone can and should take it upon her- or himself to help the fat woman by telling her what to do. The goal of such admonition is to instill in every fat woman the necessary self-discipline to lose weight, to make of her a proper moral subject, because in modern U.S. culture, we all know that deviation from prescribed norms for personal appearance results exclusively from failures of will and certainly not from any fundamental disparity between the ideal feminine form and the material realities of most women's bodies.

McNay objected to Foucault's characterization of subjects under the operation of disciplinary power as "docile bodies." But Bartky reviewed research on gender differences in bodily comportment—the way men and women walk, sit, and reach—to show that, in many ways, women in our culture really do have docile bodies, at least in comparison with men.[28] In this view, Foucault's account presented the problem not that he made disciplinary power seem too effective but that his failure to notice gender difference meant that he described disciplinary power as less effective than it really is. From the perspective of potential resistance, the disciplinary power that Foucault described had the virtue that it depended on relatively large, distinct institutions that one could readily identify. Gender discipline, by contrast, pervades the culture at the level of daily interactions among individuals in virtually every institution. But it does so without depending on the deployment of a set of discourses or practices that one could associate with a single type of institution. It also naturalizes itself as a set of claims about biological, rather than cultural, differences, such that many who suffer from it consider their suffering perfectly legitimate. How does one resist? Bartky posed acutely the problem for McNay's version of "autonomy" and "self-determination" as unproblematic concepts for feminists: "On the one hand, no one is marched off for electrolysis at gunpoint, nor can we fail to appreciate the initiative and ingenuity displayed by countless women in an attempt to master the rituals of beauty. Nevertheless, insofar as the disciplinary practices of femininity produce a 'subjected and practiced,' an inferiorized, body, they must be understood as aspects of a far larger discipline, an oppressive and inegalitarian system of sexual subordination."[29]

Bartky's feminist revision of Foucault's account of disciplinary power led her to the more difficult question "Why aren't all women feminists?"[30] McNay's insistence on autonomy as the basis for female identity suggested that all women should resist any attempt at gender-based oppression—all women should be feminists. Bartky offered a brilliant analysis according to which standards of feminine beauty constitute a specifically patriarchal version of Jeremy Bentham's Panopticon, a device for inculcating self-discipline and moral subjectivity in inmates that Foucault examined in *Discipline and Punish*.[31] In Bartky's view, the common rituals of feminine beauty, such as repeatedly examining one's makeup or agonizing over every morsel of food for fear of getting fat, constitute self-policing according to the dictates of patriarchy.[32] She put Foucault's central point to feminist uses: The most insidious forms of discipline do not rely on physical exclusion or isolation. Rather, the most insidious forms of discipline serve to convince women, or anyone else, of their own "autonomy" as the very device for distracting their attention from the rules with which they will govern themselves or for convincing them that they chose those rules and the concomitant discipline.

McNay and Bartky contributed to a feminist debate that continued throughout most of the 1980s and into the early 1990s. Martin also addressed concepts related to autonomy in her reading of Foucault. Foucault would insist on the historical, not necessary, character of the emphasis on unitary, rational identity as the basis for knowledge, and he would insist on the consequent emphasis on definitional certainty and identity as the only possible ground for knowledge. As Martin pointed out, feminist scholars made the case that this epistemological edifice of certainty and identity rested on the exclusion of women; canons of representation and rationality, like practices of domination, depend on gen-

dered practices and assumptions.[33] The insistence on retaining a traditional conception of identity—whether "rational," "autonomous," or
both—as the only possible basis for the demand that masculinist politics take serious account of women's needs only reinscribed the very system that defined women as necessarily unnecessary in the first place.

Martin's piece, first published in 1982, became the first essay in Diamond and Quinby's 1988 *Feminism and Foucault: Reflections on Resistance*.
In introducing the collection, Diamond and Quinby echoed Martin's
point in their list of "striking" convergences between many feminist theorists and Foucault:

> Both identify the body as the site of power, that is, as the locus of domina-
> tion through which docility is accomplished and subjectivity constituted.
> Both point to the local and intimate operations of power rather than focus-
> ing exclusively on the supreme power of the state. Both bring to the fore the
> crucial role of discourse in its capacity to produce and sustain hegemonic
> power and emphasize the challenges contained within marginalized and/or
> unrecognized discourses. And both criticize the ways in which Western
> humanism has privileged the experience of the Western masculine elite as it
> proclaims universals about truth, freedom, and human nature.[34]

The contributors to Diamond and Quinby's collection had found numerous important feminist projects that Foucault's work could contribute to.
In their essays in the volume, Bartky, Bordo, and other feminist scholars explored major problems for women in light of Foucault's ideas.

Not without some important modifications of these ideas, however.
Writing in *Signs* in 1988, Linda Alcoff modified poststructuralist
thought to arrive at what she called "a concept of positionality." She
began by noting the difficulties that the identity category "woman"
poses: "For many contemporary feminist theorists, the concept of
woman is a problem. It is a problem of primary significance because the
concept woman is the central concept for feminist theory and yet it is
a concept that is impossible to formulate precisely for feminists."[35] She
pointed up the dilemma with the specific example of child care, borrowed from Denise Riley. Feminists see the question of adequate child
care as a political issue that primarily affects women in our society. To
demand adequate child care in the political realm on behalf of women,
however, risks reinforcing the presumption that women are somehow
"naturally" responsible for the care of children because of some biologically determined element of female identity. But to refuse to make
such a demand in the political realm means to accede to the definition

of child care as a "private," and therefore properly "feminine," issue. Here is the dilemma of identity politics again: As a question of logic and as a question of public policy, the terms of the debate operated such that women lost either way.

Damned if you do, damned if you don't.

In Alcoff's view, feminists could not resolve this dilemma simply by adopting a poststructuralist account of identity, whether Foucaultian, Derridean, or other. These accounts position women as the undefinable, always avoiding domination by refusing positive assertion in favor of repeated negation. Critics of poststructuralists feared precisely this eventuality. But rather than reject poststructuralist analyses outright, Alcoff described a position that built on them, using Lauretis's account of identity in terms of practices. Rather than accept gender as a given, Alcoff examined the systems of representation and social practice through which we produce gendered subjectivity. This approach had the advantage of demonstrating the specific ways in which naturalized accounts of gender identity conceal the political contest involved in associating certain social roles with certain anatomical configurations.[36]

Women may be singularly concerned with child care in our society, but not because of any "natural" aspect of their identity. Rather, our society's organization of family and work results from myriad decisions and compromises, some motivated by expediency, some by ideology. That organization and its mutually constitutive practices in turn have a substantial impact on women's identities, but practices and identities do not display complete congruence, and both remain susceptible to change. Feminist political involvement became the deliberate effort to change the definitions of what constitutes appropriate practices for women or, more radically, to eliminate the distinction woman/man from among those that serve to distinguish appropriate practices for types of individuals.

Amoral Foucault?

This program bore greater resemblance to Foucault's genealogical practice than Alcoff recognized. For feminist scholars, much of Foucault's appeal stemmed from their recognition that they could translate his approach to sexuality into an analysis of gender. Rather than focus on the substance of gender roles and meanings, they would examine the processes of producing gendered meaning and attaching it to individuals. But even for those feminists who could resolve concerns about Foucault's idea of subjectivity, other issues remained. Some complained that, while the shift from identity to subjectivity might allow for greater appreciation of the processes for producing and enforcing gender hierarchies, still Foucault's criticism of universals would leave feminists with no moral standards with which to justify their resistance to those hierarchies. Feminist demands for equal opportunity and treatment, on this view, depended on universal standards of right and wrong.

McNay lodged this complaint against her "anti-Enlightenment" Foucault, but Nancy Fraser's version probably became better known in the United States. Fraser argued that Foucault's refusal to elaborate generalized normative standards constituted a significant limitation in his work because it precluded him from distinguishing between legitimate and illegitimate exercises of power.[37] Foucault objected to the use of universal norms as the basis of political struggle because he believed that those who wield such norms would substitute the certainty of universal knowledge for careful attention to the needs of the oppressed. He failed to practice what he preached on this point, but Fraser criticized the entire concept, not merely Foucault's use of it. Reading *Discipline and Punish*, Fraser insisted that in "the real world" the prisons that Foucault seemed to condemn were preferable to unreformed prisons outside the "humanist" West.[38]

For Foucault, however, such philosophical assertions as Fraser's failed to account for the specificity of the prisoners' experiences. His references to prison riots in the early 1970s raised the question that Fraser could not answer: Why would prisoners in humane prisons revolt? (Why aren't all women feminists?) The answer is that the psychiatrists and teachers, the very apparatus of the humanism that Fraser lauded, served as the mechanism for exercising disciplinary power. Further, the prisoners themselves, with whom Foucault worked extensively through the Group d'Information sur les Prisons, could scarcely assess their situations in humanized French prisons by comparing them to Soviet gulags or Salvadoran torture cells.[39] No matter how bad the prisons were thousands of miles away, French prisoners remained subject to the discipline of French prisons. The universal moral standards of humane, dispassionate liberalism allowed Fraser to overlook Foucault's most basic point about resistance: One who would determine the legitimacy of a given exercise of disciplinary power should ask those who are subject to it.

Foucault's statements on rape indicated at once his own failure to abide by this dictum and the gender blindness that motivated that failure. While discussing the issue of repression in 1977, Foucault had argued that rape should be punished, not as a sexual crime, but solely as an assault. Because the deployment of sexuality constitutes a primary means of repression in our society, Foucault reasoned, removing as many activities as possible from examination as manifestations of sexuality would serve to reduce the aggregate amount of repression in the world and deprive those who normalize sexuality of one avenue for control over individuals. In this view, rape would become analogous, for legal purposes, to punching someone in the face, an analogy that Foucault himself used.[40]

Monique Plaza, a French feminist, castigated Foucault for taking this position. For Plaza, Foucault's suggestion that we emphasize the aggressive element of rape to the exclusion of the sexual element overlooked the ways in which women suffer a disparate impact under the deployment of sexuality. As Foucault himself pointed out in *The History of Sexuality*, one definition of sex characterized it as constituting women's bodies entirely. Not every rape is merely an assault, but every assault of a woman is a rape—men's choices to attack women typically depend on disparities of power that operate according to the discourses of gender and sexuality. "We have shouted, written, debated, organized against rape," Plaza wrote. "We have appealed to the courts against rapists. All this is proof that for us rape is not an assault like any other, that being punched in the face is not the same thing as being raped."[41]

By advocating punishment of rape solely as an assault, Foucault failed to live up to his own suspicions about totalizing theory. He assumed that "sexuality" provided the only rubric under which one need analyze rape as social practice. Plaza's response suggested that the conjunction of gender and sexuality may provide important reasons for reconsidering an analysis based exclusively on the truths of sexuality. But Foucault's own genealogical claims on behalf of subjugated knowledges should have led him to conclude that intellectuals' theoretical pronouncements on punishments for rapists will most likely fail to account for the subjectivities of people who have actually suffered rape. In terms of Bartky's analysis, rape serves as perhaps the most local and intimate exercise of disciplinary power. Foucault's ostensibly gender-neutral survey of disciplinary power and the deployment of sexuality focused on institutions and broadly sanctioned practices. A gender-specific survey of disciplinary power must account for rape as a practice that, while technically lacking official sanction, still functions quite effectively to discipline women by constraining their choices. Rather than engage in theoretical elaboration on the meanings of sexuality, Foucault should have returned to the procedure that he followed in writing about prisons: Ask those individuals whose subjectivity has been constituted by the specific experience. Here Foucault backhandedly demonstrated the centrality of gender by failing to take it into account. Plaza repeated the basic feminist point insistently: Men typically fail to take women's views seriously.

Diamond and Quinby addressed the debate about the legal status of rape in their advocacy of Foucaultian analyses for feminist theorists. By including Winifred Woodhull's essay on the subject in *Feminism and Foucault*, they contributed a new twist to the debate.[42] Woodhull pointed out that feminists in the United States had recently landed on the same side of the question as Foucault. They advocated an analysis of rape as a crime of power rather than sex (although Foucault repeated without comment the suggestion of a French magistrate that rape be decriminalized, a position that no feminist, to my knowledge, has taken or will likely take).[43] U.S. feminists argued that, insofar as some would minimize rape as the conjunction of natural male aggression and irresistible sex drive, we should dissociate the crime from sex to prevent such appeals.

At this point where feminists and Foucault arrived independently at the same conclusion, however, a feminist pointed out how a Foucaultian analysis would suggest just the opposite conclusion. As Woodhull noted, the attempt to separate out the sex from rape, leaving only the violence, assumes that sex exists independently of power; Foucault argued against precisely this sort of naturalization of sex. But fealty to a supposed Foucaultian line, assuming one could give it specific content, interested Woodhull less than the practical consequences of this naturalizing move. She quoted Susan Brownmiller's feminist classic, *Against Our Will: Men, Women, and Rape*, where Brownmiller effectively argued that rape constitutes a nearly inescapable result of physiology, or "man's structural capacity to rape and woman's corresponding structural vulnerability."[44] This position seemed doubly dubious to Woodhull. She argued that Brownmiller implicitly accepted the proposition that bodies dictate sex, which in turn dictates identity. This removal of rape and all sexual matters from the realm of cultural contest struck Woodhull as singularly disempowering for women. Brownmiller had just the opposite goal, of course.[45] Woodhull's analysis came from the same impulse as Diamond and Quinby's—the desire to break the link from nature to sex to identity in favor of a political stance from which women can insist that rape, like all sexual issues, operates as a function of culture rather than biology.

This move still left considerable leeway for determining the significance of culture, as Foucault's Lapcourt example indicated. In this instance, Foucault took a position not so patently obtuse but nearly as controversial as his position on rape. Describing the deployment of sexuality in *The History of Sexuality*, Foucault related the 1867 tale of a simpleminded casual laborer in the village of Lapcourt. The parents of a girl from whom he had obtained sexual favors had him arrested, with the result that he spent the rest of his days in a hospital and became the subject of expert study. "What is the significant thing about this story?" Foucault asked. "The pettiness of it all; the fact that this everyday occurrence in the life of village sexuality, these inconsequential bucolic pleasures, could become ... the object not only of a collective intolerance but of a judicial action, a medical intervention, a careful clinical examination, and an entire theoretical elaboration."[46]

Writing in the edited volume *Up against Foucault: Explorations of Some Tensions between Foucault and Feminism*, Kate Soper castigated Foucault for his interpretation of this incident. Soper pointed out that the episode may have had a far greater impact on the girl than Foucault acknowledged. Here Foucault and most feminist theorists likely diverged, given the energy that many feminists have devoted to naming and combating men's sexual domination of women and children. Soper also noted that many antifeminists make remarks about feminists similar to Foucault's remarks about the official response to the Lapcourt incident, dismissing feminists' every concern about gender hierarchies as the petty ravings of (probably unattractive) women.[47]

Soper recognized merit in Foucault's work despite his treatment of the Lapcourt incident. But her "intemperate, even mildly hysterical" response, perhaps justifiable in its own terms, precluded a more careful consideration of the incident's significance for questions about how to understand the meanings and practices surrounding sexuality.[48] Even rereading the report on the laborer from which Foucault took his account might not settle the question of the effects that the episode had on the girl. Foucault's focus on the response of the various authorities apparently precluded any consideration of the girl's response. Most feminists would probably accord the authorities and the girl at least equal attention. But for practical purposes, her feelings remain unavailable to us.

Soper's moment of transhistorical feminist outrage on the girl's behalf prevented consideration of the effects that official intervention would have had. Foucault speculated that "during this same period the Lapcourt schoolmaster was instructing the little villagers to mind their language and not talk about all these things aloud."[49] Further, although removal of the laborer from the village prevented him from assaulting or playing with—depending on one's perspective—other girls, the official practice of focusing attention on the village idiot as the source of sexual deviance also may have diverted attention from even more traumatizing situations in which male family members abused children. Adult efforts to channel children's understandings of their sexuality did not necessarily improve the situation. Indeed, insofar as one accepts Foucault's contention that the significance of sexuality stems from cultural practice, one can moot the possibility that at least some of the deleterious effects on children of adult sexual abuse result from the response, or lack of it, from other adults.

This sort of difficulty in some sense inhered in Foucault's analysis. With his genealogical attacks on dubious universals, he occasionally hit an assumption that feminists relied on. By insisting in *The History of Sexuality* that no single locus of power exists, whether in the bourgeoisie or the patriarchy, he improved on the more reductive versions of Marxism and feminism. He also suggested, at least obliquely, that relationships of power can operate through age and class distinctions as well as through distinctions of gender or sexual practice. Here his analysis again parallels Rubin's. Rubin argued that much oppression of sexual minorities occurs under the aegis of "protecting children."[50] Foucault suggested that resisting the deployment of sexuality would entail rethinking our approach to children's sexuality.

As Diamond and Quinby argued, however, the failure to find a monolithic patriarchy did not necessarily prove that individuals of either gender could equally avail themselves of power. Foucault effectively denaturalized sexuality by historicizing it. He failed, however, to extend his denaturalizing move to include gender. According to Diamond and Quinby, the naturalization of gender proceeds through the representation of gender hierarchies in terms of binaries.[51] From Foucault's position, the contrived character of sexuality seemed obvious, the contrived character of gender less so.

Peggy Kamuf showed how deeply embedded gendered assumptions and habits can become in her contribution to Diamond and Quinby's volume. Paralleling Woodhull's strategy of rereading a feminist classic, Kamuf compared Virginia Woolf's *A Room of One's Own* to *The Will to Knowledge* (the English translation of the title *La Volonte de savoir*, the French title of *The History of Sexuality*) as a way of considering how Foucault's rhetorical strategies revealed masculine assumptions about writing and knowledge. A series of interruptions that occurred when Woolf allowed her abstract thoughts to divert her attention from the quotidian practice of being a woman became crucial to Woolf's rhetorical strategy. During Woolf's intellectual ramblings at Oxbridge, avatars of masculine privilege repeatedly reminded her that, in reflecting on her condition, she trod both literally and metaphorically on properly masculine turf.[52]

Foucault allowed certain detours during his argument in *The History of Sexuality*. But these detours served only to anticipate and dispose of objections that he considered specious. They remained purely intellectual, never physical: Foucault need never have worried that, on the many occasions when his intellectual ramblings led him to a famous library, the guardians of that library would refuse him entrance. Even in his intellectual style, then, Foucault proceeded in a characteristically masculine manner. Whereas Woolf could not conduct her research, could not even walk across the grass, without having some man deter her, deny her access to knowledge, for Foucault access to knowledge and the ability to pursue an argument in as straight (or bent) a line as he saw fit came as a matter of course. In this view, the practices of gender and the practices of knowledge look not merely congruent or parallel but exactly the same.

The contrast among Woolf's experiences with physical restraints on her intellectual mobility, and Bartky's self-policing women, and Foucault's unselfconscious intellectual mobility, including his ignorance of gender, demonstrated the difficulty with McNay's, or any other, concept of autonomy. Individual women may never have heard anyone say that they must attend compulsively to minute details of their physical appearance. Many women—not all—routinely internalize that message simply from its constant repetition through images of female beauty in the surrounding culture. Foucault's argument carried the implication that we learn the habits of gender and sexuality, we become gendered and sexed subjects, long before we develop any capacity for critical reflection on or resistance to those habits. Resistance often proves a much more complicated matter than simply reflecting rationally on, and choosing to fight against, oppression. Foucault also insisted that the use of force, of physical coercion, signals a failure of power: Relationships of power operate most smoothly and effectively precisely when the subjects enforce rules on themselves, when they become autonomous, or "self-governing."[53]

Feminists could have developed such accounts of the specific effects of gendered power relationships without relying on Foucault's description of disciplinary power. Foucault's description offered an enormously useful heuristic device for discerning those effects, however. McNay's assertion of the political necessity of female "autonomy" against Foucault's account of disciplinary power simply reinstalled generalizations that inhibited rather than enabled resistance. As Bartky's example demonstrated, self-governing women may remain resolutely antifeminist, depending on whose rules they use to govern themselves.

Joan Wallach Scott codified the poststructuralist position in this debate in her 1991 article "'Experience.'"[54] Scott suggested that "historians of difference," those writing about women, lesbians and gay men, African Americans, or any other minority group, produce enormously useful yet limited accounts of overlooked lives from the past. The limitation lies in accepting the "experience" of the individuals involved as a foundation of evidence on which to justify telling the stories of those individuals. To accept individuals' experience as foundational entails foregoing the opportunity to examine the practices and meanings that constituted the experience. Scott argued that "the project of making experience visible precludes critical examination of the workings of the ideological system itself, its categories of representation (homosexual/heterosexual, man/woman, black/white as fixed immutable identities), its premises about what these categories mean and how they operate, its notions of subjects, origin, and cause."[55]

Scott recommended that historians who would avoid accepting "experience" as foundational should "read for the literary." Historians should attend more closely to language, reading sources not as simply referential but as constitutive as well. Scott's suggestion had implications both for how one reads Foucault and for how one practices historical inquiry. Near the end of her essay, she quoted a long passage about the practice of interpretation from Foucault's essay "Nietzsche, Genealogy, History." It bears repeating if only for its indication of how Scott viewed the processes by which we elaborate the meanings of gender and sexuality.

If interpretation were the slow exposure of the meaning hidden in an origin, then only metaphysics could interpret the development of humanity. But if interpretation is the violent or surreptitious appropriation of a system of rules, which in itself has no essential meaning, in order to impose a direction, to bend it to a new will, to force its participation in a different game, and to subject it to secondary rules, then the development of humanity is a series of interpretations. The role of genealogy is to record its history; the history of morals, ideals, and metaphysical concepts, the history of the concept of liberty or of the ascetic life; as they stand for the emergence of different interpretations, they must be made to appear as events on the stage of historical process.[56]

The history of individual identity as revealed in the truth of sexuality stood, for Foucault, in synecdochic relationship to the histories of nations and cultures. Continuous history and the stable identity of the scholar reinforce one another in the historical telos of modernism. In Scott's account, pointing out the exclusions that scholars performed in order to maintain historical continuity and stable identity had proven otiose as a political project, the significant intellectual interest of the resulting stories notwithstanding. The central task had to become not solely one of describing that exclusions of gender, sexuality, race, or class had occurred but of examining *how* those exclusions occurred.

As Scott noted, encouraging historians to "read for the literary," to attend to the process of creating and eliminating meaning within texts as well as to the referents beyond texts, cut against the grain. Historians often put great store in defining their discipline against literary criticism.[57] Scott's argument suggested that, for historians who would understand not only the facts of gender and sexuality but also the processes of gender and sexuality, this distinction between history and literature would become less firm.

The intersection of feminist scholarship with Foucault's work more generally confirmed this expectation about the declining importance of disciplinary distinctions. This resulted partly from the administrative and political choices that contributed to the creation of women's studies programs: The topic guided the inquiry, with input from all disciplines welcome, at least in theory. But it was equally a result of the philosophical critique from both sides. Feminists read Foucault's assertion about the episteme of "man" quite literally. From both feminist and Foucaultian perspectives, the division of intellectual effort into history, literature, politics, philosophy, and so forth seemed like the choices of a (European, "heterosexual") man—an ethnologist or psychoanalyst—

who takes his own identity as a scholar for granted, using that scholarly identity as the basis from which to pursue dispassionately truthful accounts of the world. Scholars who began with some minority identity, or some combination of minority identities, did not enjoy the luxury of taking their identity, as either politically or intellectually competent individuals, for granted. Thus, they commonly pursued studies linked to their minority identities across disciplinary lines—for example, African American studies, women's studies, lesbian/gay studies. As Scott described in the case of women's history, and as feminist uses of Foucault's work confirmed, this revision of knowledge began with the addition of women, or a minority, to the existing, purportedly universal, categories of inquiry. Scholars increasingly found, however, that these categories were in fact best suited to the needs of the people who created them and that women and minorities would have to revise the organization of knowledge on which these categories rested.

4

Shrinking History

Queer Theory, Psychoanalysis, and Genealogy

ueer Nation appeared on the cover of the lamentably short-lived lesbian/gay quarterly *OutLook* in the Winter 1991 issue. Introducing three articles on the topic, Allan Berube and Jeffrey Escoffier emphasized that Queer Nation strove to embrace paradoxes in its political activism, that its activism took new forms, and that it revolved around issues of identity: "Queer Nationals are torn between affirming a new identity—'I am queer'—and rejecting restrictive identities—'I reject your categories,' between rejecting assimilation—'I don't need your approval, just get out of my face'—and wanting to be recognized by mainstream society—'We queers are gonna get in your face.' Queer nationalism's actions play on the politics of cultural subversion: theatrical demonstrations, infiltrations of shopping malls and straight bars, kiss-ins and be-ins."[1]

Like *OutLook*, Queer Nation did not last very long. In retrospect, it seems clear that there was a significant outburst of lesbian/gay political/cultural activity during the late 1980s and early 1990s—coincident with George Bush's administration?—beginning with ACT-UP (the AIDS Coalition to Unleash Power), whose members engaged in civil disobedience and other militant forms of protest to demand increased response to HIV/AIDS, and ending with—who knows? Don't ask, don't tell? Out of this mini–gay renais-

106

sance emerged queer theory. Film theorist Teresa de Lauretis, introducing the 1991 special issue of *differences: A Journal of Feminist Cultural Studies*, entitled "Queer Theory, Lesbian and Gay Sexualities," in 1991 described lesbian/gay culture in North America in terms that mirrored Berube and Escoffier's description of Queer Nation: "Gay sexuality in its specific female and male cultural (or subcultural) forms acts as an agency of social process whose mode of functioning is both interactive and yet resistant, both participatory and yet distinct, claiming at once equality and difference, demanding political representation while insisting on its material and historical specificity."[2]

This is not to suggest a direct connection or isomorphism between Queer Nation and queer theory. There was probably a goodly overlap in the personnel—in his brief history of Queer Nation for *OutLook*, Alexander Chee offered as his examples of queer political organizations outside of New York and San Francisco the groups at Wesleyan University in Connecticut and the University of Texas at Austin. Even the political manifestations of queerness tended to have an academic tone. Queer Nation seemed perpetually self-conscious about the common desire among participants to be as inclusive as possible—along the known lines of sexuality, gender, race, and class, but along any others that anyone cared to point to as well—and their frequent recognition that the movment was still, for the most part, one of white, middle-class, gay men—the same sorts of people (sexuality excepted) who still produce most of the theory in the United States.[3]

Herein perhaps lies the key difference between the Nation and the theory. Whatever the dominance of white, middle-class, gay men in Queer Nation, the three persons who set much of the intellectual agenda for queer theory were women, two of them lesbians. Teresa de Lauretis, Judith Butler, and Eve Sedgwick laid much of the conceptual groundwork for the emerging field in the early 1990s. Along with other queer theorists, these three scholars outlined a political hermeneutics. The key term is representation, in both senses, of course. How does the representability of gender and sexuality in the larger culture influence the political representations of women and sexual minorities? How do those representations influence the ability of different constituents—under the rubrics of "women," "homosexuals," "lesbians and gay men," "bisexuals," "transgenders," and so on—to work effectively together for common political ends, assuming that they have common political ends? How do those representations and related practices inform the subjectivities of women and minorities and constitute the array of viable political options such that those persons often find it difficult to avoid participating in, much less resist, patterns of domination? While some critics insist that queer theory is apolitical word-smithery, the film theorist, philosopher, and literary critic take seriously the role that signs and symbols play in shaping the meanings and possibilities of our culture at the most basic level, including politics conventionally defined.

Publishing in 1990, Sedgwick took Foucault's analysis of sexuality in *The History of Sexuality*[4] as "axiomatic" in order to argue that "sexuality," whatever the term refers to, depends for its significance on, and has its effects in the realm of, culture rather than nature. She directed her literary critical enterprise both extensively and intensively toward the proposition that the designation "homosexual" constitutes far less a medical category than it does the organizing principle for gender solidarity among men in our society. This led her to consider the relationship between gender and sexuality as categories for signification and as practices. Neither reduces to the other, yet, as Sedgwick argued, they often operate in conjunction. Both have political implications, but figuring out what those implications are and how they come to pass can be surprisingly difficult.

Like Sedgwick, Judith Butler and Teresa de Lauretis raised questions about the relationship between gender and sexuality in their elaborations of queer theory. Two issues present themselves: first, the substantive question of how gender and sexuality operate, alone and in conjunction, in the lives of persons and in the larger culture; second, the procedural question of how one might articulate queer theory as a mode of inquiry that deals primarily with issues of sexuality while recognizing the important role that feminist theory and gender issues played in creating the conditions of possibility for queer theory. Butler and Lauretis also dealt with a recurring question that the intellectual and cultural history of Europe and the United States pose for many queer theorists: What role should psychoanalytic theory play in queer theory or in genealogy more generally? Does psychoanalysis describe universal, or at least common, features of personhood, especially with respect to gender and sexuality, such that, however extensively modified, some version of psychoanalytic theory remains necessary even in the face of genealogical suspicion about existing explanatory categories and narratives?

Judith Butler: Genealogy versus Psychoanalysis

Butler approached these issues brilliantly with her deconstructions of male/female and homo/hetero. Her work illuminated not only the issues of sex, gender, bodies, and signification in their various interimplications and overdeterminations but also the tensions between genealogy and psychoanalysis. Butler described her first book on sex and gender, *Gender Trouble: Feminism and the Subversion of Identity*, as a Foucaultian and *"feminist genealogy* of the category of women."[5] Addressing a common topic for feminist scholars, she doubted the necessity of arriving at a generalized account of the identity category "woman" as the basis for effective feminist politics. She argued that, in our culture's hegemonic account, gender roles simply reflect in culture the biological given of anatomical sex. According to this heterosexual scheme of representation, bodies with one anatomical configuration desire bodies with the "opposite" anatomical configuration; social and linguistic implications follow from this ostensibly irreducible "fact."

Butler as genealogist refused to accept this account of the origins of gender roles. Instead, she reversed the perspective to examine how culture informs our understanding of biology. On Butler's view, the assumptions about gender and sexuality in the positive unconscious of the culture determine our conception of biological sex as the origin of gender identity. She examined the works of various authors who offer explanations of anatomical sex as the origin of gender, including French feminists Julia Kristeva and Monique Wittig, as well as Sigmund Freud and Jacques Lacan, who offers a poststructuralist version of psychoanalytic theory. She extended this argument to include scientific research into the physiological determinants of sexed anatomy as the basis for gender identity. The sciences of biology and anatomy, while purporting to describe the self-evident, irreducible ground of sex difference, betray the signs of their constitution in language and the consequent indeterminacy of their meanings.[6]

Butler wrote to address the debate that raged among feminist theorists over the ostensible necessity of a precultural ground for identity. Some feminists worried that if they must understand themselves as subjects whom culture had constituted, then they musy also lose any claim to agency and therefore to the capacity to battle gender hierarchies. In order for feminists to act politically on behalf of women, according to this argument, they must have some concrete understanding of who women are, and women must all have some biological or anatomical similarities. Butler replied that this argument depends on a mistaken conception of identity. Feminism involves "the subversion of identity," as her subtitle indicates, because a precultural identity as the basis for agency depends on assumptions that exclude women. Individuals have no identity apart from the categories available in the culture. These categories simultaneously constrain and enable subjectivity. In order to speak as a coherent subject, one must understand and represent oneself as gendered. Yet because anatomically sexed bodies do not provide a permanent foundation for gender, this process of self-understanding and self-representation must recur constantly. Butler argued that "the effect of gender is produced through the stylization of the body and, hence, must be understood as the mundane way in which bodily gestures, movements, and styles of various kinds constitute the illusion of an abiding gendered self."[7] Subjects convey gendered meanings, signify gender, at every moment.

In Butler's account, possibilities for resistance reside in this necessity for repeating the styles of gender. Butler argued that feminists lose the possibility for thinking about subversive ways to convey gendered meanings when they insist that gendered identities depend on sexed bodies as the loci of agency. No origin of gendered identity exists. Rather, daily practices of socialization result in the body's signification of gender. Effective attacks on gender hierarchies would stem, on Butler's view, not from organizing around a foundation of anatomical sex, but from proliferating into incoherence the meanings of gender by repeating the culture's existing signs of gender in subversive ways. Butler thus rejected the notion of a constitutive subject who would refuse gender identity in favor of some more egalitarian option. Instead, she posited subjects who necessarily operate through gendered signs. The subjects who repeat the signs have the capacity to alter their meaning through that repetition.

Subjectivity, on Butler's view, results from the intersection of bodies with history. The meanings of gender change over time, because no repetition of the signs that convey gender meanings can remain identical to a previous repetition. According to current hegemonic accounts of gender identity, the anatomically sexed body provides the original source of gender meaning. Butler insisted that the specification of the body as such an original source actually resulted from the historically specific meanings of gender in our culture—the positive unconscious of gender. She explicitly borrowed from Foucault in developing this argument, but she pointed out an ambiguity in Foucault's references to "the body" as the site for the inscription of cultural meaning. He claimed to eschew any reference to the body as a source of precultural identity or drives that the agents of culture only manipulate and repress. Thus, wardens produce souls in the bodies of prisoners through disciplinary practices, and psychiatrists produce sexuality through the minute examinations of sexual thoughts in confessions.

But in Foucault's discussion of the nineteenth-century French hermaphrodite Herculine Barbin, Butler claimed to find reliance on a precultural body.[8] For Butler, Foucault's definition of genealogy depended on the assumption of a precultural body. Consequently, that assumption escaped the radical historicization that he intended to pursue with his genealogical approach. According to Butler, "By maintaining a body prior to its cultural inscription, Foucault appears to assume a materiality prior to signification and form." She saw this as a significant limit on the utility of Foucault's genealogical approach for feminists bent on changing or eliminating the meanings of gender through subversive repetition. Citing anthropologist Mary Douglas, Butler argued that the specifications of the body's contours, and limitations on what objects may or may not enter the body, constitute a primary mechanism for elaborating a culture's rules.[9]

The next step for Butler's feminist subversion of identity, then, involved examining how our culture constitutes "the body" as a discrete object. One motive for her next book, *Bodies That Matter: On the Discursive Limits of "Sex,"*[10] arose from her perception of a limitation in the available conceptual tools for subverting identity. In *Gender Trouble*, she cited French feminist Julia Kristeva's notion of abjection as a beginning point for her genealogy of the body. "Abjection" describes the process by which one expels anything from oneself. That which is expelled then becomes completely different from oneself—an excretory function. This excretory function, on Butler's view, describes identity formation and the specification of bodily limits as intimately related processes: "In effect, [abjection] is the mode by which Others become shit."[11] Butler incorporated this concept of abjection into her psychoanalytic account of identity formation in *Bodies That Matter*.

Another of Butler's motives for writing *Bodies That Matter* arose from the doubts of many other feminists about *Gender Trouble*. In response to Butler's account of gender as the repetition of signs, other feminists repeatedly asked, "What about the materiality of the body?"[12] She replied to this objection by pointing out that, although the concept "materiality" may refer to nonlinguistic matter, one who invokes the concept does not thereby achieve some direct access to that nonlinguistic matter. "The materiality of the body" does not, as some feminists argued against Butler, offer refuge from the catastrophic consequences of an alleged linguistic monism or determinism. Instead of relying on references to nonlinguistic matter, Butler insisted on the recognition that, because we can attribute and discuss attributes only through language, the attribution of qualities to that matter has effect only through language. "The materiality of the body" may have some extralinguistic status, but, given the realization that no one can speak about that status except through words, the point becomes moot. Because words do not simply refer to objects or matter but also constitute them as such in the process of naming, the effort to separate out a material body from language becomes futile.[13] Hence the pun in the title *Bodies That Matter:* The materiality of bodies offers no secure basis from which to launch feminist politics, because the determination of what has substance, what consists of solid stuff, on one hand, and the determination of what is important, that which persons must take into account, on the other, are always already intertwined. It is worth noting the difficulty of explicating the pun: In playing on the relationship between the category of physical mass with extension and weight and the category of intellectually and ethically important concepts, our language offers few resources for defining one category without using terms that routinely serve metaphorically to describe the other.

The pun on "matter" reveals Butler's project of trying to understand the process by which we came to understand "the body" as referring to some extralinguistic matter in the first place. Without arguing that bodies consist exclusively of language, as some less-perceptive critics have charged, Butler and other queer theorists simply point out that our conceptions of our bodies, whether as material, or important, or neither, come to us through language; the belief in a preculturally material body as the ultimate ground of identity itself depends on the circulation of meanings in a culture. Butler's project in some sense involved turning Foucault's own genealogical project against the "body" that, in her view, implicitly grounded genealogy. It also involved the application of Joan Scott's injunction to "read for the literary," to look for the processes that constitute experience, rather than accept "women's experience" as foundational.

In Plato's *Timaeus*, Butler found an explanation of the origin of "matter" that, in her reading, excluded women as part of its foundational account of form and matter. In Butler's account, Plato's foundational exclusion of women, as well as children, slaves, and animals, exemplified the principle that any positive definition depends for its intelligibility on an excluded exterior as the ground against which the definition will signify. On this view, by excluding all those whom Plato defined as physically or intellectually incompetent, he defined philosophical discourse as the exclusive province of adult males. This principle of exclusion applied not only to conceptual identity—definitions—but also to individual identity—women, children, slaves, and animals are not persons under Plato's definition.

Here the tensions between genealogy and psychoanalytic theory became manifest in Butler's work. She began by specifying a limitation in Foucault's genealogical approach. This limit could provide the occasion for further genealogical investigation. Butler alleged Foucault's assumption of a precultural body. Foucault would readily admit that one can perform a genealogy of the genealogist. Butler's reading of Plato could have served as the basis for such a genealogy. She might have investigated the historical circumstances that enabled Plato to exclude women from participation in philosophical discourse, perhaps finding some similarity to the conditions that allowed Foucault to define his project using exclusively masculine pronouns. Such an inquiry would involve revealing gendered assumptions at the archaeological level of Western philosophy. The positive unconscious of Western philosophical discourse constituted that discourse as a masculine endeavor. This line of inquiry would continue Butler's project of moving understanding of the body from the realm of biology to the realm of culture.

Rather than pursue this genealogical inquiry, however, Butler invoked psychoanalytic theory to explain gender identity as a function of individual unconscious. She offered Lacan's version of psychoanalytic theory as a route out of unproductive debates over essentialist versus constructionist accounts of gender identity. Constructionist accounts explain gender as a result of social practices and meanings in response to essentialist attempts to explain gender as a necessary result of anatomical sex. But, as Butler noted, the constructionist position implies a measure of choice about gender identity that no one wishes to claim. She suggested instead the notion of constitutive constraint, the enabling requirement that subjects signify themselves as gendered if they wish to signify at all.[14] No individual decides for or against gender identity, because no individual inhabits society without having already become gendered.

This argument emerged from the problem of the relationship between interiority and exteriority, between the psyche and the social. Butler argued against biological determinism, for the refusal to read identity as simply an effect of physiology. As her emphasis on signification in the process of producing gender indicates, not only must gendered subjects convey the signs of gender but someone else must watch and listen as well. Gender, any other aspect of identity, identity *tout court*, is social, relational. Yet Butler's use of psychoanalytic theory effectively evacuates all exterior, social experience from the determination of gender and sexual identity. She escaped biological determinism only to set up psychoanalytic determinism. The problem becomes clear in the title of her third book on the topic, *The Psychic Life of Power*.[15] If differences in the exercise and experience of power reduce ultimately to psychic functioning, then differences of race, ethnicity, geography, age, class, or anything else become irrelevant to the process, or so Butler implies with her universalizing readings of psychoanalysis. Yet queer theorists wish to investigate how the practices of a culture constitute these experiences and via experiences constitute subjects along multiple, unpredictable, sometimes conflicting axes of identity.

Butler's choice of Lacanian psychoanalytic theory over Foucaultian genealogy seemed to stem in part from her understanding of historical inquiry and its relationship to philosophical inquiry. This understanding manifested itself in her article "Sexual Inversions" in the collection *Discourses of Sexuality*. In this essay, Butler criticized Foucault for his account of the historical circumstances that gave rise to the management of life, rather than the prevention of death, as a condition for the deployment of sexuality in the eighteenth century.[16] She quoted from the final section of *The History of Sexuality*, where Foucault described the increasing agricultural production and decreasing threat of plague that led to a significant alteration in the sovereign's traditional "right of death" over his subjects. Foucault argued that "this formidable power of death ... now presents itself as the counterpart of a power that exerts a positive influence on life, that endeavors to administer, optimize, and multiply it, subjecting it to precise controls and comprehensive regulations."[17]

Overlooking Foucault's characterization of the management of life as a "counterpart" to the power of death, Butler stated that this account fails logically because both life and death can appear only as the immanent possibility of the other. This objection rested on a misreading: Foucault did not assert that death disappeared from the scene altogether, as Butler implied with her gloss that "death is effectively expelled from Western modernity, cast *behind* it as an historical possibility, surpassed or cast *outside* it as a non-Western phenomenon."[18] Rather, he argued that "death was ceasing to torment life so directly."[19] But Butler's objection also rested on a puzzling effort to apply the conceptual analysis of philosophy traditionally defined to a properly historical question without exploring the relationship between the two disciplines and the possibility for conceptual analysis of empirical claims about past events.

Butler called the historical validity of Foucault's account into question. But the only actual evidence that she could adduce to justify her doubt stemmed from the point that a new epidemic, AIDS, had arrived since Foucault first argued, in Butler's terms, that "the category of 'sex' emerges only on the condition that epidemics are over."[20] Ignoring the point that this constituted an egregious oversimplification of Foucault's argument, one might consider his reliability as a historian. Many historians have questioned the accuracy of Foucault's historical claims.[21] But one need hardly develop extensive expertise in the history of early modern Europe to recognize that here, at least, Foucault's claims fell well within the range of generally accepted knowledge about the period. Butler's attempt to deny the accuracy of Foucault's historical argument would also seem to entail denying that, during the early modern period, national governments in the West began to develop formidable bureaucracies for managing their populations. Not only is this assertion absurd on its face but it also overlooks the basic point that the central medical research establishments in France and the United States—central bureaucracies for the management of populations—first tracked AIDS as a public health risk and isolated the HIV virus as the cause.[22]

Yet in the present context, the pressing question became not the accuracy of historical claims in the conventional sense but the type of claims that Foucault made. Here perhaps lay the crucial point in Butler's reading of Foucault. In *Bodies That Matter*, Butler defined the term "presentism" as the false universalization of culturally or historically specific terms. She insisted that one could not describe all "conceptual language or philosophical language" as presentist, because this description would entirely conflate philosophy with history. Finally, she asserted that she understood Foucault's genealogical procedure as "a specifically philosophical exercise in exposing and tracing the installation and operation of false universals."[23]

This description of genealogy looks accurate except that Foucault suspected that all universals are false, including those that ground philosophy and history as disciplines. With her argument about the relationship between epidemics and sexuality, Butler effectively philosophized Foucault's genealogy. She argued that the arrival of AIDS defeated Foucault's argument about events of the eighteenth century. One can legitimately make this argument insofar as one specifies how subsequent events belie the interpretation of a historian who remained unaware of or failed to take into account those events. But Butler offered no explanation of how the advent of AIDS influenced historical understandings of rising agricultural production and declining incidence of the plague some two hundred years before. Rather, she treated Foucault's historical claims as pure argument, a "phantasmatic history" that he created out of whole cloth simply for the purposes of buttressing his larger analysis.[24] One can also raise questions about a philosophically naive reliance on historical documents as unproblematic representations of past events, yet Butler offered no such concerns in her reading of Foucault. Even if she had, reducing historical sources entirely to self-referential texts available to the abstract manipulations of philosophers hardly constitutes an improvement over empiricist naivete.

Butler's account of Foucault's history in "Sexual Inversions" presaged at the level of scholarly practice the substantive claims that she would make in *Bodies That Matter*. In arguing for gender and sexual identities as cultural processes rather than biological givens, she posited an opaque unconscious as the primary locus for these processes.[25] Her understanding of these processes thus depends on abstract arguments with Lacan rather than on any empirical investigation of the changing cultural meanings of gender. Ironically, this opaque unconscious functioned in Butler's text much as Foucault's body did in his elaboration of his genealogical procedure: It became the unchallenged foundation of her analysis. But an important difference remained between Foucault's ostensibly precultural body and Butler's opaque unconscious. Even assuming that Foucault did rely on a precultural body to ground his genealogies, that body remained conceptually and theoretically relatively fluid. It was effectively blank, solely an outline awaiting definition from the culture into which it was born, as he made clear in "Nietzsche, Genealogy, History."[26]

The opaque unconscious, however, clearly carried an enormous amount of theoretical baggage as a concept. In some sense, Freud "discovered" the unconscious, and attempts to explain its functioning depend heavily on psychoanalytic concepts, whether primarily Freudian or Lacanian. Foucault might simply say that Butler as genealogist necessarily accepted some constitutive universals as the provisional ground for her inquiry. But with the opaque unconscious as the grounding assumption of her inquiry, Butler imported unexamined and uncritiqued the gargantuan assumptions of psychoanalytic theory into her genealogy of bodies and matter. In doing so, she reinstalled precisely the universal that she claimed to dispense with in her subversion of identity. By positing the unconscious at the level of the individual, rather than at the level of culture and history, Butler seemed to preclude the possibility for change, except as an exclusively textual process of argumentation over psychoanalytic concepts.

This exclusively textual manipulation clearly undermined Butler's own intellectual and political commitments. The conceptual move that she wished to make from body as biologically determined to body as culturally constituted both required and found its support in a concomitant shift in scholarly practice away from philosophical idealism, whether platonic or psychoanalytic. Lacanian psychoanalysis may have a deconstructive effect, but especially given Butler's point that one can deconstruct that which remains necessary, the question remained: How much had Butler really changed with her reinscription of the opaque unconscious via Lacan?[27] Butler denied the charge that her notion of performativity assumed a choosing subject that deliberately enacts gender. However, her insistence on valid universals as the stuff of philosophical analysis and her purely textual manipulation of abstract Freudian and Lacanian categories still suggest that she saw herself as a sovereign scholarly subject who commanded the field of gendered signification and escaped the historical changes that the genealogist describes.

The problem comes down to this: Butler has identified herself as a scholar with the explicitly political goal of undermining existing categories of gender and sexual identity in order to minimize the differences in access to power that those categories currently enable. She is a feminist. Yet whether she discusses the opaque unconscious, in *Bodies That Matter*, or "the psyche," in *The Psychic Life of Power*, she faces the following dilemma: either Freud and Lacan can offer "scientific" explanations of these psychic objects because the objects function in basically the same manner for all persons, in which case it becomes very difficult to understand how one would ever achieve any change in those functions and hence in disparities of power on the basis of gender and sexuality; or psychic mechanisms admit of significant alteration in their functioning according to varying cultural input, in which case it may be useful to understand the mechanisms themselves in order to change them effectively. But as a practical matter, politically engaged scholars will wish to attend to the changing cultural inputs and the relationship between these inputs and psychic mechanisms at least as much as they attend to the mechanisms themselves.

The evacuation of social factors in favor of abstractions recurs throughout *The Psychic Life of Power*. Butler's goal in that book is to understand the move by which conscience and consciousness develop through the subject's turning on itself. She begins with a discussion of Hegel's account of slave consciousness in *Phenomenology of the Spirit*. In Butler's reading of Hegel, unhappy consciousness emerges when the slave leaves the control of the master and becomes master of himself:

> The bondsman takes the place of the lord by recognizing his own formative capacity, but once the lord is displaced, the bondsman becomes lord over himself, more specifically, lord over his own body; this form of reflexivity signals the passage from bondage to unhappy consciousness. It involves splitting the psyche into two parts, a lordship and a bondage internal to a single consciousness, whereby the body is again dissimulated as an alterity, but where this alterity is now interior to the psyche itself.[28]

This passage demonstrates an ambiguity that permeates the entire discussion: How does the bondsman ever escape the master? Through what historical process did the end of slavery, whether for individual slaves or the class as a whole, come about? Clearly, Hegel and Butler use the image of a slave figuratively in order to elucidate a philosophical point—this is not literal slavery. Yet the significance of this philosophical trope for any actual political struggles around gender and sexuality remains obscure. Without participating in the anti-intellectual demand that all philosophical writing have immediate "practical" import, still one can apply a criterion of relevance that derives from Butler's own feminist and queer political/intellectual commitments. While it will undoubtedly prove significant in some sense to elucidate the mechanism by which subjects develop conscience and consciousness— become persons—that process must involve far more interaction with other persons than Butler ever considers in her discussion.

Ultimately, what Butler would achieve in *The Psychic Life of Power* is an understanding of how the psyche, by itself, invests itself with the conscience that indicates its susceptibility to operations of power. But there is no psyche by itself. At the end of the first chapter, she states that Hegelian and Freudian accounts of conscience seem to pose a question for Foucault about subjects' attachment to the very regulatory regimes that strive to discipline them, in part by eliminating the subject's attachment. In the second chapter, she feels compelled to explain the apparent logical circularity by which both Freud and Nietzsche posit the subject as both presupposed rather than formed and formed rather than presupposed. These thorny philosophical difficulties admit of simple cultural and historical explanations. Most subjects attach to regulatory regimes because they meet these regimes in the form of parents, who usually succeed in installing some version of a regulatory regime in their children long before the children have any capacity to survive apart from their parents. That they remain somehow attached, with varying degrees of conflict, to the regimes of their parents after they begin to survive apart from those parents would seem to admit of much more compelling explanation in terms of the repetition of signs and practices that Butler emphasized in *Gender Trouble* than it does in Hegelian terms.

Schools, prisons, armies, and factories at once presuppose and form subjects. They do so because, over time, they develop their understanding of what a subject should be, then elaborate norms and practices for requiring/encouraging subjects to approximate that understanding, all of which process will vary according to time, place, and institution. The answers to the questions that Butler poses are more complex than these simple sketches indicate. However, in order to flesh out such brief characterizations into answers to the questions Where do persons come from? and Where do queers come from? scholars will need to move more toward the empirical and less toward the psychoanalytically metaphysical.

Indeed, one of the great accomplishments of feminist and queer theory has been the move away from a disembodied, fully rational subject as the beginning point for philosophy. Butler seemed to forget her own deconstruction of such a subject in *Gender Trouble* when she attempted in *The Psychic Life of Power* to understand the subject in the completely abstract, idealist terms of Hegel and Freud. Part of Foucault's utility for feminist and queer theorists must stem from his insistence on grounding his inquiries into subjectivity in empirical information. Empirical work cannot proceed apart from constant conceptual clarification and revision, especially given the genealogical/queer theoretical point that the concepts that inform and enable empirical work themselves have political implications—this is not a naive positivism. Butler herself, writing with Scott in the introduction to *Feminists Theorize the Political*, put the point well: "This interrogation does not take for granted the meanings of any terms or analytic categories, including its own. Rather, it asks how specific deployments of discourse for specific political purposes determine the very notions used."[29] Every genealogist's inquiries begin from a particular cultural and geographical spot, and recognition of such beginnings helps queer theorists to avoid the sorts of generalizations that become disciplinary requirements for conformity.

Ironically, Butler's use of psychoanalytic theory becomes just such a generalization. In *The Psychic Life of Power*, she ultimately strove to reconcile Freud and Foucault by reading each through the other. Again, the primary issue is political: In subjects constituted by culture, in a process that produces persons through subjectification, how does resistance occur? If, as Foucault argued, nothing in the subject exists outside of the power that produced that subject, then how can some of these subjects choose to resist the producing power? Butler describes the two ways that Foucault specified in *The History of Sexuality*: first, subjects can resist through the idea of a "reverse-discourse" in which they use the very explanatory scheme that produces them as particular types of subjects in order to resist that categorization. The classic example that Foucault pointed to was gay liberationists' deliberate use of psychiatric discourse to prove that psychiatrists, using their own standards, could not vindicate their claims that all "homosexuals" necessarily suffer some psychopathology.[30] Second, subjects can invoke competing discourses or legitimating narratives against the discourses that oppress them.[31] Here one might point to the various civil rights movements in the United States: Beginning with the African American movement and continuing through women's and gay liberation, they have invoked the ideals of liberty as enunciated in the nation's founding documents in order to delegitimize discursive practices that had justified their subordination.

The process of subjectification is always incomplete and uncertain. Butler echoed her argument in *Gender Trouble*, stating that the possibility for resistance resides in the inevitable failures and need for repetition of practices of subjectification. For some reason, however, this explanation, by itself, failed to satisfy Butler. She went on to state, "From a psychoanalytic perspective, however, we might ask whether this possibility of resistance to a constituting or subjectivating power can be derived from what is 'in' or 'of' discourse. What can we make of the way in which discourses not only constitute the domains of the speakable, but are themselves bounded through the production of a constitutive outside: the unspeakable, the unsignifiable?"[32] Certainly, if we take the African American civil rights movement as an example, simply pointing to the availability of rights discourse in the Declaration of Independence and the Constitution does not fully explain the emergence of a movement in 1955, when Rosa Parks refused to stand up so a white man could sit down on a Montgomery city bus. And even this begs agreement on a beginning date for the civil rights movement: Why not 1941, with A. Philip Randolph's call for a march on Washington, or 1905, with the beginning of the Niagara Movement?[33] Why 1955? Why not 1855? 1875? 1776?

But surely the answer to this question is historical not psychoanalytic. Neither historian nor psychoanalyst will ever specify every element of the consciousness or conscience that led Parks to resist the laws of segregation; some aspect of the incident will always remain opaque. But Butler's approach to this opacity involves the elaboration of an untestable, culturally obtuse universal hypothesis. Foucault offered two useful correctives to the sort of universalizing move that Butler would make here. First, he refused to offer generalized explanations of the requirements for resistance or any idealist telos toward which "liberation" must aim. Any such requirement or telos will eventually become disciplinary itself, because true believers will demand from other oppressed persons conformity to their ideal, even if the requirement or telos is irrelevant to the situation of such persons. Butler might avoid this objection by insisting that, rather than describe any substantive requirement or direction for resistance, she would describe the mechanism by which resistance occurs. But discussions of supposed psychoanalytic mechanisms still evacuate difference. Psychoanalytic theory assumes, rather than demonstrates, an "opaque unconscious," allowing it to become the sort of discursive talisman around which true belief, not critical inquiry, tends to accumulate.

Second, insofar as discourses that subjectify and enable resistance entail a constitutive outside and insofar as we can determine some relevance for that constitutive outside to the persons who would resist, with

Foucault's reading of psychoanalysis in *The Order of Things*, he suggested a locus for this exterior. According to Foucault, "man" as the organizing principle of knowledge arose in the space that biology, economics, and philology created.[34] A specific limiting concept defined the possibility for each discipline: death in the case of biology, desire in the case of economics, and the word as law in the case of philology. These three limiting concepts gave "man" as empirical object of knowledge and knowing subject his definition. Any understanding that "man" could acquire of himself would come through the study of these three limits: "man" as subject to death, desire, and law. In most of the human sciences, scholars searched for knowledge about "man" by looking where they found the best light: They described actions and statements that already appeared in representations, those over which the sovereign subject appeared to exercise control. Scholars in the human sciences thus hoped to bring the laws of human finitude fully to consciousness.

Freud disrupted this search by positing and claiming to study the unconscious. There he found the unrepresentable origin of those limits—death, desire, and law—that delineate "man" as subject and object of knowledge. Psychoanalysis thus occupied the paradoxical position of simultaneously apotheosizing and opposing the human sciences. At the level of archaeology, where discursive rules constitute possible objects of inquiry, psychoanalysts approached directly what other scholars in the human sciences approached only obliquely. Psychoanalysts operated at the limit of representation, bringing the unrepresentable operations of "man's" limits into discursive representation. Foucault described the politically as well as intellectually disruptive effects of psychoanalytic theory, especially in Freud's initial formulation. With psychoanalysis, Freud opposed the scientific chain of heredity and degenerescence that grounded the science of eugenics generally and Nazi schemes for racial purity specifically.[35]

Foucault's genealogy of the deployment of sexuality effectively historicized Freud's science.[36] Foucault expanded Freud's argument about the confessional demand to tell all as the avenue to the truth of the unconscious into a historically constituted cultural imperative. On Foucault's view, Freud made a crucial first step in denying, with his positing of the unconscious, the possibility of bringing "man's" constitutive limits fully to consciousness. Freud necessarily remained embedded in the episteme of "man," however, as he demonstrated by positing that unconscious within the terms of the sovereign subject. The subject becomes split under a psychoanalytic description, lacking complete self-mastery because of the operations of the unconscious. However, that subject retained its unity as the object of Freud's inquiry, through which he worked to specify the relationship between conscious and unconscious. For Foucault, the operation of "man's" constitutive limits occurred not in the psychological unconscious of the individual but in the historical "unconscious"—what Foucault called the "positive unconscious"—of the culture. "What I would like to do," he wrote, "is to reveal a *positive unconscious* of knowledge: a level that eludes the consciousness of the scientist and yet is part of scientific discourse."[37] In these terms, queer theorists would like to reveal how assumptions about gender and sexual identity informed the positive unconscious of our culture not simply with respect to scientific inquiry but also with respect to virtually every aspect of the culture. On this view, assumptions about gender and sexual identity inform our perceptions and understandings of the world at the most basic level, and they inform our conceptions of who is or is not a person.

Or, as Butler pointed out, queer theorists and other activists must assert some claim to terms such as "woman," "lesbian," "gay," and "queer," because those terms inform personhood, identity, subjectivity—whatever term one chooses. Whether one endures the term "queer" as an epithet or brandishes it as a tool of empowerment depends heavily on its meaning, on the history of its usage and the expectation of its future meanings. But it also depends heavily on the history and subjectivity of the individual who chooses whether to use it. No individual or group of activists can unilaterally control the meaning of a term, but that observation does not recommend unilateral disarmament through a refusal to contest meanings.[38] Butler's efforts to redefine the terms of psychoanalytic theory exemplify her own efforts in this direction, but the problem remains: Even with such resignifications as "the lesbian phallus," Butler's deployments of psychoanalytic theory work at odds with the deconstructive goals of her project.[39]

Teresa de Lauretis: The Historical Psyche

For queer purposes, if psychoanalytic theory can retain any utility at all, it needs more thorough reworking. Feminist film theorist Teresa de Lauretis has produced one such reworking. Psychoanalytic theory is only one of many conceptual frameworks that she has relied on. She noted that other feminist film theorists had written about sexualized female stars and other cinematic techniques that represent women as sex before Foucault wrote about the "technologies of sex" in *The History of Sexuality*. Lauretis argued, much as Butler did, that gender identity results from practices of representation, especially self-representation. She used Foucault's notion of "technologies of sex" as a way of describing the vast array of practices, images, and meanings in our culture through which we represent gendered identities.[40]

Lauretis adopted critical concepts from numerous scholars, taking those concepts as far as she could toward an understanding of how gender and sexual difference operate in our culture. But after pointing out the failure of any male critical intellectual to incorporate gender in his attempt to explain oppression, she eventually struck out on her own. Thus, for Lauretis, however useful Foucault's notion of technologies of sex and Louis Althusser's account of ideology may be, they both ultimately fail to explain how gender categories legitimate domination.[41]

Lauretis saw a larger problem among some male literary and film critics of the 1980s. Rather than simply ignore gender, certain male critics seemed to use Derridean deconstruction as a critical strategy for what Lauretis considered antifeminist ends. Citing Derrida, they arrived at a proposition similar to Butler's and Lauretis's: Language and gender identity constitute one another. Males write great literature and build great buildings by relegating females to the background, where they perform the necessary but mundane tasks of maintaining life on a daily basis. Similarly, linguistic meaning as a masculine process of signification depends on a feminine background that remains necessarily excluded from meaning as an enabling condition for that process of signification. According to Lauretis, males who wished to use their Derridean formulation of this hypothesis in order to critique great literature conventionally defined had begun to represent themselves as critiquing from the position of feminine absence. Thus, the assertion of femininity as a function of signification allowed men to manipulate "the feminine" as a category while resolutely ignoring the lives of actual women.[42]

This feminist objection to the practices of male critics provided a point of continuity between the motivations and scholarly practices of *Technologies of Gender* and Lauretis's earlier book, *Alice Doesn't: Feminism, Semiotics, Cinema*. Lauretis began *Alice Doesn't* by arguing that women necessarily think and write in a fundamentally gendered system of representation. Feminists cannot escape the confines of patriarchal representation in language, cinema, or anywhere else. They have access to personhood only on masculine terms. Consequently, they must work to represent themselves subversively in patriarchal terms, to write the language yet still resist its tendency to naturalize gender hierarchies. Through her reflections on the possibility for feminist theory and plausible goals for feminist theorists, Lauretis had already concluded in effect that utopian political schemes promising an end to gender hierarchies, or any other kind of hierarchies, would prove useless to her.[43]

Critical reflection for Lauretis served not to specify a path toward a gender-free utopia. It served instead to describe the practices and representations that produce and reinforce gender hierarchies. For Lauretis, cinema offered a primary medium for reading and critiquing representations of gender. She argued that "cinema both exemplifies and employs, even perfects, that technology of sex."[44] Not only in the content of cinematic representation but also in its techniques Lauretis found profuse indications of how our culture creates and incites conformity to the meanings of gender and sexual identity. Cinema instantiates the discourses of gender as they operate in the positive unconscious of the culture.

Cinema also offers a metaphor for the situation of feminists who necessarily speak and write in the master's language. Lauretis referred to the concept of the "space-off," that which the viewer cannot see on the screen but, given what the viewer does see, must exist beyond the scene. Feminists must move back and forth, from screen to space-off, from the representations of gender that appear on screen to women's experiences that do not, that cannot, appear on screen, because they fail to conform to existing canons of representation.

For Lauretis, lesbian desire offered a compelling example of women's experiences that occur in the space-off. She returned to psychoanalytic theory in *The Practice of Love: Lesbian Sexuality and Perverse Desire* in order to create a self-representation that would provide theoretical justification for her own desire. She hoped to explain lesbian desire in terms other than the "sexual indifference" that, in her view, has characterized all other such attempts. "Sexual indifference" for Lauretis has the punning effect of referring both to the conflation of female desire with male desire and the removal of the specifically sexual element from female desire. She argued that existing efforts to explain lesbian desire rely on either some version of a masculinity complex, thus conflating lesbian desire with male heterosexual desire, or some version of a return to identification with the mother, thus evacuating the specifically sexual character of lesbian desire.[45]

Unlike Butler, however, Lauretis did not read Freud as describing universal psychic mechanisms. Rather, she read Freud's "passionate fictions" in order to produce "passionate fictions" of her own, fictions that, whatever use they might have for others, helped her to understand her own desire. Lauretis did not write an entire book solely to explain her desire to herself; she found representations of lesbian subjectivity in cinema and literature that perform the principles that she derived from her reading of psychoanalytic theory.[46] More intriguingly, Lauretis found in both lesbian desire and psychoanalytic theory possibilities that appeal to feminists. According to Lauretis, both offer the possibility for female agency, social and sexual, in a way that no other theory in our culture does.[47]

Lauretis took the unusual tack of relating lesbian desire and psychoanalytic theory to Charles Peirce's semiotics. She did so in order to explain how subjects negotiate the intersection of their interior psychic processes and external representations of sexuality. For Lauretis, the virtue of combining psychoanalytic theory with semiotics lay in the limitations of each. From Freud she derived an account of instincts, including sexual instincts, as originating within the body and requiring some sort of action from the subject to gratify the instinctual demand. She stressed Freud's acknowledgment that, although the instincts originate within the body, external stimuli may have a significant effect in shaping them.[48]

Despite the apparent inconsistencies between psychoanalytic theory and semiotics, Lauretis found a homology between them. That homology lay in the similarity between Freud's account of instincts and Peirce's account of habit change. The subject of semiosis constantly negotiates an external world of signs, which have "significate effects" on the subject. The most profound such effect is a habit change, in which a series of signs has the significate effect of changing the subject's characteristic patterns of behavior and action. The habit changes that Peirce described can have an impact on the instincts that Freud described, thereby creating what Lauretis called "*a process of sexual structuring.*" For Lauretis, this theory has the virtue of accounting for the production of subjects in a general way while recognizing the "contingencies of both a personal and a social history."[49] Freud offered a description of psychic regularities that in many respects resonated with Lauretis's understanding of her own desire. However, she wished to explain these psychic regularities in terms that would take into account the role of culture in shaping subjectivity, especially sexed subjectivity. She wished to avoid the ahistorical implications of positing gender and sexual identity as functions of an opaque unconscious.

According to Lauretis's reading of Freud, fantasy plays a crucial role in sexuality. Fantasy involves the mental image of an object that will gratify sexual instincts. That object always represents a displacement from the original source of satisfaction, breast milk. Lauretis compared this displacement of the original object into a fantasized sexual object to Peirce's distinction between a dynamic object and an immediate object. The dynamic object is the real thing to which a sign refers. The immediate object is the sign's representation of the dynamic object, the meaning that the sign conveys to the observer. Thus, whereas the dynamic object exists independently of the sign, the immediate object is a function of the sign and depends for its meaning on the context in which the observer sees the sign.

The stories and fantasies of the surrounding culture, then, can become the immediate objects that produce habit changes as modifications of sexual instincts. Lauretis gave the example of the Oedipus complex. She argued that its pervasiveness in Western culture as a story, not necessarily as a description of actual events, explains its centrality for Freud's theory of sexuality. As a representation, the Oedipus story can have an impact on the processes of sexual structuring in our society if we understand it as the immediate effect of a sign, in Peirce's theory, that structures the fantasized sexual objects of Freud's theory. The important aspect of Freud's theory for Lauretis thus became not the particulars of the Oedipus story but the process of producing sexual instincts: the displacement of the real object into a fantasized one, where that process involves initially the gratification of survival instincts (milk as food = dynamic object), but also the impact of stories and representations from the larger culture in informing the object of gratification in fantasy (leather jackets as fetishes = immediate object).

In the final pages of *The Practice of Love*, Lauretis suggested a certain parallel between Freud's and Foucault's accounts of sexuality. She argued that, whereas Freud had described intrapsychic processes, Foucault described interpsychic, or social, processes through which subjects come to understand themselves as sexual. Peirce's semiotics provided Lauretis with a theory to explain the conjunction of the intra- with the interpsychic. She also found a striking congruence between the practices of "self-analysis" that Foucault described in Volumes 2 and 3 of his history of sexuality and Peirce's idea of "self-analyzing habits."[50] On this view, Foucault's exploration of the practices by which ancient Greek and Latin men came to understand themselves as desiring subjects became his effort to specify different content for the stories of sexual fantasy in our culture. Lauretis described Foucault's version as a "non-Oedipal world, beyond the Fall, perversion, repression, or Judeo-Christian self-renunciation, and sustained instead by a productively austere, openly homoerotic, virile ethics and practice of existence."[51]

In some sense, then, Lauretis fleshed out the formal parallel between Foucault's history of sexuality and Freud's psychoanalytic theory. Her description of Foucault's "openly homoerotic, virile ethics" seems hardly calculated to appeal to feminists, especially lesbian feminists. But, as she pointed out at the beginning of *The Practice of Love*, the stories that currently provide the official content of lesbian desire rest on "sexual indifference." If, for Lauretis, the importance of Freud's theory of fantasies of displaced objects as central to sexuality lay in its description of a process rather than its reliance on a particular story, then psychoanalytic theory becomes a potential avenue for understanding how new stories and representations of lesbian desire will have the effect of overcoming sexual indifference by bringing female desire—specifically, lesbian desire, women's sexual desire for other women—out of the space-off and onto the screen.

Eve Sedgwick: The Queen Mother of Queer Theory

Psychoanalytic theory also places the narrative and particular—stories of particular fantasies and fetishes—at the center of sexual practice and identity. In this respect, Lauretis took the universalizing edge off of it and implicitly agreed with Eve Sedgwick's Axiom 1 from *Epistemology of the Closet*: "People are different."[52] Sedgwick prefaced this observation with a brief discussion of the difficulty of sorting out the revelatory from the banal among various statements of the obvious that she had stumbled across while writing her book. But she concluded that, politically and intellectually, our culture wreaks considerable havoc with the presumption that authoritative categories are more important than individual self-perception in managing and categorizing sexual practice and identity.[53] A feminist scholar like Butler and Lauretis, Sedgwick had examined "homosexuality" first as a central disciplinary mechanism for gender solidarity among men and second as one of the interpretive keys to modern, Western culture.

In *Between Men: English Literature and Male Homosocial Desire*, Sedgwick coined the term "homosociality." "Homosociality" denoted the continuum of relations in which persons of the same gender cooperate to mutual ends. The extremes of that continuum for men—in Sedgwick's view, the most macho, mainstream friendships and the most intimate gay male relationships—lie farther apart and define themselves more explicitly in opposition to one another than the comparable extremes for women. She argued that "the historically differential shapes of male and female homosociality—much as they themselves may vary over time—will always be articulations and mechanisms of the enduring inequality of power between women and men."[54] Homophobia— the paranoid disavowal of any "homosexual" connotation or practice— arose much more commonly and characteristically in the modern era among nongay men who bonded around their own interests than it did among similarly interested women. On this view, sexual identity serves to police the boundaries of gender identity: A "real" man must always take care to avoid any hint of the "homosexual" as he participates in "homosocial" rituals that revolve around the exchange of women through marriage (but that may display prominently a certain ass-slapping homoeroticism).

In *Epistemology of the Closet*, Sedgwick addressed the essentialist/social constructionist debate that then raged among lesbian and gay scholars. She began that book with the assertion that she would take Foucault's conclusions as "axiomatic."[55] If scholars such as Butler and Lauretis had nudged discussion of sexual identity categories away from the realm of nature and toward the realm of culture, Sedgwick administered a definitive shove in that direction, profoundly altering the terms of the debate. She did so by making two crucial moves. First, she pointed out the dubious character of lesbians' and gay men's hopes for "nature" as a political panacea. As people on the political right worked to define the debate over lesbian/gay rights in terms of moral choice, and therefore the presumptive immorality of choosing same-gender erotic practices, lesbians and gay men increasingly responded that sexual "orientation" was a function of biology for which they could not legitimately suffer moral condemnation. But, Sedgwick noted, "increasingly it is the conjecture that a particular trait is genetically or biologically based, *not* that it is 'only cultural,' that seems to trigger an estrus of manipulative fantasy in the technological institutions of the culture."[56] Biology will not serve as refuge from politics precisely because those who command the political and epistemological heights of our culture want, above all, to alter biological givens.

Sedgwick did not, however, argue in favor of the social constructionist position. The essentialist/constructionist debate posed a problem for Sedgwick in that it centered on the issue of etiology: Both positions offered an answer to the question, Where do lesbians and gay men come from?, both at the level of biological and cultural generality, and at the level of individuals. But Sedgwick found the impulse to eradicate existing lesbians and gay men and prevent the production of them in the future so fundamentally embedded in our culture that any question about etiology seemed dangerous. A concrete answer, in favor of either culture or nature, would in all likelihood provoke the "estrus of manipulative fantasy" that Sedgwick feared, with disastrous consequences for lesbians and gay men.[57]

In her second move, then, Sedgwick replaced "essentialist/constructionist" with "minoritizing/universalizing" as a more appropriate binary for understanding the significance of lesbian and gay identities. She preferred these terms in part because the participants in the constructionist debate had arrived at conceptual gridlock but also because she saw her terms as evoking the question "In whose lives is homo/heterosexual definition an issue of continuing centrality and difficulty?"[58] Does the definition of "homosexuality" matter only for those who might wish to adopt it as an identity category of their own, the minoritizing view, or does it serve as half of a binary, "heterosexuality/homosexuality," that fundamentally informs our entire culture, the universalizing view? Typically taking a universalizing view herself, Sedgwick backed away from the question, Where do lesbians and gay men come from? to ask instead, How does the constitution of lesbian/gay, or "homosexual," identity contribute to the power/knowledge regimes through which all persons become constituted in this culture?

Knowledge about "homosexuality" centers on the image of the closet, a sort of conceptual transfer point between revelation and ignorance. The effects in meanings and politics of this play between knowledge and ignorance constituted central questions for Sedgwick. In an interesting twist on Foucault, Sedgwick pointed out the usefulness of ignorance to the powerful and thus the limitations on the traditional Enlightenment project of escaping the dead hand of power by increasing knowledge.[59]

Sedgwick offered not a science of society leading to liberation but a set of interpretive propositions about the operations of certain representations and meanings. Although she argued that the meaning effects of the homosexual/heterosexual binary spread into a long list of other binaries, she did so not in pursuit of universal, totalizing theory. Whether her proposition proved tenable (its "truth" does not pose a decidable question) would rest on a slow accumulation of readings that engage interpretive skills and attend to details that neither ordinary nor educated opinion has valued or developed before because, as Butler pointed out, an important feature of the deployment of individual identity is a refusal to recognize the historical processes by which individuals come to have identity—processes of subjectification.[60]

Perhaps more troubling to the liberation-minded, Sedgwick's deconstructive project promised no necessary political salvation. Indeed, Sedgwick pointed out the frustrating irony that deconstructing the mutual dependence of homo- and heterosexuality by demonstrating the irreconcilably contradictory character of the definitions involved simply revealed the utility to the powerful of dependence and contradiction.[61] The whole project operated within the context of irreducible indeterminacy.

That observation does not mean that the project lacked utility. Rather, no one, Sedgwick included, could tell from the beginning where it would end up. Despite this uncertainty, in the introduction to *Epistemology of the Closet*, Sedgwick made two moves that characterize queer theory. First, she emphasized the connections among politics, categorization, representation, and reading. Her "antihomophobic" project began from the observation that, while homophobia plays a central role in disciplining both women and men in our culture, an important element of that discipline is an enforced silence about the homophobia itself and the persons whom it serves to silence. Thus, whereas reading novels alone will not ensure political change, reading the messages of gender and sexuality wherever they appear—and they appear everywhere: classic texts of philosophy or literature, film, television, billboards—is a crucial first step in understanding the operations and effects of the oppression that antihomophobes would battle.

Second, Sedgwick described her own commitments in the theoretical/political debates among feminist, lesbian, and gay scholars, but she also readily acknowledged that persons with opposing commitments contributed vitally to the possibility of her own project and to the possibility of reducing (eliminating?) homophobia. No single model of political/cultural/intellectual action will guarantee the desired results, so far better to allow as much leeway as possible for various persons to pursue their own tactics. Sedgwick preferred to take a universalizing, gender transitive approach—to claim that homo/hetero definition is crucial for the entire culture and that it characteristically involves movement across gender distinctions. But she recognized the value of those who take separatist, minoritizing, positions, claiming that queers should remove themselves on a gender-segregated basis from a seemingly inevitably heterosexist, homophobic culture.

For Sedgwick, her intellectual work performed political work. She described *Epistemology of the Closet* as an "extended introduction," in doing so somehow performing her concern with the performative character of speech acts, including silences, around the subject of "homosexuality."[62] Speech acts have a performative dimension insofar as the meaning of words depends not solely on reference but on the fact of their utterance ("I hereby pronounce you . . ."). Speech acts perform the very acts that they describe. Sedgwick could not predict reliably what would happen, but she decided to speak and discover the consequences—a sort of epistemological or academic coming out.

In some contexts, the meaning and political effects of the closet as open secret become visible, if not necessarily immediately clear, simply by posing the question. Sedgwick noted the difference between questions of sexuality and questions of race or gender for the politically fraught matter of canon formation. The standard dismissal by the monoculturalists comes in the form of the pseudoargument that trained scholars can find no persons with the stipulated characteristic who have produced great literature. Sedgwick posed the dismissive question in terms appropriate to lesbian/gay studies:

> Has there ever been a gay Socrates?
> Has there ever been a gay Shakespeare?
> Has there ever been a gay Proust?
> Does the Pope wear a dress? If these questions startle, it is not least as tautologies. A short answer, though a very incomplete one, might be that not only have there been a gay Socrates, Shakespeare, and Proust but that their names are Socrates, Shakespeare, and Proust.[63]

Remove the authors for whom the significance of same-sex eroticism was a crucial issue but has become an open secret, and one eviscerates the canon. Perhaps anticipating the problem of military service for federal policymakers, Sedgwick characterized the approach in the class-room to this issue as "*Don't ask; you shouldn't know.*"[64]

The question of performativity arose again in Sedgwick's discussion of the term "queer." She raised the possibility that the meaning of the term may depend crucially on whether one uses it to describe oneself or someone else. The standard for determining the presence of queer-ness became not empirical but performative: In order to prove oneself "truly" queer, one need only have the impulse so to designate oneself. Similar questions of performance surround the closet. The statement "I am a lesbian" derives its significance not solely from the referential value of the purported correspondence between the term "lesbian" and a discreet, specifiable identity category but also from the concomitant performance of coming out of the closet.[65]

But this account suggests a much cozier fit between "queer," on one hand, and "lesbian and gay," on the other, than most queer theorists wished to allow. Clearly, in popular use, "queer" has become a synonym for "lesbian and gay," as the book of quotations *Queer Notions: A Fabu-lous Collection of Gay and Lesbian Wit and Wisdom* demonstrates.[66] In coin-ing the term "queer theory," however, Lauretis explicitly intended to "mark a certain critical distance" between it and "lesbian and gay stud-ies."[67] Lauretis saw at least two problems with the term "lesbian and gay studies": Insofar as it lends itself as a substitute for "homosexual," a term that takes the male as exemplary and the female as simply a minor vari-ation, it tends to reinscribe the invisibility of specifically lesbian experi-ence/sex/writing/subjectivity. And it serves to create yet another discrete set of identity categories that should automatically become primary in the scholarship/politics/lives of those who fit the category. But this was the white, middle-class model of identity and its politics, in which the minority aspect could become the exclusive focus because all other aspects conform to the norm. For Lauretis, instead of adding on "black" to "lesbian and gay," the term "queer" allowed for the possibility of keep-ing open to question and contest the element of race—or class, age, or anything else—and its often complicated, unpredictable relationship to sexuality. Rather than revise definitions to conform to experience, "queer" deliberately left definitions open and undecided.

Roughly two years after the publication of Lauretis's "Queer The-ory," Sedgwick approached much the same point from a slightly dif-ferent direction, with her discussion of "queer" in "Queer and Now." Sedgwick offered a long list of characteristics that one can supposedly deduce about any individual solely on the basis of the person's "sexual identity," including her or his biological sex, gender, and sexual practices as well as those of her or his partner. "Normatively," Sedgwick noted, "it should be possible to deduce anybody's entire set of specs from the initial datum of biological sex alone—if one adds only the normative assumption that 'the biological sex of your preferred partner' will be the opposite of one's own. With or without that heterosexist assumption, though, what's striking is the number and difference of the dimensions that 'sexual identity' is supposed to organize into a seamless and univocal whole. And if it doesn't?"[68] The gender or sex of one's sexual object choice is one "spec" that may, by failing to line up correctly, produce a "queer." But Sedgwick's analysis allowed "queer" to encompass many other possibilities besides "lesbian" and "gay." Indeed, Sedgwick did not identify herself as a lesbian but did identify with gay men and implicitly took up a "queer" subject position of her own.[69]

The term "queer" connotes a certain failure to live up to expectations. On Sedgwick's definition, it could retain this connotation even in a society that included "lesbian" and "gay" among the officially approved, and therefore expectable, sexual identity categories. But, as David Halperin stated, "queer" also connotes a much broader failure of definition: "As the very word implies, 'queer' does not name some natural kind or refer to some determinate object; it acquires its meaning from its oppositional relation to the norm. Queer is by definition *whatever* is at odds with the normal, the legitimate, the dominant. *There is nothing in particular to which it necessarily refers.*"[70] In an important sense, "queer" served as the conceptual connection between the politics of difference that some feminists, lesbians, and gay men had cultivated and the philosophical language of difference that Foucault, among others, initiated. Placing personal identity radically into question raised significant questions about conceptual identity, "truth," and the philosophy that chases it.

And placing personal identity radically into question also raised serious questions about liberatory models in which the truth of individuals will delegitimize oppressive uses of power—the "coming out" model that lesbian/gay rights activists continue to use, by both choice and necessity.[71] Butler, Lauretis, Sedgwick, and Halperin (to name only a few) made connections between reading and interpretation, on one hand, and politics, on the other. Sedgwick began her discussion of queerness with data on lesbian/gay teen suicide and the observation,

"This society wants its children to know nothing; wants its queer children to conform or (and this is not a figure of speech) die; and wants not to know that it is getting what it wants."[72] Thus, for queer youth, survival itself became a problem, a problem that Sedgwick and, she suspected, others dealt with through interpretation of the messages that seemed univocal to their normal peers but looked disconcertingly, or enticingly, plurivocal to queer youth: "I think that for many of us in childhood the ability to attach intently to a few cultural objects, objects of high or popular culture or both, objects whose meaning seemed mysterious, excessive, or oblique in relation to the codes most readily available to us, became a prime resource for survival."[73] Reading and interpretation proved crucial to Sedgwick's survival into queer adulthood. Whether this was so literally in the sense of preventing her from killing herself as the ultimate act of nonconformity or figuratively in the sense of allowing her the psychological and cultural space to persist in queerness, rather than lapse into conformity, matters little for present purposes even though it clearly mattered definitively for Sedgwick herself. What matters here is that reading and interpretation—especially reading "against the grain," in Sedgwick's terms—were crucial for queer survival and therefore for queer politics.

Sedgwick's elaboration of queerness draws attention not only to the rhetorical aspects of categorizing persons but to the point that the process begins at birth. For various reasons, as she noted in "How to Bring Your Kids Up Gay,"[74] the lesbian/gay civil rights movement has tended to pay relatively little attention to children and the dangers that protoqueers face growing up. Yet at the very moment that gay liberation seemed to secure its most essential victory—the elimination of "homosexuality" as a diagnosis from the American Psychiatric Association's official *Diagnostic and Statistical Manual of Disorders*—some psychiatrists conducted a quiet rearguard action: They installed the diagnosis "gender identity disorder of childhood" as a way of recouping ground for sexism and heterosexism that their colleagues lost with the abandonment of "homosexuality." In order to find in this new diagnosis an avenue for the elimination of queerness, one need not claim that all lesbian and gay adults displayed gender-atypical behavior as children, although Sedgwick points to evidence suggesting that such behavior is common. In Sedgwick's reading, the point of the diagnosis seems to be that, while good liberal or progressive shrinks want to show how hip they are by admitting the existence of well-adjusted, sane lesbian and gay adults, they still hope to prevent the production of such persons in the future.

More Queers Than You Can Close a Closet Door On

Halperin extended Sedgwick's analysis in his essay "The Queer Politics of Michel Foucault." He began by describing the central frustration of lesbian/gay rights activism: The "heterosexual" norm abides by no standards of logic or morality in perpetuating itself as normal and therefore as the desirable, "natural" opposite to undesirable, "unnatural" "homosexuality." He made this point in part by offering a long quotation from *Epistemology of the Closet*, in which Sedgwick related the story of a hapless schoolteacher who lost his job in 1973 for being gay. In adjudicating his lawsuit against the school board, the trial court found that the teacher had compromised his potential contribution to the mission of public education by bringing excessive attention to his "homosexuality" through his interviews with the press. Therefore, the school board could legitimately fire him. The appeals court reversed the decision of the trial court, claiming that the teacher's interviews constituted protected speech under the first amendment. The teacher had no standing to sue the school board, however, because he had not included in his application for employment his service as president of his college's homophile organization. Because he had withheld information that would have led the school board not to hire him in the first place, he had no basis for complaint when the board fired him upon discovering the information. Therefore, the school board could legitimately fire him.[75]

Damned if you do, damned if you don't.

Homophobia—the radical disavowal of all "homosexuals" in the figurative sense, fear of the same in the literal sense—demonstrates the incoherence of Western philosophical logic all the way back to its very beginnings. The law of the excluded middle no longer applies when one is busy eradicating the conditions of possibility for "homosexual" identity: Homophobes get to have their cake and eat it too.[76] They give with one hand, removing "homosexuality" from the *DSM*, and take with the other, creating the new "disease" "gender identity disorder of childhood." Let's be nice to queer adults, because they can mobilize politically on their own behalf (and they throw great parties), but let's intensify the pressure on queer children, who have less capacity to defend themselves. Logic is optional. If you really see nothing wrong with queer adults, why strive to prevent children from growing up queer? Whether an authorized—white, "heterosexual" male—subject adheres to the principles of formal logic depends on circumstances, contingency. Logic itself is contingent. As Halperin put it, "Sedgwick's account recalls us, specifically, from our natural impulse to try and win, move by move, the game of homophobic truth being played against us and to respond to each fresh defeat in this losing game by determining to play it harder, better, more intelligently, more truthfully." Instead, according to Halperin's reading of Sedgwick, we should "stop playing long enough to stand back from the game, to look at all its rules in their totality, and ... examine our entire strategic situation: how the game is set up, on what terms most favorable to whom, with what consequences for which of its players."[77] Not only must we step back to consider the rules of the game; we must also recognize that the game is specifically a rhetorical one, a game designed for the purpose of deploying meanings. The textual investments that Sedgwick cultivated to ensure her survival were specifically "formal."[78]

For queer theorists, language plays a crucial role in producing persons. They do not argue for linguistic determinism or monism. Rather, they note that our understanding of the world comes to us through language, with the result that, whatever else may exist in the world independently of language, our knowledge of those things is always already bound up with the terms that we use to describe them. More, the terms we use and the discursive rules that govern our usage participate in the constitution, as such, of the objects that we recognize in the world. This observation is crucial for our understanding of the process of producing persons and the relative value that our culture assigns to different persons depending on which identity categories they seem to fit into.

This constitutive and evaluative function of language depends to some extent on the organizational reductiveness of categorization. Queer theorists wish to emphasize the blooming, buzzing, observable multiplicity of desires, pleasures, acts, and fantasies that beggar our conceptual vocabulary of identities. That the empirical effortlessly overwhelms the conceptual may not serve as argument for dispensing with the conceptual altogether, but it certainly enjoins us to hold very lightly our categories of sexual identity and our prescriptions for how those identities and the persons whom we consign to them should operate.

Because categories continue to function in the face of criticism, however—partly because many persons are invested in their continuation—

pointing out the inadequacy of categories is not sufficient. Queer theorists also see the need to examine the functional modes of identity categories and figure out ways to undermine them.

5

A Georgia Sodomite in King Henry's Court

The Rhetorical History of "Homosexuality" in Law and Politics

Queer theory has its critics, external and, perhaps inevitably, internal. David Halperin wrote his book, *Saint Foucault: Towards a Gay Hagiography*, explicitly in response to the charge from gay philosopher Richard Mohr that some scholars seemed to have lost their critical faculties on the topic of the "social construction" of "homosexuality," which position Mohr and Halperin agree on attributing in its origins to Michel Foucault. In keeping with the characteristically queer practice of appropriating pejorative terms for affirmative uses, Halperin wrote, "I may not have worshipped Foucault at the time I wrote *One Hundred Years of Homosexuality*, but I do worship him now. As far as I'm concerned, the guy was a fucking saint." Halperin elaborated on this claim by describing the similarities that he saw between Foucault's position, or reputation among U.S. scholars since his death in 1984, and Halperin's own position as a U.S. scholar identified with Foucault. Attacks on the two of them in Halperin's view demonstrated vividly the continuing vulnerability of any queer person, even one who works in the university havens of good liberals, who refuses the comforts of the closet. Halperin came to admire Foucault for his understanding of the ever-shifting politics of sexuality in Western culture.[1]

By the early 1990s, these politics had produced scholarship ranging from the most theoretically abstruse to an anthology expressly designed to offer accessible readings for classroom use.[2] It is perilous to offer generalizations about a body of work that begins by questioning categories, but one might begin with two basic propositions that most queer theorists would agree to: first that issues of sexual definition pervade every aspect of the culture, even where they seem most visibly absent. Eve Sedgwick, of course, began *Epistemology of the Closet* with this claim, and Michael Warner makes a similar claim in his introduction to *Fear of a Queer Planet: Queer Politics and Social Theory*.[3] Secondly, again borrowing from Sedgwick, among others, in matters of sexual definition, the categories do not reduce to the neat binarism of "heterosexual/homosexual" or even to the equally neat "trinarism" (?) of "hetero/homo/bi." The experience of sexual alterity takes many forms of practice—differences of object choice, centrality to self-definition, gender, race, class, age, even being from Oklahoma—some of which come to identify persons and some of which do not.[4]

Mohr offers a useful starting point with his vigorous dissent from the major intellectual moves that enabled queer theory. He echoed other critics by calling Foucault's account of bodies and sexual inscriptions "idealist." According to Mohr, on Foucault's view, "'true' bodies are whatever bodies are thought to be."[5] Introducing *The Material Queer: A LesBiGay Cultural Studies Reader*, Donald Morton made a similar charge, although in different terms. He distinguished between "textual" studies under the influence of poststructuralism and cultural studies in the more specific sense of a concern with "the reproduction and maintenance of subjectivities," especially as developed by the Birmingham School, which resisted the "overtextualization" that "textual studies" supposedly performs.[6] Some charges of overtextualization parallel charges of idealism in that both presuppose the omission of "real" or "material" aspects of persons' lives in producing their subjectivity.

Launched at Foucault, the claim is simply absurd. While it may be that, in U.S. universities, readings of Foucault have tended to emphasize the discursive elements of power over all others, still it seems a bit peculiar to hurl "idealist" as an epithet at a man who initially elaborated his understanding of power through a book on prisons. Mohr seems to have missed the point that, in *Discipline and Punish*,[7] Foucault emphasized discursive organization, but discursive organization of architectures and practices that clearly have a very concrete impact on prisoners' bodies and have that impact effectively only insofar as they are well organized according to certain discursively elaborated principles.

Foucault's *History of Sexuality*[8] lacks an institution as imposing in its concreteness as the prison, but in the case of sexuality, Foucault emphasizes the relational character of the power that discourse enables. Nowhere does he claim that bodies or sexuality are "whatever [they] are thought to be." Rather, he claims that authorities—priests, physicians, psychiatrists—inscribe sexuality on bodies through repeated interaction with their subjects. Despite his extensive training in the traditions of Western philosophy, Foucault nowhere took up the idealist/materialist dichotomy, presumably because he considered it false. "Discourse" and even "thought," in Foucault's writing look distinctly nonidealist, articulated as they are through, affecting as they do, and affected as they are by concrete institutions and practices.

For Mohr, for Morton, for Halperin, and for virtually every other participant in debates about queer theory, the question of "idealism" remains pressing because of the political implications that queer theory carries. While thay offer very different solutions to the problem, Mohr and Morton agree in charging "idealist" queer theorists with the bad habit of believing that their textual manipulations necessarily have some political impact. But it seems that, whatever their failings, queer theorists are at least correct insofar as they suggest that among the most confused categories in contemporary Western culture must be "the political," the boundaries of which shift unpredictably in response to myriad pressures but nowhere so queerly as when the issues deal with gender and sexuality.

Queer theorists themselves worry that queer theory may become little more than self-deluded, apolitical wordsmithery. Writing about "Identity and Politics in a 'Postmodern' Gay Culture," in *Fear of a Queer Planet*, Steven Seidman expressed the concern that attention to binaries of gender and sexuality, to discursive practices divorced from their institutional locations, verges on "textual idealism."[9] Seidman's concern mirrors Mohr's criticism. Mohr sees only the discursive, "idealist" aspect of Foucault's account of disciplinary power and the persons that it produces. Seidman frets about the tendency of poststructuralist critics of identity politics to abstract the discursive aspects of power from their institutional locations.

Unlike Mohr, Seidman appreciated the insistence of poststructuralists that identity is the result of unstable social (institutional and discursive) processes, always in need of repetition (compare Butler), rather than a transcultural, ontological fact, as Mohr argues. Seidman reiterated what many queer theorists note: The ontological approach to identity demands the abstraction of each minority element, its hypostatization as the defining characteristic of one's personhood—race, class, gender, sexuality, age, geography, and so forth—and an additive approach to persons with multiply minority identities.[10] Despite his express contempt for, and presumptive opposition to, racism, Mohr seemed entirely unfamiliar with the work of many persons—especially black, lesbian feminists—who insist that the experiences of "homosexuality" and "womanhood" vary importantly on the basis of race, or that any of these categories varies according to class, or that race and class vary according to the others. Mohr insists on the possibility of defining "homosexuality" such that no cultural specificity remains, leaving only the essential features of the identity. He fails, however, to explain just what could remain in an identity category absent all cultural specificity. Mohr claims the possibility for a "God's-eye view," but he does not explain how he arrived at such a perspective.[11]

Like Boswell's dissent from the orthodoxy of social construction among gay male historians, Mohr's critique of social construction has the benefit of demonstrating how little difference exists between the two positions in important respects. Mohr disputes the salvational potential of biological determinism not, as Sedgwick does, because he fears the likelihood of efforts to alter biological "givens." He does so because he insists, quite rightly, that discrimination against queer persons presents a moral issue: In the context of U.S. political and legal institutions, there is no justification for such discrimination. The claim that some aspect of queer identity justifies discrimination, like the claims that Jews poison wells or steal babies, results from a post hoc attempt to justify, rather than causing, the decision to discriminate. Also like Boswell, however, Mohr refuses the possibility that the definition of the concept "homosexual" in any way enables such discrimination and prejudice.

Mohr's position ultimately becomes incoherent on its own terms. He argues that discrimination results from social practice and that empirical information will have little impact in changing pejorative stereotypes of lesbians and gay men, because these stereotypes lack significant empirical content to begin with. At the same time, however, he insists that the social determination of prejudice has no impact on the "real," "natural" category "homosexuals."[12] Whether one is or is not "homosexual" seems to depend, for Mohr, exclusively on sexual practice, with no reference whatsoever to the subjectivity of the person practicing. Thus, Mohr cannot explain journalist Frank Browning's example of a casual sex partner who, while routinely having sex with men, remained happily married to a wife whom he claimed to love and committed to an otherwise highly conventional family life centered around his daughter. Is this man "homosexual"? Apparently so, according to Mohr's definition—or perhaps he is "bisexual"—although the man refused gay identity for himself.[13] Browning offered this personal anecdote to demonstrate the point that putting a name on a practice, whether the name is "homosexual," "gay," or "queer," will have some impact on the approach that various persons take to that practice, including their willingness to continue engaging in it. Mohr leaves quite opaque the question of what purchase, intellectual or political, he gains with his perspective. Comparing definitions of "homosexuals" to definitions of widgets, Mohr misses the performative aspect of sexual identity that Sedgwick pointed to in her discussion of closets and her definition of "queer": Widgets never say, "I'm a widget," but persons do say, "I'm gay," or, in some circumstances where we knowing queers would expect otherwise, they say, "I'm not gay," as Browning points out.[14]

In defending the category "homosexuality" as "real" and "natural," Mohr ended up taking a strangely idealist position of his own. According to Mohr, "A boy who wants to be with males, likes the way they look and smell, wants to touch and rub up against them, and is excited by physical contacts with them will find his developing sexual attraction to men realized through various channeling influences laid out by social norms, especially as these are embedded in the beliefs and actions of the men whom the boy finds exciting and in the techniques and instrumentalities through which the boy learns to fulfill his desires."[15] This sounds to me suspiciously like a process of subjectification according to discursive practices—learning the meanings of an identity category through interaction with authoritative practitioners. Regardless, it certainly seems that this blissfully unproblematic process of "homosexual" identity formation reflects more Mohr's thoughts than it does the "material realities" of gay life for many boys.

What if this boy, growing up in the United States during the twentieth century, finds his "homosexual" identity constituted through years of "therapy," or even incarceration, as part of his parents' concerted efforts to "cure" him of the dread diseases "gender identity disorder" and "homosexuality"?[16] Or, perhaps more likely, what if the boy grows up in a carefully controlled and officially asexual family environment where information about same-sex desire leaks in only obliquely and confusingly. Or what if the boy stumbles onto the right Boy Scout troop or football team and learns—literally gropes his way?—to express his desires through mutual exploration with equally uninformed peers. Or what if he grows up hearing that his life will be difficult enough as a black man in a racist society, so the last thing he should do is compound his problems by being (publicly) gay. Or what if he grows up hearing constantly about "homosexuality" in the context of repeated denunciations from his family's esteemed preacher, to the effect that all "homosexuals" will burn eternally in hell. In this case, of course, arguments about the "realness" or "social construction" of the boy's developing sexual awareness may well become moot when he decides that God hates him, so he might as well kill himself.[17]

And what if this exemplary boy is a girl?

This brings us back to Eve Sedgwick and her techniques of queer interpretation as a means to survival. As with Judith Butler's "opaque unconscious," one may grant, for argument's sake, Mohr's "real, natural homosexual" then ask what purpose the concept serves. Arguing about ontology may prove fruitful for philosophers, but it has come to seem otiose to queer theorists. Textual manipulations do not *necessarily* have any political impact, but they *may* have political impact, and they may enable readers and authors to perform political acts conventionally defined. To dismiss such impact out of hand makes as little sense as to insist on the political efficacy of all queer theory. Sedgwick described as "formalist" the interpretive practices that contributed to her survival as a queer. She recognized that formalist criticism supposedly entails a failure to consider the specific content—emotional, psychological, historical, political—of the text.[18] Similarly, formal analysis of discursive power—a distinctively "postmodern" critical practice—supposedly entails political quiescence.

Halperin rehearsed the numerous charges that good, liberal intellectuals have lodged against Foucault, according to which Foucault's suspicions about the usefulness of "liberation from oppression" as a prescription for political activism led inescapably to the conclusion that resistance is impossible. Such criticisms proved neatly Foucault's own point about the blindness that comes with theoretical certitude. Halperin pointed out that the necessarily quiescent implications of Foucault's argument in Volume 1 of *The History of Sexuality* quite failed to stop members of ACT-UP—many of whom read Foucault, especially *The History of Sexuality*, avidly—from blocking off the Golden Gate Bridge and disrupting both the New York Stock Exchange and the CBS Evening News.[19] Quiescence indeed.

ACT-UP begat Queer Nation. The political efficacy of queer theory by no means stands or falls with the livelihood of Queer Nation, a short-lived loose network of chapters (compared with ACT-UP, which is, at least in some cities, alive and well).[20] But both groups did originate very concrete political practices that relied on categorical resignification and confusion deployed through subversive use of canonical representations. At the simplest and most widely dispersed level, these practices manifested themselves in the politics T-shirts. One favorite depicted Superman kissing Dick Tracy. The caption read, "Clark wants Dick. Dick wants condoms." Even the most macho of superheroes is potentially queer and, as such, potentially available for conveying safe-sex messages. Even the most ordinary terms may have queer uses, as in the pun on "Dick" or the favorite lesbian saying from 1992 (and again in 2000?) "Lick Bush."[21] And one can wear a T-shirt, and therefore carry one's politics, just about anywhere—an important feature of activism for a usually invisible minority, as the popular "No one knows I'm gay" and "I'm not gay, but my boyfriend is," emblazoned on T-shirts, reflect. Queer politics here enacts Sedgwick's queer theoretical point that queerness, while officially invisible, is around every corner—if you look from the right angle—and it depends on practices of knowledge and representation.

But queer politics cannot be reduced to sayings on T-shirts. In their chapter in *Fear of a Queer Planet*, Lauren Berlant and Elizabeth Freeman elaborated on the politics of Queer Nation. In this essay, Berlant and Freeman describe Queer Nation's statements "I hate straights" and "Bash back" as indicators of a queer refusal to abide by the terms of traditional, liberal politics.[22] The goal, for Queer Nation, was not the right to privacy but the creation of public spaces in which queers could be overtly, safely queer. Thus, Queer Nationals claimed to hate straight persons for blithely taking such space for granted and for insisting that queers could win such space for themselves by being "reasonable" and by practicing the politics of "moderation." The threat to bash back, to respond violently to the violence of gay bashing, dramatizes the failure of homophobic municipal administrations to "protect and serve" all citizens equally, while challenging the stereotype of gay men as "pansies."

Perhaps the exemplary queer protest is the kiss-in. ACT-UP pioneered the die-in, in which protestors fall to the ground as if dying. Evoking the classic civil rights tactic of sit-ins, die-ins dramatized the extraordinarily high mortality rates from AIDS for the edification of those persons (straight, bureaucratic, or both) whose response to the AIDS crisis was, in ACT-UP's estimation, grossly inadequate. Kiss-ins, in which large numbers of same-sex couples kissed each other in public places, had the decidedly queer effect of making same-sex desire seem at once outrageous and frighteningly normal by making it visible where it should remain officially invisible. Queer Nation found other tactics with which to pursue this strategy of evoking queerness in the faces of nonqueers: visibility actions in which same-sex couples spent the evening frequenting straight bars, acting just like the straight couples, or shopping in queer regalia at suburban shopping malls—the province of the Suburban Homosexual Outreach Program, or SHOP, a focus group of the San Francisco chapter of Queer Nation.[23] The point was to insist on the presence and legitimacy of queers even outside the safe but constrained space of urban gay ghettoes, relying on hegemonic representational codes to make queerness at once spectacular and ordinary. The categorical confusion of queer theory on display at better stores near you.

Queering Canons

The great virtue of "queer" lay precisely in its undefinability, which included a certain unpredictability in the implications and consequences of deploying the concept. The point is precisely to refuse the accepted identities, the expected and predictable alignments or divisions among reading, interpretation, scholarship, scholarly identity, and politics—to name only the most obvious categories that queer theorists have muddled with their inquiry. Queer activism in the form of Queer Nation may have proven short-lived, but queer academic activism continued, accelerated, and proliferated during the 1990s. The politics, like the scholarship, took unusual forms, however. Almost all of the scholars in this chapter on historical representations of gender and sexual identity categories identify themselves as literary critics or theorists. Again, historian Joan Scott recommended that historians of difference—nonidentity—"read for the literary." But literature occupies an ambiguous position in the pantheon of sources for historical evidence, and—from the perspectives of most historians—literary scholars do strange things when they study history.

For example, literary critic Jonathan Goldberg recently published three volumes: *Sodometries*, which he authored, and *Queering the Renaissance* and *Reclaiming Sodom*, which he edited.[24] *Sodometries* and *Queering the Renaissance* represented the latest literary scholarship on the English Renaissance, or the late sixteenth and early seventeenth centuries. Both volumes also contained extended discussions of the U.S. Supreme Court decision in the 1986 case *Bowers v. Hardwick*.[25] For a historian, this presents a problem. No one would deny the important connections between the English Renaissance, the period in which British people first colonized North America, and the modern United States. But the chain of relevance should run in the other direction. We might expect a discussion of recent U.S. Supreme Court decisions to include references to the English Renaissance. Discussions of English Renaissance literature, however, should not contain references to recent U.S. Supreme Court decisions.

But the Supreme Court decision in *Bowers v. Hardwick* dealt with sexuality, or the allegedly immutable truth of the self. More specifically, a bare majority of the highly esteemed justices voted to uphold a Georgia statute prohibiting "homosexual sodomy." Janet Halley's chapter "*Bowers v. Hardwick* in the Renaissance," in the volume *Queering the Renaissance*,[26] contrasted two positions on the issue: The Supreme Court assumed that sodomy constitutes a self-evident, stable, transhistorical designation for a particular behavior that defines a sexual identity category. In contrast, Goldberg, quoting Foucault, had asserted that "sodomy" represents "an utterly confused category"[27] the very confusion of which allowed the justices to invoke the term as they saw fit.

Halley's essay helped to clarify the mutual relevance of the English Renaissance and *Bowers v. Hardwick*. The justices based their permission for official prohibitions of sodomy on an ostensibly unbroken legal tradition stretching back to King Henry VIII, who adopted the first secular prohibition of sodomy in the Anglo-American canon in 1533. In a legal sense, then, Michael Hardwick, the Georgia sodomite, committed in 1986 the very act that King Henry VIII prohibited in 1533. Or so the justices assumed.

At one level, the accuracy of the justices' account admitted of falsification using good old-fashioned empirical investigation. One could simply examine the requisite documents to determine if that political entity known as the state of Georgia has, since its inception, maintained some law prohibiting sodomy. Only the task of determining if the Georgia law conformed to King Henry's original intent, to borrow a favorite term of judicial conservatives, would remain. The justices, or their assistants, performed just such an examination, as the extensive footnotes on pages 192 through 194 of the decision attest. They found no actual statute prohibiting sodomy in Georgia before 1816, apparently defeating the court's own claim that "sodomy was a criminal offense at common law and was forbidden by the laws of the original 13 States when they ratified the Bill of Rights." In 1784 Georgia's General Assembly had adopted the common law of England as its own, however. Thus, insofar as the sodomy law of 1533 constituted a part of that common law in 1784, the justices could accurately describe Georgia as having participated in a legal tradition stretching over some 453 years.

That this decision attracted considerable attention from lesbian/gay activists and legal scholars should come as no surprise. The attention that literary scholars have paid to it wants explaining, however. The scholarly production that resulted from the appearance of a Georgia sodomite in King Henry's court reflected a fascination with representations of sexuality and the paranoia that those representations can produce. To state this fascination in the terms of the present inquiry: The justices assumed that the terms "homosexual" and "sodomy" signified reliably and univocally, referring to phenomena whose meaning has remained stable for at least several hundred years. The act to which "sodomy" refers, in turn, designates a class of persons, because this particular sexual "perversion" defines its practitioners' very being. Goldberg, Halley, and others, by contrast, suspected that probably no term signifies reliably and univocally, certainly not over extended periods of time, and that any ranking of terms according to their instability and plurivocality would surely place "homosexual" and "sodomy" near the top. Further, the assumption that "sodomy" as act defines "homosexuals" as persons is a relatively recent conceptual move, certainly more recent than Henry VIII.

Having quoted Foucault to the effect that sodomy constitutes "an utterly confused category," Goldberg went on to argue that sodomy represents categorical confusion. Instead of assuming that "sodomy" refers unproblematically to a discreet, specifiable activity, Goldberg read sodomy as an interstice at which oppositions meet—a term that marks the point at which ostensibly mutually exclusive meanings connect, at which discrete categories collide. In the Renaissance, "sodomy" separated the disorderly from the orderly; in the modern period, it separates the homosexual from the heterosexual. Taking the justices of the Supreme Court at their word, "sodomy" the term refers to much more than does sodomy the act, today just as it did in Renaissance England. The orderly and the heterosexual may well perform acts that fall under the denotation "sodomy," but those acts will go unrecognized as such insofar as they fail to threaten the social boundaries that constitute orderliness and heterosexuality. As if to confirm Goldberg's analysis, some ten years after carrying the day before the Supreme Court, and shortly after having another court dismiss a lesbian's lawsuit against him for having fired her because she was a lesbian, former Georgia Attorney General Michael Bowers admitted that he had committed adultery while enforcing standards of sexual propriety against queers. He also admitted that such behavior made him a hypocrite, no doubt atoning for his sin thereby.[28]

The critical practice known as new historicism provided a partial basis for Goldberg's deconstructive readings. Since roughly 1982, some literary scholars have challenged formalist modes of criticism by insisting on the profound embeddedness of literary texts in their historical contexts and the inescapable textual mediation between scholars in the present and their objects of inquiry in the past. New historicist critics challenged the older separation of literary texts from other sorts of texts. Plays, poems, and novels, on this view, offer no direct reflection of reality, but neither do textual representations from other genres. Literature, then, can contribute as much to our historical understanding as can other types of sources. Equally, our historical understanding must contribute to our reading of literary texts.

The problem of deciding what constitutes a historical phenomenon remains, however. One can historicize only that which changes over time. As Goldberg demonstrated in *Sodometries*, many new historicist critics tended to read Renaissance literary and other texts as if the sexual categories they rely on have remained unchanged over the intervening four hundred years. In doing so, they took basically the same approach to the question as the justices did. But for new historicist literary critics to do so seems more peculiar than for justices to do so. The growing mounds of empirical evidence for the historical variation of sexual identities categories aside (see Chapters Two and Three), new historicist literary critics claimed as a major source of intellectual inspiration the very same Foucault whom Goldberg quoted in order to establish the point that sodomy constitutes a confused, historically variable category.[29]

New historicists most frequently took from Foucault arguments about the operation of disparities of power among individuals. In doing so, they hoped to assess the political function of a given text or texts with respect to the culture from which it came. But Goldberg argued that critics who invoke a Foucaultian account of power differentials routinely failed to appreciate Foucault's point that sexuality can constitute particularly effective sites for the operation of power among individuals. This failing he hoped to remedy with his own readings of English Renaissance texts, some literary, some not.

Goldberg offered an interesting example of how counterhegemonic analyses of identity categories also tend to challenge disciplinary boundaries. If *Queering the Renaissance* looked odd for its temporal leaps, it looked just as odd for its disciplinary leaps. Although most of the contributors to the volume worked in university English departments, other disciplinary locations represented in the text include law, history, comparative literature, women's studies, and gender studies. Perhaps as an indication of where intellectual production would find itself soon, the one graduate student whose work appeared there listed her administrative location as the "Humanities Center at The Johns Hopkins University," where she "works on the technologies of representation and gender in late medieval and early modern cultures."[30] Did she call herself a literary critic, a historian, neither, both?

Do we assume that, by dint of having contributed an essay to a volume entitled *Queering the Renaissance*, the author must identify herself as a queer theorist, or a queer? Insofar as we understand "queer" to connote instability and indeterminacy of definitions and identities, this is not the question to ask. The queerness of *Queering the Renaissance* consisted not in the identities of its contributors but in their scholarly practices. It consisted in reading literary, historical, legal, private, or any other kinds of texts "against the grain" in order to illustrate the illogical rhetorical and historical logic of "sexuality." It consisted in insisting on the importance of astute interpretation, of attention to texts and the textuality of practices as crucial elements in any successful political resistance to the domination of homophobia and heterosexism under the deployment of sexuality.

And, especially for Goldberg, queer theory consisted in examining representations of sodomy. "Sodomy" under Goldberg's Foucaultian definition, "that utterly confused category," seemed almost synonymous with "queer." One might be tempted to isolate their domains of meaning by calling "queer" the identity and "sodomy" the act. But such definitional certitude precisely undermines the definitional uncertainty that is the virtue of both terms. The categorical confusions that sodomy represented for Goldberg spin off in multiple directions. He performed a certain disciplinary sodomy in *Sodometries,* most clearly in Part 3, "'They Are All Sodomites': The New World."[31] There he read not "literary" texts but "historical" sources. This distinction plays on the presumption that "historical" sources refer to "real" events, whereas "literary" texts describe only "imaginary" events, which, however suggestive, cannot substitute for "facts."

Goldberg revealed another facet of the distinction between the "literary" and the "historical," however. He read accounts of Spanish conquests in the New World not simply as descriptions of events but also as signifiers of gender, race, and class. In their descriptions of American sodomites, European observers revealed far more about themselves than about their new subjects. Reading an account of Vasco Núñez de Balboa's feeding some forty sodomites to his dogs, Goldberg argued, "Post facto, preposterously, the body of the sodomite takes on the status of an origin, serving as the cause and justification for what was done to the Indians, but its originary status is troubled not merely by being presented as an aftereffect but also because, cross-dressed, it is a double body and the only truth it testifies to is the preposterous nature of colonial accounts, that the ideological production of the text will never justify the atrocities of the European invasion of the New World."[32]

Goldberg's reading of Balboa performed numerous queer functions. It reinstalled the violence perpetrated on Native Americans as the founding act of European control over the Americas, thus undermining the happy narrative of progress toward freedom that underwrites scientific history. Representations of sodomy and the cross-dressed bodies that perform sodomy also served to reverse our epistemological expectations. A literary reading of an observer's firsthand account (albeit translated from Spanish into English) belied the presumptive "truth" of such immediate observations. The account that Goldberg read does not contain the truth of the events that it describes. It reveals only the preposterous attempt to justify violence and domination. Here is interpretation in the sense that Foucault defined in, and that Scott cited from, "Nietzsche, Genealogy, History."[33]

Here is also queer interpretation. Goldberg conflated the supposedly distinct critical practices of formalist deconstruction and new historicism by reading a historical text in and for its historical contexts, while pointing out that the narrative trajectory of the text itself operates in oppositional tension with the historical and ethical significance of the events that it describes. He relied on the officially apolitical Foucault to read properly "private" information about sexual practices as crucially determining the politics of conquest. And he insisted that the central category in his interpretive framework, "sodomy," would not admit of categorical definition. The political significance of a historical text becomes clear through a literary analysis that contrasts the text's own narrative politics—Balboa doing the work of God by destroying sodomites—with the larger story of growing suspicions about attempts to justify murder and conquest by reference to Christian and/or republican eschatology.

On Goldberg's queer reading, the immorality of sodomy constituted retrospective justification for the enormity of Spanish depredations in the New World only for those of a common ideological bent. Foucault worked to challenge just this sort of progressive metanarrative in which the white enlightened bring salvation, civilization, and democracy to the benighted natives, in Goldberg's text, or to the insane and the criminal, in Foucault's texts. In his reading of the Spanish conquest, Goldberg used sodomy to disrupt the presumption of the linear movement of time. In the same way that Foucault used "episteme" to connote a historical space in which discursive regularities operate, Goldberg posited an interpretive space for sodomy in the early modern period, with which he juxtaposed representations and relationships of power. In doing so, he undermined history as "ideal significations and indefinite teleologies."[34] Ideal significations succumbed to the sodomitical interpretation of a queer theorist who refused the progressive teleology of American history as the triumph of Christianity, reason, and democracy over the darker races.

But Goldberg did not adopt Foucault's arguments about sexuality uncritically. He cited *Epistemology of the Closet* to argue that *Bowers v. Hardwick* belied the sharp distinction that Foucault posited between acts and identities. On its face, Georgia's sodomy law aims solely at acts. In practice, however, if authorities enforce the law only on particular sorts of people, a prohibition of acts can serve to police identities: The law produces persons. If the only persons who get arrested under a sodomy law happen to do their thing with others of the same gender, the prohibition of sodomy as act contributes to the definition of "homo-sexuals" as persons. In other words, it contributes to the supposedly sharp distinction between the categories "heterosexual" and "homo-sexual": Officials recognize sodomy as such only insofar as persons of the same gender are doing the act. One could read this as the performative element of the law. In prohibiting a category of acts that it purports only to describe, the statute thereby serves to create that category of acts—by distinguishing the acts in question from others—and to create an identity in the bargain.

As Halley pointed out in her Renaissance reading of *Bowers v. Hardwick*, the justices herniated themselves to adjudicate Georgia's sodomy law as defining a class of persons, "homosexuals." According to the justices, "The issue presented is whether the Federal Constitution confers a fundamental right upon homosexuals to engage in sodomy."[35] But, as Halley explained, the Georgia statute prohibits acts that it defines as sodomy without distinguishing the gender or sexual identity of the participants. Further, although Hardwick undeniably did the deed with another man, the claim as he presented it to the justices—that the statute violated his Constitutional guarantee of privacy—made no reference to the gender of his partner. Thus, the justices used the act of sodomy to define a class of persons, "homosexuals," concealing their own act of definition with the claim that they simply described the issue that Hardwick put before them. That they may have done so ingenuously, sincerely believing the connection between acts and identities that they helped to cement, only proves the point more vigorously: Highly educated persons steeped in the traditions of jurisprudence suddenly lose their ability to read the plain language of a statute when an opportunity for queer bashing presents itself through the automatic conjunction of acts with identities.

Halley used this circumstance to make a point similar to Sedgwick's. The justices relied on a reading of the history of sodomy, or prohibitions of sodomy, to reach their decisions. By conventional standards, as many scholars have noted, the justices proved in this instance very poor historians. Concurring with the majority, Chief Justice Warren Burger cited Derrick Bailey's *Homosexuality and the Western Christian Tradition*[36] but not Boswell's *Christianity, Social Tolerance, and Homosexuality*, a much more recent work in which Boswell took pains to engage and disagree with Bailey.[37] However, Halley insisted that queer historians could more reliably prevent such homophobic readings of history as pleased the justices if they gave up the fruitless search for the origins of modern "homosexual" identity. Instead, they should concentrate on the ways that varying understandings of the relationship between acts and identities have influenced efforts to define, and thereby control, sodomy.

This looks much like the practical effects of Foucaultian genealogy. Scholars who have relied on Foucault not simply for substantive clues about the history of sexuality but also for procedural clues about how to approach the topic have tended to focus increasingly on institutions and practices rather than on individuals. That is, rather than worrying about who became "homosexual" when, we should examine the institutions through which people defined acts as normal or deviant and the practices that they used in creating and enforcing these definitions. We should "read for the literary." Or, in Halperin's version, we should stop playing the game long enough to examine the rules with care.

This distinction may look exceedingly fine, but it makes all the difference. As Halley explained, when the justices grounded their permission for sodomy statues in a continuous tradition that extends not merely to the U.S. Constitution or King Henry VIII but also—in Justice Burger's words—to "millennia of moral teaching," they represented themselves as conservatives bound by historical necessity.[38] This historical bridge over which the justices escaped the monster of innovation will support their weight only when it rests on the founding assumption of a continuous connection—definitional, legal, historical, moral, psychological—between sodomitical acts and homosexual persons. The justices assumed that what sodomy is now it always has been and ever shall be.

Halley showed that, even taking the state of Georgia alone, one could easily find considerable debate and confusion over how to define sodomy. The statute that Hardwick challenged dated to 1968, when the legislature specified the body parts involved in any act of sodomy. Such specification resolved difficulties with judicial interpretation of a less-specific statute from 1833. Judges had interpreted this ambiguous law to prohibit fellatio as well as cunnilingus by a man but not cunnilingus performed by a woman on another woman. Halley argued that the justices evaded this morass of sodomitical instability by assuming the continuous presence of a homosexual person as the subject of all of these acts. Here she agreed with Goldberg, both in pointing to an ostensibly stable, unitary homosexual identity as the glue that holds together an otherwise fragmented history of sodomites and in arguing that this conjunction of sodomy and homosexual identity required a revision of Foucault's scheme. As Goldberg suggested, if sodomy remained available in 1986 as the defining characteristic of homosexual identity, then Foucault's narrative of a shift from acts to identities looked untenable.

Goldberg noted that, in defining the question as the right of homosexuals to engage in sodomy, the justices implicitly sanctioned heterosexual sodomy by assuming that heterosexuals never do that sort of thing. Goldberg then read this definitional move as their use of sodomy to define "homosexual" identity. This constituted a distinction without a difference. "Hetero" and "homosexual" alike may commit sodomy, but it matters only when homos do it, because it defines only "homosexuality," not "heterosexuality." Here Goldberg found the proof of Foucault's mistake: "Sodomy," an act, remains available to define "homosexual," an identity. At the same time, however, Goldberg recognized that the basis for this distinction between homo and hetero depends entirely on the assertion of the difference, on a speech act, a judicial performance. In order to escape suspicion as a sodomite, one need only state one's identity as a "heterosexual." The homo/hetero distinction thus revealed its performative character.

But the situation that Goldberg described also admits of just the opposite interpretation. Clearly, sodomy remains available as a category of acts that authorities can associate with types of persons. But, as both Goldberg and Halley suggested, the governing image has become that of the "homosexual" person. The reason that the Supreme Court could easily overlook mounds of evidence for the definitional instability of sodomy lay in the reliability of the identity category as a retrospective container for the mess. Foucault may have mistaken the situation when he suggested that the discourse of persons displaced the discourse of acts entirely. However, the discourse of identities and its categories "homosexual" and "heterosexual" served as the governing principle of interpretation for the justices. They could only recreate through citation the simultaneous permission for "heterosexual" sodomy and prohibition of "homosexual" sodomy once the deployment of sexuality had produced the discourse of identity in which the act came to define the identity. The ideal signification, "homosexual," in this case, governed a retrospective teleology that encompassed and reduced the confusion of definitions of sodomy.

Goldberg's argument with Foucault provides an opportunity to clarify our understanding of how discursive practices define subjects. Foucault may well have used indefensibly broad terms in stating his claim in the *History of Sexuality*. However, one can read his statement about the shift from acts to identities as referring primarily, if not exclusively, to the perspective of physicians. Remembering Foucault's own insistence that no central organizing mechanism or site for power exists, we will more readily accept the proposition that medical and legal discourses do not necessarily work seamlessly in tandem. Thus, the unequivocal assertion from many physicians that "sodomites" are really "homosexuals," who should be treated rather than punished, will by no means automatically vitiate a long-standing legal tradition. No doubt, in the United States, legislators at the federal level have relied on expert medical advice in devising categories of sexual deviance in immigration policy, to cite one example.[39] But legislators and judges have also resisted physicians' efforts to arrogate complete responsibility for dealing with sexual deviants, as the persistence of sodomy statutes attests. Medicine and law constitute distinct, by no means fully independent but certainly often competing sites from which to exercise discursive power. Once again, Foucault's broad statements about the character of modern power have proven more reliable than the narrower claims he made about the history of sexual identity categories.

Perhaps the debate over the shift from sodomy-as-sinful to "homosexual"-as-species relied on an inappropriately linear conception of change. Foucault wrote in *The History of Sexuality* about "the tactical polyvalence of discourses." In defining this rule of method for his study of the deployment of sexuality, Foucault stated, "We must not imagine a world of discourse divided between accepted discourse and excluded discourse, or between the dominant discourse and the dominated one; but as a multiplicity of discursive elements that can come into play in various strategies."[40] Under the deployment of sexuality, a variety of discursive elements and strategies can coexist, perhaps combining, or competing, or both at different times. Halperin's argument for a queer politics of interpretation confirmed this point. The logic of heteronormativity can easily contain its own contradictions and effortlessly deploy them against "homosexuals" precisely because of discursive tactical polyvalence. If the medical discourse fails to get you going, the legal discourse can get you coming. (Or, in the case of the hapless schoolteacher, the legal discourse will find a way to get you coming or going.) Perhaps most confusingly of all, Goldberg's and Halley's doubts about Foucault's narrative of a shift from acts to identities raised the possibility that historical change does not operate in only one direction: Does the esteemed justices' careful use of acts to identify persons in *Bowers v. Hardwick* constitute merely regress, as opposed to progress, or was it some sort of lateral move, or loop, that opened up an entirely new field of interpretation and contest?

In Halperin's terms, then, Sedgwick, Halley, and Goldberg contributed to queer politics with their queer readings of Supreme Court decisions by revealing the rules of interpretation that the justices used to justify prohibitions of "homosexual sodomy." Further, for Sedgwick and Goldberg as literary critics, in contrast to the legally trained Halley, their queerly sodomitical readings of Supreme Court decisions revealed a performative aspect as well. One does not ordinarily think of literary critics as having authority to interpret the logic of Supreme Court justices. Canons of interpretation for Supreme Court justices are properly legal, not rhetorical. Both justices and literary critics engage in an intellectual pursuit called "interpretation" (although "conservative" justices may deny that they do even that). But in an orderly world, the categories of genre would reliably distinguish proper interpretive texts for justices from proper interpretive texts for literary critics. Only sodomitical queers would disregard this generic distinction and apply literary modes of interpretation to legal questions. But judicial opinions are exercises of discursive power par excellence and therefore crucial sites for a queer interpretive politics that aims to map the tactical polyvalence of discourses. Further, according to the justices' own opinion, the mere assertion of legal rights for "homosexual" identity constitutes a category error, a rebellion against "millennia of moral teaching." Why, then, expect that "homosexuals" would refrain from performing textual sodomy, given their predilection for sexual sodomy? In for a penny, in for a pound.

Lest one suspect that the interpretive sodomy of literary readings of judicial opinions constitutes nothing more than clever word play, two decisions since *Bowers v. Hardwick* merit consideration. Ten years after *Bowers*, the Supreme Court decided *Romer v. Evans*.[41] In that decision, the Court struck down Colorado's Amendment Two, which repealed existing local lesbian/gay civil rights laws and prohibited the state or any of its municipalities from enacting such laws in the future. The Court's decision made no explicit reference to recent scholarship in lesbian/gay studies or queer theory. However, Matt Coles of the American Civil Liberties Union's lesbian/gay civil rights project has argued that the most important factor distinguishing *Romer* from *Bowers* is not so much the treatment of legal issues as the justices' underlying attitudes toward lesbians and gay men.[42] In other words, a decade of "coming out," of deliberate disclosure on the part of lesbians, gay men, and bisexuals seems to have begun redefining sexual identity categories. Coles suggests that in 1986 most if not all of the esteemed justices could state that they knew no queers. In 1996, however, fewer of them could legitimately make such a claim.

The connection between queer theory and judicial decisions may still seem tenuous at best. But note that, at least according to Coles's argument, the justices' evolving attitudes toward lesbians and gay men results not from increasing "enlightenment" or "reason" but simply from greater exposure to actual persons. The categories are experiential, not logical. More direct evidence for the relevance of queer theoretical discussion to judicial decision making comes from U.S. District Judge Eugene Nickerson's decision in *Able v. U.S.A.*, a challenge to the Department of Defense's "Don't ask; don't tell" policy. Without delving into the niceties of the social construction debate, Nickerson relied extensively on Boswell's *Christianity, Social Tolerance, and Homosexuality*, implicitly ascribing to Boswell a social constructionist position and citing him as agreeing with Halperin on the status of gay persons in ancient Greek and Roman societies.[43] More remarkable still, Judge Nickerson quoted Sedgwick's statement from *Epistemology of the Closet* that "the closet is the defining structure for gay oppression in this century," in order to buttress his claim that lesbians and gay men suffer significant discrimination as a class and therefore merit increased scrutiny under the equal protection clause of the Fourteenth Amendment.

Performing Disciplinary Sodomy

Foucault's definition of "the tactical polyvalence of discourses" contained Goldberg's quotation, the reference to sodomy as "that utterly confused category." Just how confused, in the context of any effort to construct a continuous definition stretching from the sixteenth century to the present, became clearer from other essays in *Queering the Renaissance*. In "The (In)Significance of 'Lesbian' Desire in Early Modern England," Valerie Traub demonstrated one important failure of continuity. The "homosexual" identity that the justices relied on to contain sodomy supposedly applies equally to men and women. But Traub described a document from the eighteenth century in which the definition of sodomy made no mention of women. From this and other sources, Traub concluded that desire between women signified, or failed to signify, as an issue of gender roles rather than of sexuality. Confirming Foucault's broad assertion about the recent provenance of sexuality as the organizing rubric for desire in all of its manifestations, Traub argued that desire between women attracted men's attention only when the women usurped some male prerogative or threatened to interfere with the exchange of women in marriage and reproduction. Women's desire for each other became sodomy only when it threatened gender (read: social) disorder.

Traub's article also confused disciplinary boundaries with her reliance on both "fictional" and "nonfictional" sources to support her argument. Traub posed the question of women's desire for each other in the context of antitheatricalists' condemnation of cross-dressing on the stage. The distinction between history and literary criticism got silently elided on a page that began with a discussion of the significance of cross-dressing women and ended with a quotation from Shakespeare.[44] In Traub's description of the significance of the tract by John Disney with which she began her discussion, she gave a clue to her elision of this distinction: "If we recognize in Disney's tract not the idiosyncrasies of an individual but the discourse of a culture, we gain a point of access into the historical obscurity of early modern women's erotic desires for one another."[45] Where thought silently thinks, the constituent ideas of the episteme will appear as reliably in fictional as in nonfictional texts.

Traub's argument became Scott's method in reverse. Shakespeare as evidence for "lesbian" desire—not lesbian desire because, like Carroll Smith-Rosenberg's nineteenth-century women, Traub's early modern women had no such category available to them—constitutes not reading for the literary but reading from the literary. Traub investigated desire that did not depend on man, either in the literal sense or in Foucault's sense of the knowing subject and object of inquiry. The distinction between "factual" and "fictional" sources played little role in her inquiry, because literary sources can reveal as much, or more, about the organization of knowledge and modes of thought in a given culture as nonliterary sources do. Existing disciplinary divisions reflect the assumption of universal man in the human sciences: man's economic activities, his linguistic skills, his bodily needs, his literary production. Area studies—women's, African American, lesbian/gay—reflect the effort to bring all of these elements together for the purpose of understanding identities other than generic "man."

Alan Bray, a civil servant by profession, hewed closer to ordinary historical practice in his discussion of sodomitical confusion, "Homosexuality and the Signs of Male Friendship in Elizabethan England."[46] He argued that sodomy in Elizabethan England covered a wider range of sexual acts than just those between persons of the same gender. It also constituted not merely a sexual crime but a political and religious crime as well. The circumstances in which sodomy might easily occur also provided the context for a highly commendable relationship, the close friendship between two men. According to official definition, no two types of relationship could less resemble one another, as Sedgwick argued in her definitions of the extremes of homosociality. Observers leveled the charge of sodomy, Bray argued, only when a particular friendship in some important respect violated the canons of the institution. He offered the famous example of Edward's generosity to his favorite, Gaveston, in Christopher Marlowe's play *Edward II*. Edward's offense lay not in any specific sexual act but in his bestowal of noble presents on the common Gaveston. He violated the social order, with sexual misconduct serving simply as the most vivid possible symbol for his crime. Sodomy marked the divide between order and disorder.

Bray's analysis here resembled Sedgwick's account of her project at the beginning of *Epistemology of the Closet*. We might read this observation about the centrality of homo/heterosexual definition for understanding Western culture backward, arguing from Traub and Bray that any understanding of early modern English culture remained inadequate insofar as it failed to trace out the differences between the meaning of the term "sodomy" then and now.

Failure to understand sodomy in early modern England returns us to the esteemed justices of the Supreme Court. Perhaps not surprisingly, Sedgwick offered her own reading of the *Bowers v. Hardwick* decision in the introduction to *Epistemology of the Closet*. She focused on the broader issue of knowledge versus ignorance as they play out against one another, or play out synergistically, in the majority opinion. In Sedgwick's reading, the justices' posture represented a claim of knowledge not only about the law but about the intent of the plaintiff. They couched that claim of knowledge within a moat of ignorance, or "transparent stupidity," to use Sedgwick's terms, the specifics of which, as they raise historical questions, we have already examined.[47]

But, as Sedgwick pointed out, the justices also claimed knowledge of the plaintiff, he who committed sodomy and thereby created certain presumptions about his identity. Justice Byron White wrote that "to claim that a right to engage in sodomy is 'deeply rooted in this nation's history and tradition' or 'implicit in the concept of ordered liberty' is, at best, facetious."[48] This unsupportable claim that Hardwick facetiously pursued his case to the Supreme Court (raising, of course, the question of the spirit in which the justices chose to hear the case), in Sedgwick's view, relied on the paranoid fantasy that gay people can somehow read the minds of straight people. One might also detect here the operation of the social scientific procedure of defining the object of inquiry as fully available to the consciousness of the knowing subject by dint of that subject's reliance on the universal principles of scientific method. "Conservative" justices, especially, remain fond of "neutral principles" as their guides for legal interpretation.

Justice White's unsupported claim also depended, in Goldberg's view, on the assumption that the justices all define themselves as heterosexual, or nonsodomites. Their competence to adjudicate the question of a "right of homosexuals to engage in sodomy" rested on the implicit representation that they would never do such a thing themselves, indeed that they definitionally could not do such a thing, because they represent themselves as heterosexual. Lee Edelman argued in his literary reading of the *Bowers v. Hardwick* decision that representation matters far more in such debates than do actual acts. Edelman suggested that the decision dealt as much with the question of reading and interpretation as it did with sodomy. The justices' concern for "ancient roots" and things "fundamental" reflected the fear that, had they found a "right of homosexuals to engage in sodomy," they would have performed a sodomitical reading of the Constitution and acquiesced in their own metaphorical sodomizing.[49]

In arguing that the legal issue concerned the public representation of sodomites rather than specific acts of sodomy committed in private, Edelman echoed Goldberg's argument about the hope of defeating sodomy statutes with an argument from privacy rights. Reading debates over National Endowment for the Arts funding for photographer Robert Mapplethorpe, protections for gay men and lesbians in the District of Columbia, and the *Bowers* decision, Edelman concluded that many officials see in public representations of sodomy the threat of a complete reversal of public order. He noted that the district attorney in Georgia refused to prosecute Hardwick even as he asserted the legit-imacy of the statute criminalizing Hardwick's behavior.

Goldberg argued that even the minority decision in *Bowers*, declar-ing the Georgia sodomy statute an invalid invasion of privacy rights, offered cold comfort to lesbians and gay men. Their line of reasoning, on Goldberg's view, resembled the majority opinion in equating acts with identities, thus allowing only a private but no public space for the identity that accompanies the privately permissible act of sodomy. Gold-berg asserted that "both majority and minority views in the *Hardwick* decision agree that if homosexuals have any place at all it is in the closet. (The majority would have that closet barred and padlocked, of course)."[50] Identity categories result from practices of representation, which in turn admit of public contest, or politics. These practices deter-mine what public authorities will recognize and what they will ignore, and on what terms. Permission for acts but not public representations continues the practice of moving the debate out of the political arena into the realm of the "private."

These literary readers of a Supreme Court decision share an inves-tigative motivation that Foucault described in defining his genealogi-cal stance. Reading Nietzsche, he stated that "'effective' history differs from traditional history in being without constants. Nothing in man—not even his body—is sufficiently stable to serve as the basis for self-recognition or for understanding other men. The traditional devices for constructing a comprehensive view of history and for retracing the past as a patient and continuous development must be systematically dis-mantled. Necessarily, we must dismiss those tendencies that encourage the consoling play of recognitions."[51] Neither "sodomy" nor "homo-sexual" serves to designate a constant of human behavior or identity. If we would understand fully the meanings of these terms, we must sus-pend as thoroughly as possible the assumption of their simple referen-tiality. We must look instead for the struggles and debates through which these terms acquired their meanings.

These literary critics disrupted the justices' recognitions of sodomy in order to challenge the knowledge claims the justices had made about sodomitical acts and homosexual persons. The critics' readings offered interpretations, not explanations, hermeneutics rather than science. Foucault began *The History of Sexuality* by disparaging the hopes of those who looked for the coming revolution in reliable knowledge of the self revealed through sexuality. Knowledge, on Foucault's view, offers no revolution, no salvation. Knowledge of a more or less rigorously scientific sort first helped officials distinguish the homosexual from the sodomite. And, as Foucault pointed out, that very scientific knowledge, or the discourse that enabled it, also provided the basis from which the modern lesbian/gay rights movement began to resist the dominations of both medicine and law.

Literary critics, historians, and philosophers in the late 1980s and early 1990s increasingly read medicine and law, however, precisely because they increasingly suspected, with Halperin, that to counter knowledge claim for knowledge claim would only perpetuate, not alter, the games of truth that we play under the deployment of sexuality. Perhaps the clearest example of this assumption came in Goldberg's reading of the dissenting opinion in *Bowers v. Hardwick*, especially insofar as that reading contained Goldberg's own dissent from the liberal orthodoxy that "privacy" offers the best ground from which to legitimize lesbian/gay civil rights. Goldberg took no comfort from the minority opinion in *Bowers*, because he detected a formal congruence in the arguments that both minority and majority used. Like Queer Nation, Goldberg wished to assert the legitimacy of public displays of queer or sodomitical pleasures. He argued that to insist only that people denominated "homosexual" should have the right to perform sodomy in private perpetuates the assumption that "sodomy" as conduct defines "homosexuals" as persons. Disputes and distinctions that remain within these terms, in the long run, may not help. Instead, Goldberg and other queer theorists interpreted medicine and law from the outside, the better to resist and critique their practitioners' claims to expert knowledge. Political change, on this view, depends not on more knowledge but on different games of truth.

Writing in *Fear of a Queer Planet*, Halley examined the relationship between privacy and equal protection from inside the discipline of law as well. When she suggested limits to the efficacy of textual, deconstructive criticism, she expressed a more nuanced version of the concern that Seidman and Mohr raised. She did not dismiss such practices wholesale as Mohr did. Rather, in her reading of cases involving equal-protection claims by lesbian and gay litigants, she found that the definitional incoherence of shifting identity categories as revealed by deconstructive readings actually formed a useful part of the strategies that judges employed in denying those claims. In the 1991 case *Jantz v. Muci*,[52] the reasoning of one federal judge differed from that of several of his peers. He found that the alleged constitutionality of sodomy laws under *Bowers* did not automatically prevent "homosexuals," the class of persons defined by the act of sodomy, from making claims under the equal-protection clause.

For Halley, while it was a fine thing to have a decision distinguishing equal protection from the privacy issue under *Bowers*, still the logic of the *Jantz* decision exhibited a troubling congruence with the logic of previous decisions denying equal-protection claims. The federal judge in *Jantz* found a "homosexual" identity defined not in terms of sodomitical acts but in terms of a central, immutable characteristic of personhood—essentialism, in the terms of earlier debates among feminist and gay scholars. This idea of a natural, precultural identity troubled Halley. She noted that, whatever the legal accomplishments of the specific decision, the underlying logic was not terribly different from the logic of defining immutable identity in terms of sodomy: "The internal logic of the personhood definition would not be fundamentally offended if one proceeded to add to it the only additional requisite of the deviance definition: that the persons essentially committed to homosexual personhood are thereby also essentially committed to sodomitical action."[53]

Like Sedgwick, Halley worried about judges positioning themselves as neutral "heterosexuals" who could make knowledge claims about proper definitions of "homosexual" persons. Part of the definitional move involved what Halley called the "bribe" of heterosexuality: The legal, administrative, physical, and definitional expulsion of "homosexuals" has the effect of constituting a community as "heterosexual" even as claims to natural or essential identity categories allow these "heterosexuals" to ignore their active role in the expulsion process. Meanwhile, the expulsion reinforces incentives to remain publicly "heterosexual" for anyone who might harbor designs of proclaiming a "homosexual" identity. Although the *Jantz* judge chose not to participate in the expulsion, he continued to occupy the position of one who would define categories of sexual identity for others. Halley closed her essay in *Fear of a Queer Planet* by calling for new approaches to equal-protection litigation that would fundamentally change the terms of the debate.

Similarly, Cindy Patton argued in *Fear of a Queer Planet* that the time had come for a fundamental reconceptualization of identity politics. She wrote that "the crucial battle now for 'minorities' and resistant subalterns is not achieving democratic representation but wresting control over the discourses concerning identity construction. The opponent is not the state so much as it is the other collectivities attempting to set the rules for identity constitution in something like a 'civil society.'"[54] This conclusion resulted from her reading of right-wing efforts to disqualify the claims of lesbians and gay men to authoritative knowledge about their own sexual identities. These efforts took place in the larger context of far-right activists' redefinition of themselves as members of a minority who persisted in championing what they portrayed as moral positions that had once commanded majority adherence in the United States, before the fall from grace of the 1960s. As Patton explained, the brilliance of the far Right's redefinition lay in their appropriation of the logic of civil rights protest to represent themselves as suffering a diminution of their civil rights as conservatives while also denying that lesbians and gay men could legitimately claim civil rights protections under legal doctrines designed to remedy discrimination on the basis of race.

The issue among competing political groups then comes down to their ability to cite successfully the precedents and traditions of the political culture. On Patton's view, the coming-out logic that many lesbian/gay activists deploy appeals not to a natural or essentialized version of gay identity but to a moral requirement for action. According to activist logic, anyone who comes out of the closet as lesbian, gay, bisexual, or transgender has a moral responsibility to participate in political action that will minimize the influence of the far Right while promoting the public policy agenda of the queer rights movement. The New Right and the lesbian/gay civil rights movement identify themselves in opposition to—which is to say, in relation to—each other, compensating for the unlikelihood of attracting significant numbers of new members by encouraging members of other social groups to disidentify with the opposition.

Patton has described brilliantly the way in which traditional practices of political organizing have acquired new meanings in the context of what she calls "postmodern governmentality." She defines identity in this context as "a rhetorical effect that (1) elides its construction, (2) implies or renarrates a history, (3) produces a deontic closure, and (4) operates performatively within a field of power in which citational chains link symbols and political subject position."[55] In other words, discourses of government define the field of possible relationships among subjects, as well as between subjects and the state. Queer activists strive to tell a story about queers that will motivate the queers to action while legitimating their claims to minority status in the tradition of U.S. civil rights protest and delegitimating the claims of right-wing activists to superior moral understanding of "homosexuality."

Queer Inside as Well as Out

Just as the question of nonqueer persons and groups defining themselves is an issue for queer theorists, the internal definitions of queer theory are also important. Butler's 1994 article "Against Proper Objects" addressed this point.[56] It began with an attempt to describe the distinctive domains of feminism and lesbian/gay studies that the editors of *The Lesbian and Gay Studies Reader* offered in introducing their collection. Butler took issue with the editors' statement, "Lesbian/gay studies does for *sex* and *sexuality* approximately what women's studies does for gender."[57]

Butler pointed out that such definition of the "proper objects" of study for lesbian/gay studies and feminism overlooked two major points: First, the editors effectively reduced "sex" as anatomy to "gender." Although feminist scholars had long worked to establish some distance between the social meanings of gender difference and the anatomical differences that supposedly ground these social meanings, still the relationship between sex and gender remained an important point of contest for feminists, not the basis of a simple assimilation of one to the other. Second, by claiming sovereignty over questions of "sex" as the set of acts that grounds the deployment of "sexuality," the editors overlooked an enormous body of work in which feminists debated the relationship between sexual acts and gender definition. For Butler, "A characterization of feminism as an exclusive focus on gender thus misrepresents the recent history of feminism in several significant ways."[58]

More broadly, the definition of proper objects entails some refusal to recognize historical specificity. When the editors of *The Lesbian and Gay Studies Reader* defined "sex" and "sexuality" such that those domains became the proper objects of study for lesbian/gay studies, the editors ignored significant aspects of the history of feminist scholarship. Butler emphasized that "what is at issue here is clearly *not* a question of what the editors of the volume intend, given that all three have made strong contributions to feminist scholarship, but rather . . . a set of political and historical implications of the analogy between feminism and lesbian/gay studies which have been difficult to discern for many of us who work within and between these domains of study."[59] Or, to use Foucault's description of disciplinary power, the editors' choice was intentional and nonsubjective. They certainly intended to arrive at a definition of the proper domain for lesbian/gay studies, its proper objects, but they did so within a historical and intellectual tradition over which they could not exercise complete control. Their intentional definition necessarily carried unintended consequences, which Butler felt compelled to point out.

Butler felt compelled to point out these unintended consequences because she feared the loss of important features of the history of feminism. For Butler, definitional certainty, the specification of proper objects, would come at too high a price in lost historical contest and variation. Traub specified more concretely how this process had already begun to operate among scholars in the field of English Renaissance studies. In a move similar to the one that Butler described, Traub pointed to an emerging confrontation between feminist theory and queer theory according to which queer theory claimed "sex and sexuality" as its proper object, in distinction to gender as the proper object of feminism. Even more problematically, however, this definition of proper scholarly objects enabled a general disinterest in, or repudiation of, feminist theory by younger scholars who no longer saw the relevance of feminism. For Traub, this refusal to recognize the importance of feminist analysis for the development of queer theory depended on the same logic of gender according to which her male counterparts who studied sexuality in Renaissance England tended to assume, rather than investigate, the invisibility of women's desire for other women, and according to which the term "queer," insofar as it came to equal "homosexual," became thereby implicitly male.[60]

This problem gave weight to the arguments of those feminists whom Butler describes as emphasizing sexual difference over gender. According to this distinction, some feminist scholars considered emphasis on the social categories of gender politically disempowering. They insisted that social categories have meaning only within a symbolic field in which men produce meaning against a backdrop of invisible and unspeakable femininity. Every assertion of femininity or of women's identity, on this view, is always already an erasure of that identity, because it is an assertion that men make within a symbolic economy that they control and that depends on the exclusion of the female. In "Against Proper Objects," Butler associated this position with Lacanian psychoanalytic theory, which emphasizes the psychic aspects of sexual difference as constituted and mediated through language and symbolic interaction.[61] In this article, however, she recognized the problem that Lacanian psychoanalysis presumes an origin of the symbolic that effectively becomes unchanging and unchangeable. She argued for a conception of the symbolic that recognizes its interactions with social categories. Yet, at the same time, the emphasis on sexual difference as somehow importantly connected to the social meanings of gender helps to prevent the assertion of sex and sexuality as the proper objects of lesbian and gay studies in a manner that perpetuates the invisibility of anything feminine, including feminism.

In opposing proper objects for lesbian and gay studies or for feminism, Butler demonstrated the value of discrete categories and historical continuity for maintaining the status quo. She ended her essay by pointing to the active disavowal of feminist alliances among some gay male leaders for whom gender hierarchies are not only legitimate but valuable.[62] On this view, the very definitional instability of the term "queer" could become the gender- and race-blind utopia of white males. Laura Alexandra Harris made this point in her discussion of "queer black feminism." For Harris, "Queer, as it is often claimed by academically powerful white masculinity, sometimes suggests and describes its political constituency as seductively fluid, unmarked, ambiguous, and chosen. This fluidity sounds dangerously like the status of white masculinity to me."[63] Feminist scholars have long noted how the masculine category functions as the default or definitive version of any category, with the feminine marked as the exception. The very words that we use reveal this process: man and wo-man, male and fe-male. The danger of "queer" as free-floating signifier was that, under the weight of historical precedent, any "unmarked" category might simply reinstall white, male subjectivity as normative.

Attempts to define "queer" or to leave it undefined raised issues of historical determination and agency, especially around the issue of race. Again, Lauretis's undefinition of "queer" offered race as a definitive category that would remain as an open question in its relationship to sexuality.[64] Reading Lauretis, however, Evelynn Hammonds disputed both Lauretis's characterization of the relationships between race and sexuality and scholars' knowledge of these relationships. Hammonds argued that Lauretis had chalked up the relative absence of African American queer scholarship to the personal choices of African American queers, thus underplaying the importance of institutional racism and homophobia in the academy and the society as a whole.[65] Hammonds elaborated the enormous difficulty for black feminists of articulating any conception of black female sexuality, given the weight of historical precedent according to which a culture dominated by white racist imaginings categorized hypervisible black women's bodies as always oversexed and immoral. This categorization rendered black women's own experiences of their sexuality invisible and unhearable. In that context, many race women chose to remain silent, and in some cases enforce silence on other black women, on the subject of their sexuality in the hope of establishing the superiority of their own moral characters.[66]

In Hammonds's account, black women clearly made choices about concealing their sexuality, but Hammonds insisted on the historical determination of the circumstances in which those women made their choices. She noted that the concerns of some race women to appear morally superior led them to characterize black lesbians as traitors to the race. Attempts simply to add "black" to the category "lesbian" thus failed to take into account the fundamental ways in which race informed and determined the array of choices available to black lesbians—the problem Lauretis hoped to address by distinguishing "queer theory" from "lesbian/gay studies." But this historical determination of black lesbians' options did not remove the possibility for agency. Whatever the problems with definitions, or undefinitions, of "queer," still the concept offered an opportunity that Hammonds took advantage of. "At this juncture," Hammonds wrote, "queer theory has allowed me to break open the category of gay and lesbian and begin to question how sexualities and sexual subjects are produced by dominant discourses and then to interrogate the reactions and resistances to those discourses."[67]

Queer interpretation of identity categories thus offered some avenue to political resistance. The necessarily disempowering implications some feminists saw in deconstructions of identity that rest on recognition of historical determination got quite as lost in Hammonds's queer black feminism as did the necessarily quiescent implications of Foucault's work in ACT-UP demonstrations. Hammonds made the connection between interpretation and politics explicit: "The work of black feminist critics is to find ways to contest the historical construction of black female sexualities by illuminating how the dominant view was established and maintained and how it can be disrupted. This work might very well save some black women's lives. I want this epidemic [AIDS] to be used to foment the sexual revolution that black Americans never had. I want it to be used to make visible black women's self-defined sexualities."[68] Attention to the discursive and institutional procedures for producing black women's silence about their sexuality may prove useful in helping black women who found themselves caught in the AIDS epidemic to articulate an understanding of their sexuality as the basis for containing the spread of the epidemic.

Harris also found "queer" useful as a concept. She deployed it with a vigorous specificity to explore how class, race, and sexuality could require modifications of feminism. Harris asserted of herself, "I can be an academic feminist; I can be a black feminist; I can be a dyke feminist. But I can't be any of them really without first 'passing' the boundaries set up in each, without confronting the assumptions of each, without recombining the advantages and disadvantages of each, and without being a queer in each."[69] For Harris, "queer" served not as an unmarked category but as the basis for marking and resisting the unacknowledged boundaries of other categories, especially the category "feminism." Feminism played an important role in Harris's adolescence, but both her identification as a feminist and the recognition of her female role models as feminist required some struggle. She learned only relatively late about many of the iconic names and ideas of feminist scholarship and politics. Her own feminist identifications came through such unlikely figures as Cher and her working poor immigrant mother, whom Harris suspected of laughing with her friends at the attitudes of educated, white, middle-class feminists of the 1970s.

A history about "the truth" of feminism in the 1970s would result in a story whose trajectory would exclude much of Harris's experience during that decade. This "truthful" history would begin with a clear definition of "feminism" that would specify the proper objects of study. Like other resistance movements, feminism produced advocates who wish to write its history as an ideal signification embedded in an indefinite teleology of progress. But feminism defined in such abstract terms would exclude the experiences of women who played important roles in the constitution of Harris's feminist subjectivity: "I do not want to argue over who remembers what right any more. Instead I want to record what feminism meant for me, to me, with the understanding that I do so because *I am grateful* it was there. I need to claim my feminist past for the future, not be told I never had one, and therefore feminism needs to be reconfigured to include that past and define that future. Often, this entails recognizing women whose voices were not articulated through feminism or whose politics were not formed correctly according to feminism."[70] Note that, at the level of method, Harris's genealogy of feminism might look little different from a good history. Harris insisted on the importance of gathering detailed information from a wide variety of sources in order to provide reliable information on the production of feminist subjectivity. The difference lies in the definition of the object of study.

Harris's approach to the history of feminism might be called "presentist" in that she offered her own position as a queer black feminist in the present as the end point from which she would look back to see what did and did not contribute to feminist thought and subjectivity during the 1970s. It might more productively be called a "history of the present" in Foucault's sense.[71] This history of the present rejects the search for origins that Foucault disparaged in "Nietzsche, Genealogy, History" in that it takes practices and subjects in the present as the starting point, looking to the past to discover how these practices attained their justifications and these subjects their significance. The search for origins assumes the existence of a category's essential form in the past. The history of the present assumes that present practices and subjects turned out as they did because of fragmented and unpredictable journeys.[72]

The genealogy of queer theory is itself heterogeneous. Neither Harris nor Hammonds, as queer black feminists, cited Foucault in her discussion of queer theory. We can no more predict the sources of Harris's or Hammonds's queerness than we can the sources of their feminisms. Identities in the form of carefully specified categories discipline the scholar and the object of study in advance. Even as "queer" increasingly became synonymous in public representations with "lesbian and gay," it still retained, in certain circles, the possibility to launch critiques of ideal identity categories. These critiques may come from within the category itself, as one who would claim that category must also specify and reckon with the ways in which the historical constitutions of the category tend to exclude some who would occupy it. Such queering from within depends on the "patiently documentary" work of queer genealogists who document the unexpected, disparate, unidentified experiences that move toward the category in question but arrive from the queerest of directions.[73]

Conclusion

On the Cost of Telling the Truth

Your body's alive, but no one told you what you'd feel.

—Melissa Etheridge

The relationship between rationalization and excesses of political power is evident. And we should not need to wait for bureaucracy or concentration camps to recognize the existence of such relationships.

—Michel Foucault

So we return again to the question What do queers want? The answer is perhaps no clearer at the end of this book than it was at the beginning. But we now have at least a preliminary catalog of propositions to consider. First and foremost, definitions of gender and sexual identity are distinct but closely related, and they vary considerably over time. Second, gender and sexual identity are integral to a process that we might call government. Again, we must use the term "government" in its broadest possible sense, to mean everything from state policy to individual deportment.

But from a feminist and queer theoretical perspective, were state policy and individual deportment ever really so far apart? Recall Linda Alcoff's discussion of child care: Because the questions of who should take primary responsibility for the daily business of caring for children, why, and with what desired outcome are concerns that impact on the governing of our society at the micro and the macro levels and at every level in between, they have become increasingly politicized since World War II. The increasingly histrionic pronouncements of traditionalist conservatives over the past thirty years or so, especially on issues of gender and sexuality, demonstrate the point: They see explicit political debates over women's role and status, child care, abortion, and lesbian/gay civil rights as threatening departures from long-standing traditions that should remain so deeply embedded in the culture as to elude question altogether. Such is the threat of historical research, especially by women who doubt the necessity, and the utility, of conservative policy preferences: They can demonstrate that traditions vary considerably more than conservatives wish to admit.[1]

Building on the work of historians, and historically minded literary critics, anthropologists, and sociologists, queer theorists began to ask after the processes of governing deportment in terms of representations and practices. Eve Sedgwick wrote about teen suicide as a question of knowledge and power—powerful conservatives in Congress do not wish the U.S. public to know that lesbian and gay teens are significantly more likely than their non–lesbian/gay peers to attempt, and to succeed at, suicide. These members of Congress see a threat to their power in the circulation of representations of queer adolescents. A given teen's choice to commit suicide may itself be a function of power and knowledge—either the knowledge, gained from authoritative adults, that one's desires are evil or the involuntary disclosure of information about these desires. Information about queer teen suicide plays a major role in the contest over queer identity: Some members of Congress figuratively accomplish their goal of denying the existence of queer teens by suppressing information on the topic, thereby contributing to their literal goal by retarding prevention efforts. Authoritative members of the American Psychiatric Association wish to retain some measure of control over the production of queer adults through the mechanism—crude, perhaps, but probably effective in some cases—of diagnosing gender identity disorder in children.

In an important sense, political contest boils down to telling competing stories. The avatars of the "ex-gay" movement tell a particular sort of story about themselves, a very old story of redemption: I once was lost (in the sin and depravity of "the gay lifestyle"), but now I'm found (redeemed by the savior, Jesus Christ, into a life of wholesome, Christian heterosexuality).[2] Lesbian, gay, bisexual, and transgender civil rights activists, by contrast, tell a seemingly newer but increasingly effective story of personal authenticity: The story of the United States of America is a story of individual rights, of each person's opportunity to live her or his life according to the dictates of individual conscience, free from tyranny of the majority. Discrimination on the basis of sexual orientation or gender expression serves no legitimate purpose; it only infringes on the rights of lesbian, gay, bisexual, and transgender persons to express, to live their lives according to, who they really are. Stories structure fantasies, which structure sexuality, which structures identity—or so the story goes under the deployment of sexuality. But what is the relationship between identity and government?

The United States continues, after two hundred twenty-three years, as the apotheosis of the liberal state. Under our Constitution, free citizens contest law and policy with the goal of achieving the optimum balance of liberty and equality. So it is that, at least since 1952, "homosexuals" have protested what they consider to be unjust treatment.[3] In keeping with the libertarian expectation that government exists to protect the fundamental rights of individuals, most queer activists have argued for nondiscrimination on the basis of sexual orientation—and, more recently, gender identity or expression—from privacy rights. They have insisted that sexual orientation and practice are personal matters that have no bearing on one's competence as an employee, parent, or tenant; consequently, these factors should not enter into any decisions about the right of queer individuals to occupy these positions.

In effect, queer activists use the same logic that Supreme Court Justice Harry Blackmun used in his *Bowers v. Hardwick* dissent: "This case is about 'the most comprehensive of rights and the right most valued by civilized man,' namely, 'the right to be let alone.'"[4] Any government that claims to protect the liberty of its citizens must begin with the presumption that they have the right to their personal choices about how to live their lives. The burden of proof should rest with government to demonstrate the necessity and efficacy of restrictions that burden individual choices. In practice, the government of the United States has often honored this principle only in the breach. The apostasy of Michel Foucault and queer theorists comes in wondering if the repeated failure of liberal institutions and their defenders to live up to their principles with respect to queers might not indicate the exhaustion of the liberal episteme in theories of government, the opportunity to rethink these questions from the ground up, starting with an understanding of how we become beings with gender and sexuality to begin with.

But queer activists' new story of individual rights seems highly effective over the long run. In ten years, we have substituted *Romer v. Evans* for *Bowers v. Hardwick*. Blackmun dissented in *Bowers* because the majority held that Georgia's law prohibiting sodomy was Constitutional—the zone of protection surrounding individuals' private choices did not extend to "a fundamental right" for "homosexuals to engage in sodomy."[5] Ten years later, however, six Supreme Court justices rejected the idea that the supposed legitimacy of government prohibitions of sodomy necessarily legitimized virtually any other restriction imposed on the class "homosexuals" whom the act allegedly defines—the position that the leading conservative activist on the court, Justice Antonin Scalia, took while dissenting in *Romer*. According to the majority opinion, by repealing existing lesbian/gay civil rights ordinances and forbidding the future enactment of such ordinances, Colorado's Amendment Two bore no discernable relationship to any legitimate governmental purpose. Even as pundits of all stripes describe the U.S. electorate as increasingly conservative, lesbian, gay, bisexual, and transgender activists continue to grow in number, organization, and power. It might seem highly counterproductive for queer theorists to shoot academic darts from our ivory towers at this politically effective engine of personal authenticity. After *Romer*, the question becomes even more acute: What do queers want?

What Does It Mean to Be Equal?

Foucault's description of disciplinary practices and the truth of the self in sexuality lead to the counterintuitive conclusion that individuals need to have their identities and experiences explained to them. Especially in his last two books, *The Use of Pleasure* and *The Care of the Self*, Foucault increasingly turned to the "games of truth" through which men in Western cultures have explained themselves to themselves as desiring subjects.[6] For Foucault, the minute attention to desire as a field for moral inquiry and specification constituted an intellectual problem. "In short," he wrote, "it was a matter of seeing how an 'experience' came to be constituted in modern Western societies, an experience that caused individuals to recognize themselves as subjects of a 'sexuality,' which was accessible to very diverse fields of knowledge and linked to a system of rules and constraints."[7] Foucault wished to stand back from this experience, insofar as a subject who was constituted by some version of that experience can do so, in order to understand its historical deployment.

Foucault criticized the claims of sexual liberationists because they posited the free expression of every individual's sexual nature as the solution to moralizing sexual repression. Foucault insisted that, even in the absence of politically motivated moralizing on the subject of sexuality, individuals would remain subjects, would continue to derive their subjectivity from some cultural source. He argued for a model of enlightenment according to which we abandon the quest for a society free of power, recognizing instead that the moral implications of any exercise of power will remain always ambiguous and labile, requiring an attitude of perpetual suspicion and critique. The trajectory of Foucault's work as refracted through the prism of queer theory in the 1990s points toward resistance to an increasingly rationalized model of identity that even many lesbians and gay men see as potentially liberatory.

We might pose the question as a reconsideration of what it means to be "created," as in "All men are created equal." Clearly, Thomas Jefferson assumed that some omnipotent deity, a "Creator," did the creating. On this view, the Creator establishes the important aspects of our identity at or before birth. From this act of Creation, we build our political practices and institutions—hence the desire among many queer activists to establish that queer identity results from some biological determination, from some act of Creation, suitably updated for our scientific age. We are equal, in this sense, because queers get their identities at the same time and in the same way that nonqueers do.

This point illuminates Scott's argument in "'Experience.'"[8] She argued that historians who accept an individual's experience as the foundation for a story about that individual thereby lose the opportunity to examine the practices and meanings that constituted the experience. Such historians describe the games of truth in which the individual played without examining the rules of the games and how the rules came to govern the games. Scott's suggestion that historians "read for the literary" serves as a means for exploring how individuals had their experiences explained to them. This constitutes reading for the literary in the broad sense that the process involves attaching meanings to events through signification: The boy who has a homoerotic thought or encounter will learn the perils of "homosexual" identity from the book, physician, or priest he consults or—should he make his desires public or prove unable to disguise them—from the teasing of his peers. Any connection between homoerotic thought or practice and "homosexual" identity depends on the culturally constituted explanation and attachment, not on a "natural" or otherwise inevitable connection between thought or practice and identity. But the exploration of explanations for experience also constitutes reading for the literary in the historically specific sense that literature has commonly provided a particular refuge of sorts for feminists, lesbians, and gay men who found scientific explanations of their subjectivities inadequate.

Joyce Appleby, Margaret Hunt, Lynn Jacob, Murray Murphey, and many others continue to insist that, in order to maintain its intellectual respectability, history must hew as closely to science as possible. John Boswell believed that a scientific determination of the causes of lesbian/gay identity would solve the essentialist/constructionist debate among historians. The experiences and theories of other feminists, picking up Foucaultian genealogy along the way to queer theory, raise instead the possibility of a rhetorical and moral critique of science as the epistemological gold standard and ultimate arbiter of political dilemmas in our culture. This is antiscience in Foucault's sense—opposition not to the content and methods of science but to the way in which claims to scientificity confer power in our culture. Judith Butler cataloged the persistence of passionately gendered research into a possible physiological seat of gender difference, despite the repeated failures of such research.[9] Queer theorists ask, Why do the claims to equal opportunity and treatment of lesbians and gay men depend on the biological stamp of approval, certifying that they just can't help it?

In 1991 Simon LeVay, a gay man, gained notoriety by publishing his research on alleged differences in brain structures between "homosexual" and "heterosexual" men.[10] LeVay, wrote, "In my view, the scientific evidence presently available points to a strong influence of nature, and only a modest influence of nurture" in determining an individual's sexual identity.[11] Perhaps LeVay's position indicated progress. The tale has become commonplace among lesbians and gay men of going to the library in search of some explanation for one's "perverse" desire only to find that the scientific accounts of "homosexuality" invariably described a psychopathology. Without making overt value judgments, LeVay offered a scientific explanation for the etiology of "homosexuality."

Before LeVay wrote, and continuing afterward if queer theorists have anything to say about it, lesbians and gay men turned from science to literature—to representations in the form of stories—in order to find a different truth of themselves. During the 1970s, literary scholars played a major role among those who led the lesbian feminist movement, both academically and politically. Lesbian feminist politics developed with an abiding interest in and commitment to literary representations of lesbian and feminist subjectivity. First-person narratives provided an avenue for challenging the knowledge of experts who claimed that feminist, lesbian, or gay identity necessarily constituted psychopathology.[12] Literary representations in films as well as in books, removed from the epistemological constraints of "science," could serve the purpose that Teresa de Lauretis described as providing fantasies of lesbian desire that do not perpetuate sexual indifference. They could also function as genealogies, countering the abstractions of scientific research into gender and sexuality with the specificity of individual lives.

Scientific research free of explicit ethical considerations holds dangers for nonlesbian feminists as well. A growing number of feminist scientists has elaborated increasingly sophisticated critiques of efforts to locate the physiological seat of gender difference. The publication of LeVay's research purporting to find differences between "heterosexual" and "homosexual" brains prompted Anne Fausto-Sterling to add a chapter to the revised edition of *Myths of Gender: Biological Theories about Women and Men*. She had argued throughout the book that attempts to trace complex human behaviors to single biological causes, whether genetic, hormonal, or structural, were profoundly misguided. She related LeVay's research to her primary focus on gender differences by pointing to the utility of homophobia for maintaining gender roles.[13]

Some, including Gayle Rubin and Foucault himself, would insist that "homosexuality" constitutes a problem unto itself. Fausto-Sterling has overstated the extent to which debates about lesbian/gay rights simply reflect anxieties about gender. Nothing precludes the possibility that women could achieve full equality in our society while a generalized prohibition on same-gender erotic activity remained—women and men might operate under an equal prohibition. Fausto-Sterling's basic point remains, however: Attempts to find biological bases for either gender difference or sexual orientation reflect the desire to shift political decisions into the realm of science.

Not surprisingly, Foucault saw the epistemological status of science as an issue of power. Addressing the alleged scientific status of Marxist inquiry, Foucault insisted that claims to the status of science have more to do with distributions of power in modern Western culture than with epistemology. French Marxists, he implied, would wrap their political preferences in the mantle of science as a way of exerting more power.[14] In the United States, along with reducing our political theory to "political science," we routinely try to displace political issues into the realm of scientific inquiry for resolution. The intellectual and political trajectories of Marxism and liberalism often reveal far greater similarities than we might expect.

As Irene Diamond and Lee Quinby pointed out in their Foucaultian discussion of the feminist sexuality debates,[15] science promises control. Phenomena that we can subsume under the operation of universal laws we can also manipulate. For LeVay and many lesbian/gay political activists, compelling evidence for a biological seat of sexual orientation would provide the deciding factor in favor of legislation prohibiting discrimination on the basis of sexual orientation. Stated in these terms, the position seems ironic: Scientific evidence will provide sufficient control over political debates to carry the principle that one may not discriminate against an individual on the basis of a characteristic over which the individual has no control.

According to Lee Edelman and Jonathan Goldberg, however, sodomy signifies lack of control. Opponents of lesbian/gay civil rights fear precisely that "homosexuality" threatens the end of civilization.[16] On the other hand, Sedgwick argued that the guiding impulse of the scientific rationality that LeVay champions could easily result in a programmatic effort to eliminate lesbians and gay men altogether by altering whatever genetic or structural factor seems to cause "homosexuality." The value of control depends heavily on the moral trajectory within which one asserts it. This observation raises the very difficult question of a given group's ability to maintain control over the trajectory within which they hope to exercise control over their own identities. A gay man who hoped to advance lesbian/gay civil rights began research into brain differences between "homosexual" and "heterosexual" men. Taking for granted the purity of his motives, what reason does anyone have to believe that he will retain control over the uses to which his research gets put? The word "homosexuality" itself is significant: Doctors invented it to describe an illness, and researchers continue to use it to abstract a type of behavior from the daily lives of individuals who may practice it. I say "may" practice it, because the connection between behavior and identity will not admit of precise specification. In the language of identity, a noun that classifies a large group of individuals by abstracting a set of sexual acts apparently makes sense. In the language of difference that poststructuralist philosophers and queer theorists work to elaborate, the coercions inherent in such abstract classifications become increasingly obvious.

Sedgwick's fear would seem preposterous except that we know that such efforts at elimination have happened before. Her fear might seem like academic hysteria, but in May 1997 *The Advocate*, the oldest gay newsweekly in the United States, published a cover photo of a fetus with the caption "Endangered Species: This Child Has the Gay Gene. Will He Be Aborted Because of It?"[17] Suddenly the traditional political goals of liberalism seem to conflict: abortion rights versus lesbian/gay rights. Is the debate over rights and liberty an adequate discourse for adjudicating between parents who wish to control their child's identity and activists who wish to combat the extirpation of their identity? Sedgwick also asserted that the homo/hetero distinction and the play of secrets and revelations that constitute the "epistemology of the closet" are central categories for any understanding of Western culture.[18] This assertion, too, looks absurd on its face. Scholars and activists who claim for themselves and their civil rights movement a central place in Western culture seem risibly self-aggrandizing. However, responses to the claims of the lesbian/gay civil rights movement and to Foucault's intellectual production reveal a fascinatingly histrionic congruence that merits consideration. Why is dispassionate, rational debate about issues of gender and sexuality so difficult?

An episteme enables a certain set of questions and precludes others. The switch from one set of questions to another comes not with the satisfactory resolution of those questions but with the exhaustion of their relevance. Feminist and queer theory and politics have the effect of exhausting the relevance of the set of questions that became important with the episteme of "man." Clearly, we have achieved enormous and important gains in minimizing discrimination on the basis of race, gender, and sexuality since the mid-1960s. Nevertheless, the difficulty of carrying the argument against discrimination on the basis of irrelevant characteristics in the context of a political and epistemological system that ostensibly rests on universal statements about human identity increasingly suggests that the system contains numerous historically and culturally specific assumptions at the most fundamental level. If a universal system of values that will allow everyone equal opportunity remains possible, this ain't it.

Or, after more than two hundred years of practice in the bastion of government "of the people, by the people, and for the people," it becomes increasingly obvious that ostensibly universal principles of justice and right cannot eradicate the historical, cultural determinations of identity. Such are the terms of the Foucault/Habermas debate. Jurgen Habermas hopes to install universal principles of communicative rationality as the basis for eradicating, or at least controlling, the historical determinations of German identity, specifically those historical determinations that relate to the Nazi period.[19] Foucault insists that no such control is possible. Habermas, in turn, described Foucault as a "young conservative"—not a young Nazi, to be sure, but someone who opposed the program that Habermas believed would preclude the possibility of a recrudescence of fascism—because Foucault expressed doubts about the political eschatology of liberalism.[20]

Nazis as dystopic reference point for contemporary political debates help to broaden the issue beyond Habermas and Foucault. At the opposite end of the political spectrum from Habermas, some right-wing activists have associated gay people with fascism. Lon Mabon—director of the Oregon Citizens' Alliance and the driving force behind two viciously anti–lesbian/gay state referenda in Oregon—stated during an election campaign that many leading Nazis, including perhaps Hitler himself, were "homosexuals" and that the Nazis' rise to power depended crucially on support from "homosexual" rights advocates.[21] Here one should read as an archaeologist. Any similarity between critiques of Foucault and attacks on lesbian/gay rights stems from coincidences among local strategies directed toward diverse ends. Clearly Habermas has not joined in conspiracy with Mabon; indeed, Habermas presumably would repudiate both Mabon's goals and his tactics. But the archaeologist will study such coincidences by suspending consideration of the specific content and goals of the discourses in order to bring their formal congruences to the fore. Foucault apparently had in common with lesbian/gay rights activists that they all threatened the historical telos that gave meaning to the cultures in which they lived.

The question concerns identity. Germans must discuss the foundations of their national identity publicly and rationally or risk allowing a historical determination of that identity to return them to the politics of particularism and irrationalism. Oregon residents must specify the terms of proper U.S. identity by voting in favor of a referendum that would write into state law the definition of lesbian/gay identity as "abnormal, wrong, unnatural, and perverse."[22] Lesbians and gay men must resist such attacks by "coming out of the closet"—that is, by revealing the truth of their identities to the voting public and by relying on scientific explanations of those identities where possible.

This necessary conjunction between identity and freedom begs for genealogical examination. In a late interview, Foucault posed the question "How much does it cost for reason to tell the truth?" He stated, "If I 'tell the truth' about myself, I constitute myself as subject by a certain number of relationships of power, which weigh upon me and which I lay upon others."[23] The question for present purposes becomes, How much does it cost feminist, lesbian, and gay scholars to tell the truth? Does LeVay's reliance on biological science promise a liberating truth or one that will bind us yet more closely to a discourse in which "sexuality" governs the truth of subjectivity?

Butler's notion of abjection becomes useful here. Having earned infamy as avatars of evil on earth, Nazis now serve the process of abjection, of eliminating from among "us" any undesirables, who become "them." Any "us," whether the Oregon Citizens' Alliance or the group's lesbian and gay opponents, can establish a positive identity by abjecting the negative image of the other with the epithet "Nazi." Abjection functions as a technique of "subjectification" in Foucault's sense, a game for establishing the truth of the self. LeVay's research plays a similar role. The historical truth of fascism shows us what we must not be, whereas the biological truth of sexuality shows us what we cannot help but be. Empirical research reflects on the nature of "man." Once we find the biological seat of lesbian or gay identity, only those persons whose bodies possess that feature may claim the identity in question. The problem stems from the formal congruence between the present practice of abjecting through the use of "Nazi" as an epithet and the Nazis' own practices of technologized abjection.

But abjection, in turn, only exemplifies the larger strategy of trying to specify in advance the substantive criteria for the achievement of liberty. On its own terms, the identity that justifies claims to truth and liberty under the Enlightenment dispensation is purely formal and universal—it applies to everyone. In practice, the conjunction between, on one hand, liberty and truth and, on the other hand, a rational, autonomous identity has meant that one must choose to forego a wide range of options for action and/or identity in order to qualify for equal treatment and opportunity (insofar as those identities are a matter of choice, which they often are not). The conjunction between foregone options and rational, autonomous identity is contingent, historically specific; it is not natural and necessary, as its proponents claimed. The historical experience of African Americans, women, and queers in demanding equality suggests that the allegedly universal identity that undergirds our claims to liberty and truth actually reflects culturally and temporally specific assumptions about who should be free.

"Liberty" and "truth" defined in terms of philosophical ideals allowed for the equation of equality with sameness. The determination of who got liberty and who could produce truth depended on an antecedent, abstract definition—in purely formal terms—of proper identity. But equality becomes an issue only among persons who are different—non-identical. Identical entities are equal by definition. Foucault's query about the cost of telling the truth and his statements about subjectivity as tying individuals to their identities raised the possibility that any given individual may not remain much at liberty while living up to the injunction to maintain a single, consistent identity over the course of a lifetime.

Foucault's contribution to the debates over rational identity versus subjectivity lay in demonstrating the contingent character of the games of truth that we take for granted as necessary. Such games involve the constitution of humans as objects of knowledge but also as subjects, as individuals with particular qualities that enable them to produce true statements about their objects of inquiry. Foucault examined the question at the level of disciplinary power. He pointed to the contrast between the analysis of law and right in terms of the sovereign and the simultaneous spread of disciplinary power through institutions and practices of surveillance. Close on the heels of the revolutionaries who deposed the king in the seventeenth and eighteenth centuries came the administrators and physicians who ensured the usefulness of individuals to society through the tabulation of populations, inquiries about and elaboration of rules for public health, and the specification of normal and perverse sexualities.[24] The particular content of the classifications "normal" and "perverse" mattered far less than the techniques for their specification. With the demise of the central sovereign, sovereignty and the exercise of power moved outward into the population as a whole. We do this to each other on a daily basis, and we should reflect on what we do in these terms.

The demise of the sovereign depended on the constitution of autonomous subjects. Foucault saw no point in combating the exercise of disciplinary power with references to rights. The type of subject who can legitimately claim such rights became the question in his genealogies. LeVay would make such subjects of lesbians and gay men with his research into brain structures, but at what cost? As only an initial query, what happens to those subjects who experience themselves as gay but who lack the requisite brain structure or gene? Will they, like the French hemaphrodite Herculine Barbin during the deployment of sexuality in the nineteenth century, be required to change identities so that their subjectivity and their empirically verified brain structures will align according to administrative sanction? Will the establishment of genetic orthodoxy in matters of sexual identity give rise to a new bureaucracy that assigns, along with gender and footprint, sexual orientation on each birth certificate? What of those who find later in life that their experience does not match their category?[25] Even without the increasing visibility and importance of the transgender movement—of persons whose gender identity does not match their anatomy—in the broader scope of queer politics, such rationalization of identity would depend heavily on violence, whether physical or psychological.

To ask these questions entails placing the entire epistemological and ethical edifice of Western culture under question. That edifice rests on the assumption that universality and rationality will typically serve the needs of justice. The enormity of this question perhaps helps to explain the vigor with which opponents enter the lists in these debates. Identity, in the sense of the morally competent, autonomous subject and in the sense of congruence between categories of representation and reality—individuals and truth—governs our understanding of the world at the most fundamental level. Practices precede and exceed their justifications—even in the absence of a robustly articulated philosophical justification for that understanding, the practices that it enables continue apace through their historical accretion of meaning.

The threat Foucault's work posed stemmed from the challenge he offered to the universalizing impulse that underlies this epistemological and ethical framework. Scientific knowledge serves as our epistemological gold standard, even for historians such as Appleby and Murphey, because scientists elaborate universal laws—generalized statements about how the world works that provide some measure of predictive certainty. Foucault suggested that we assign considerable epistemological and ethical value to science because of the historical a priori that govern the modern episteme. The human sciences, on this view, simply will not admit of elaboration in terms of universal laws, even though the episteme requires that human scientists strive to provide precisely that form of justification for their work. They can only try to answer the questions that the episteme poses for them.

Habermas, McNay, and many other scholars worried that Foucault would pull the epistemological foundation from under their ethical edifice of liberation. Foucault committed two deadly sins: He questioned the value of "modernity," and he offered no vision of what would replace it. The game of truth that Foucault's critics believed they were playing required the assertion, through epistemological universality, of authorial control over one's own discursive universe, which must also provide some representation of how the world will look once the author's ethical design governs it. If any positive, stable identity requires some abjection, then good liberals want to persuade themselves that, whoever is the other whom they turn to shit, those shits deserved it because they violated our robustly justified, universal moral rules.

Here we must return to Habermas's concern for a recrudescence of Nazi politics through the irresponsible elaboration of German national identity in cultural and linguistic terms. Rather than abject the Nazis, rather than assure ourselves of the unity and coherence of our own, morally superior, identities by drawing sharp distinctions between the Nazis over there and us over here, we should read archaeologically for regularities that have governed both their thought and ours, read genealogically for indications that deployments useful to the Nazis remain useful to us.

Genealogy begins with discontinuity. Thus, we must for the moment focus our attention not on the Nazis' treatment of Jews but on their treatment of "homosexuals." This is so emphatically not because of any claim that the Nazis' persecution of "homosexuals" was in any sense equal to or worse than their persecution of Jews, overlooking for the moment the important set of people who belong to both categories. Rather, the Nazis' persecution of Jews admits of far too ready assimilation to a long, familiar history of persecution that has befouled European history for centuries. Foucault as genealogist suggested that knowledge of a subject may in some respects impede understanding of it. The magnificent erudition of Jewish scholars, impressive as scholarship and indispensable as a bulwark against the indefatigable impulse to eliminate Jews from the earth, renders depressingly familiar a phenomenon that, for present purposes, must become disorienting in its unfamiliarity. "The object was to learn to what extent the effort to think one's own history can free thought from what it silently thinks, and so enable it to think differently."[26] The object is to consider the extent to which the comforts of certain identity simply perpetuate the practices of the past.

Thus, *The History of Sexuality* again provides the text with which to begin. Foucault has suggested, and other scholars have confirmed, that persecution of "homosexuals" differs markedly from persecution of Jews in being a relatively recent phenomenon in the Christian West.[27] The Nazis' persecution of "homosexuals" provides not a depressing confirmation of long-standing practice but a disorienting application of old and new principles to an identity category of relatively recent provenance.

Queer theorists' readings of the *Bowers v. Hardwick* decision offer a useful interpretive guide for thinking about Nazi persecution of "homosexuals." The esteemed justices of the Supreme Court posited a conjunction of "homosexual" identity with the practice of sodomy, then used that conjunction as the principle of continuity that undergirded a supposed long-standing moral proscription of "homosexuality" in Western culture. Queer theorists challenged that conjunction and the continuity that rested upon it. But both readings have in common that they led to the conclusion that the liberal metanarrative of progress toward freedom and democracy (however we define these terms) depended for its coherence on the abjection of "homosexuals" as those identities that we accidentally and regrettably produce from time to time (how much easier simply to abort them), identities that lack essential elements for full participation in our grand experiment in liberty. Recall Justice White's words: "To claim that a right to engage in sodomy is 'deeply rooted in this nation's history and tradition' or 'implicit in the concept of ordered liberty' is, at best, facetious." The esteemed justice's act of definitional fiat leaves begging a conception of ordered liberty that excludes the right to decide one's most intimate associations free of state interference, but let us not quibble. Ordered liberty is not the same as license, which emerges both etymologically and socially from the same root as liberty but is a perversion, a diversion from the straight and narrow path.

Sodomitical license, by definition, is a threat to liberty from within. Even in the final liberation of the concentration camps that marked the triumph of Allied liberty over Axis tyranny, "homosexual" prisoners did not benefit. Robert Plant, a historian of "homosexuals'" experiences under the Nazis, explains: "Some American and British jurists of the lib-eration armies, on learning that an inmate had been jailed and then put into camp for homosexual activities, ruled that, judicially, a camp did not constitute a prison. If, therefore, someone had been sentenced to eight years in prison and had spent five of these years in jail and three in a camp, he still had to finish three years in jail after liberation." Lest we congratulate ourselves too quickly on the differences between our Enlightened justice and Nazi injustice, first we must examine the areas of overlap between them. "In at least one instance, a homosexual camp detainee was given a stern lecture by an American colonel, informing him that the United States also considered what he had done criminally offensive. For homosexuals, the Third Reich did not fully end with its defeat.... Although they were no longer compelled to wear the stig-matic pink triangle, they felt marked for life. And like so many victims of the Third Reich, most gays never recovered emotionally from the Nazi boomtowns of hell."[28] To borrow an image from Nancy Fraser, for "homosexual" survivors of Nazi persecution, the punch of human-ism was anything but emancipatory.

Fraser would reply as she did to Foucault after reading *Discipline and Punish*: "Pace Foucault," she wrote, "the reformed prison is preferable to the gulag, the South African or Salvadoran torture cell, and Islamic 'justice'; ... in *this* world—which is the real world—humanism still wields its share of critical, emancipatory punch."[29] The relative merits of French prisons may increase the comfort of the liberal intellectuals who live outside them, but Fraser failed to clarify why prisoners in French pris-ons are supposed to care about what happens in Soviet gulags and Sal-vadoran torture cells. In the case of sexuality, however slow Western lib-erals may be to live up to their own principles with respect to discrimination on the basis of sexual orientation, lesbians and gay men fare much better in the United States and Europe (the Third Reich excepted) than they do elsewhere in the world. And if I were a disem-bodied, rational identity who faced the choice of what nation to settle in, Fraser's reply would prove compelling. But, without mirroring Carte-sian excess in the opposite direction—I fuck, therefore I am—I still face the more "realistic," embodied task of continuing to live my life in a political system and an identity category neither of which I chose but both of which I have spent over thirty years getting used to. From that perspective, Foucault's suggestion of exploring the limits of thought (and of practice) with the goal of overcoming them makes much more sense.

What seems most striking about Plant's scenario from "liberated" Germany is not that some lesbian and gay scholars have begun to question the ethical and epistemological underpinnings of thought that would lecture and detain survivors of Nazi concentration camps but that so few have done so. That relatively few lesbian/gay scholars have taken up the Nazis' persecution of "homosexuals" no doubt stems in part from the relative paucity of historical writing on the subject. Plant reviewed this remarkable omission in the introduction to his book, pointing to several examples in which well-informed, highly regarded observers of the Third Reich left from descriptions of Nazi atrocities only their treatment of "homosexuals." Worse still, as Plant relates, is the idea—common to far more people than only the right-wing fringe of U.S. politics—that the Nazis themselves, Hitler included, were probably "homosexual."[30] This gives the process of abjection a new twist: The authors who explained the Nazi experience in the immediate aftermath of the war purged both the Nazi and "homosexual" identities from the liberal West by smearing the shit of each on the other.

The self-understanding of historians reveals itself as much in their omissions as in their assertions. Apparently the primary point of contact between liberalism and fascism is the desire to eliminate, or at least imprison, "homosexuals." Events since World War II, at least in the United States, suggest that liberals can adjust their beliefs, as they have had to do in the past, in response to political demands from an oppressed minority. Significant changes in the treatment of lesbians and gay men have occurred since Harry Hay founded the Mattachine Society and Del Lyon and Phyllis Martin founded the Daughters of Bilitis, in the early 1950s.[31] But in *Saint Foucault*, Halperin described the extremely subtle procedures by which even, perhaps especially, those intellectuals whose "liberal" or "radical" political credentials are beyond dispute use "homosexual" identity to delegitimize the intellectual production of "homosexuals." As with the liberal, Western jurists who supervised the liberation of Nazi death camps, for intellectuals in the present day, all the rules are off when one writes about a "homosexual" life. "No wonder, then, that the vulgarity that normally attaches to ad hominem attacks (not to say bashings), at least in intellectual circles, and that normally constitutes a disincentive to engage in them, seems almost magically to dissipate—for reasons that Foucault himself explored throughout his writings in the 1970s—in the vicinity of an insufficiently normalized subject. (Only those tainted by accusations of complicity with Nazism—more tainted by such accusations, I mean, than gay men already are in the straight-liberal imagination—are easier to deprive of their claims to a serious hearing.)"[32] This process is similar to the process that feminist scholars have long noted in which any woman's objections to unequal treatment meet with immediate dismissal as the rantings of hysteria. The cure in both cases is, of course, sexual: What hysterical (read: feminist) women and "homosexuals" of any gender need to straighten them out, to render them discursively and socially acceptable subjects, is a good, normalizing fuck.

One begins to wonder why so many people find it so difficult to live up to the basic proposition that "all men are created equal." Perhaps it is because that definition of "man" is, as Foucault and feminist and queer scholars suggest, historically specific, rather than universal, as its proponents claim? The observation is heavily overdetermined. Philosophically, in Foucault's terms, "man" as subject and object of knowledge governs our episteme, but historical events beyond the control of any individual or group promise the demise of the present episteme. In terms of gender, feminists since Mary Wollstonecraft and Elizabeth Cady Stanton have decried most men's singular failure to abide by their own universal declarations of human rights. In terms of sexuality, if, as Butler argues, any definition—any assertion of identity—demands the exclusion of a constitutive exterior and, as a chief justice of the U.S. Supreme Court argues, it is possible for humans to enjoy ordered liberty even as the state prohibits an entire category of sexual expression to a category of persons defined by that sexual expression, then we might conclude that sodomitical "homosexuals" represent the constitutive, excluded exterior that allows for the assertion of the liberal subject as identity. Feminist, lesbian, and gay scholars have demonstrated the centrality of gender and sexual difference to the games of truth by which our culture constitutes knowing subjects. They have raised the possibility that feminist, lesbian, and gay activists who call for inclusion simply reinforce the system that excluded them in the first place. The specific content of the abjected identity matters less, on this view, than the process of abjection and subjection itself and the connection between identity and political participation.

What Does It Mean to Be "Created"?

Or, instead of focusing on the question of equality, we might turn to the question of creation. What does it mean that all men are *created* equal?

What if, instead of taking our creation as a given, as the primordial fact from which we must reason, we began with the proposition that humans create their own identities—not in the sense of a heroic act of self-creation but in the sense that the types of categories, and the array of options within those types, that we must fit into in order to function as persons are the products of human history and culture, of economic, religious, political, and scientific practices, representations, and beliefs? What if we acknowledge that on a daily basis we subject each other, and our students, clients, and patients (especially insofar as we are institutionally and discursively author-ized professionals—teachers, professors, social workers, mental health pro-fessionals, physicians, lawyers, ministers, priests) to the normalizing disci-pline of gender and sexuality (and race, class, religion, region, and so forth) and that we should pay attention to those disciplinary practices to make them consistent with our stated political preferences?

One implication of Foucault's archaeological method is that the same concept or practice may have radically different meanings depending on which side of the epistemic divide one looks from. This is another way, emphasizing change over time, of putting the basic point that empirical evidence can look very different to different people depending on the conceptual frameworks that they bring. The point becomes important given the question of the type of political change that we can expect. Both Marxian and liberal eschatologies point to the ultimate achievement of some perfect, or at least ideal, state at which point government will either cease to exist or run perpetually at idle, requiring no further tuning. Whether a given Marxist or liberal chooses to invoke the concept of rev-olution, the basic goal is a drastic improvement in the substance and operation of government and law over what we have now. Echoing Fou-cault, legal scholar Larry Backer argues that the desire for revolution reflects a fantasy of transformation through substitution of a new world order, which will be the final world order, the moment of "repose." Instead of revolution, Backer advocates "a subversive assimilationist proj-ect whose goal is a modulation of values *within and not outside* our cul-ture. This requires the embrace of law as a tool ... and an object."[33]

As we move away from the conservative ideal, in which ostensibly long-standing cultural practice governs virtually all social relationships, statutes and case law become increasingly important for the process of governing these relationships. This is especially the case where queers present totally new issues, such as lesbians who claim custody of or vis-itation rights with children whom they have no biological tie to, but who they participated in rearing while partnered with the children's mother.[34] But even "traditional" families can no longer assume the degree of privacy they once could, as their inner workings become subject to increased scrutiny because of changing ideas about child abuse, spousal abuse, and marital rape—feminist issues all.[35] But as Foucault argued, law and, more generally, government do not simply prohibit; they also produce.

Again, we can compare *Bowers v. Hardwick* with *Romer v. Evans*. With their characterization of the question before them—"the issue presented is whether the Federal Constitution confers a fundamental right upon homosexuals to engage in sodomy"—the justices of the majority chose to equate the act of sodomy with the identity "homosexual."[36] In Butler's terms, this speech act performed the creation of "homosexual" as an identity. The justices' act of creation was hardly original. Rather, they perpetuated a tradition dating back at least to 1869 (although, as we have seen, the exact details of this tradition remain a matter of considerable contention among historians). But all such speech acts demand repetition, because none is definitive or eternal. The *Bowers* majority refused to recognize their own role in performing the conjunction of sodomy and "homosexuality," even though Justice Blackmun, in his dissent, pointed out how this particular speech act required a gross failure even to read the statute in question, which prohibited all acts of sodomy, without reference to the gender or sexual orientation of the participants.[37]

Romer v. Evans looked like a vast improvement. It struck down an antigay state constitutional amendment on equal-protection grounds. Recall the reservations that Goldberg and Edelman expressed about arguments for queer rights from privacy—even the dissent in *Bowers* permitted the expression of queerness only in private: "the right to be let alone." Better than having the sex police in your bedroom, no doubt, but what of Queer Nationals' right to sit in straight bars unmolested, as openly queer couples, and to shop as nonqueers do at shopping malls? What of the right to demonstrate queer identity outside of one's bedroom? Here we must make the important point that, just as nonqueers express their nonqueer identities in ways that have nothing to do with genital activity, so queers should have the same opportunities. This is called equal protection.

Halley argued that the *Bowers* decision contains within it an unacknowledged requirement that the Supreme Court recognize equal-protection claims on behalf of queers. The majority, backhandedly recognizing its authority to create via citation of law, noted that "the Court is most vulnerable and comes nearest to illegitimacy when it deals with judge-made constitutional law having little or no cognizable roots in the language or design of the Constitution." In such circumstances, they argued, "the Judiciary necessarily takes to itself further authority to govern the country without express constitutional authority."[38] Consequently, as Halley pointed out, the justices left queers to the mercy of the democratic process in their efforts to repeal sodomy laws and to resist the disparate enforcement of those laws against queers.[39]

But the justices' own reservations about their authority in no way imply complete self-abrogation. Halley quoted from Justice Harlan Stone's famous footnote to his 1938 decision in *United States v. Carolene Products.*[40] In footnote four, Stone elaborated three possible reasons for judicial scrutiny of legislation on the basis of equal protection. Other than clear violations of the Constitution's express provisions—"the language or design of the Constitution," in the *Bowers* formulation—Stone specified two other categories of problems that could provoke suspicions of unconstitutionality: laws that interfere directly with the political process and laws that have the effect of interfering with the political process by placing exceptional burdens on minority groups.[41] In some sense, Halley seemed to anticipate, with her article originally published in 1989, the Court's equal-protection review in *Romer* seven years later. She argued that, in order to participate effectively in the political process of deliberating on the merit of sodomy laws, queers must have the right to participate openly in discussions of sodomy without fear of discrimination. If all efforts to advocate the legalization of sodomy will expose the advocate to discrimination, then—in the interest of protecting the political process—the advocate deserves the highest level of equal-protection scrutiny from the courts.

Stone's footnote four contains the famous formulation "discrete and insular minorities," from which the Court has since developed a tripartite scheme for review in equal-protection cases. This scheme consists of suspect classifications, with race as the exemplar, a level at which legislation will almost certainly fail to pass Constitutional muster; quasi-suspect classifications, with gender as the exemplar, at which level government must work very hard to justify its classifying acts but stands a fighting chance of doing so; and, at the lowest level, classifications that need meet only a rational basis test showing some rational relationship between the law in question and some legitimate governmental purpose. Nearly any law can survive this level of analysis.

Political scientist Evan Gerstmann has criticized this entire tripartite scheme as a conservative effort to escape the full implications of the Fourteenth Amendment's equal-protection clause. He insists not only that the scheme itself is invalid but also that it has functioned to relegate queers, among other groups, to the bottom of the Constitutional heap—creating, through law, a "constitutional underclass."[42] But what of *Romer v. Evans*, our queer equal-protection victory? In that decision, the majority described Colorado's anti-queer Amendment Two to be that rarest of beasts: a law that bore no rational relationship to any legitimate governmental interest. It failed even the rational basis test, thus allowing the justices to avoid deciding the question that everyone wants decided: Do lesbians and gay men constitute a suspect class for purposes of legislation? Many federal courts have held that they do not, reasoning as Justice Scalia did in his *Romer* dissent that, if government may prohibit sodomy and sodomy defines the class, then government may regulate the class in nearly any manner it sees fit.[43]

Here we might distinguish between the libertarian version of equal protection, beginning with the assumption that identity comes from a Creator and remains basically fixed for life, and the queer version of equal protection, as Halley and Gerstmann have developed it. Gerstmann argued that the tripartite structure of equal-protection review contributed substantially to the political success of Amendment Two. He offered polling data to indicate that Colorado citizens, in the main, do not harbor the "animus" toward queers that the *Romer* majority attributed to them as explanation for the discriminatory intent of Amendment Two. This point turns on the infamous "special rights" argument, which Justice Scalia swallowed hook, line, and sinker in his dissent. The purpose of Amendment Two, so the argument goes, was not to disadvantage queers but merely to prevent them from gaining any sort of favored status. Large majorities of Colorado citizens apparently supported the very nondiscrimination laws, including sexual orientation as a category, that Amendment Two repealed. They adopted this apparently contradictory stance only because advocates of Amendment Two succeeded in persuading them that civil rights legislation, and the scheme of suspect and quasi-suspect classifications from Constitutional jurisprudence, had the effect of conferring "special rights" on certain minorities.

Of course, this is nonsense. As the *Romer* majority noted, the rights in question are by no means "special." Rather, we have enacted specific legislation and supported Supreme Court decisions protecting these rights for specific categories of persons precisely because, unlike the majority, these persons cannot take these rights for granted.[44] As the spate of highly publicized advertisements placed by conservative, anti-queer activists demonstrated, the debate tends to revolve around the question of whether lesbians and gay men can change their sexual orientations.[45] That is, the debate revolves around the relationship between acts and identities or, more precisely, around representations of the relationship between acts and identities, since no definitive evidence yet exists to establish what that relationship is. Even if such evidence seems to lurk in the wings, its production and distribution will still depend on schemes of representation, and we have good reason to doubt its reliability for purposes of settling political debates—and the violence of discrimination persists right now. Opponents of nondiscrimination legislation that includes sexual orientation insist that civil rights laws apply only to characteristics that persons cannot change—race and "sex" in the sense of gender. If queers can change, so the argument goes, then they can demand neither legislation protecting them from discrimination nor Constitutional protection from legislation that requires discrimination.

As Halley demonstrated, however, immutability is not the primary criterion that the Court considers in adjudicating equal-protection claims. Instead, it considers the potential impact on the political process: Does legislation that singles out minority groups have the effect of preventing them from equal participation in the political process?[46] In the case of sodomy laws, Scalia says no. Taking what we might call a conservative libertarian stance, he portrays sodomy as the act that defines the category. On this logic, one can simply avoid adopting the identity "homosexual" by refusing to engage in the activity sodomy: a simple matter of rational individuals' free choice. Most queers realize—and if they do not, they will find out quickly—that the surrounding community, because of reason and tradition, condemns same-gender sexual activity. Those who wish to avoid such condemnation will simply choose to forego the activity. The choice to commit sodomy indicates, on this view, a failure of reason such that the sodomite may legitimately suffer legal sanction.

The great virtue of queer theoretical readings of identity, even such psychoanalytically informed readings as Butler's and Lauretis's, is that they remind us that the relationships among desire, identity, and politics are never so simple. As Cindy Patton points out, however, psychoanalytic and other deconstructive readings of identity, of gender and sexuality as a process of subjectification through the repetition of culturally constituted signs, often fail to make explicit their connection to political contest.[47] The point here is not that of critics who charge queer theorists with a full-scale retreat from political contest but a call for more careful, explicit consideration of how queer theory will operate in the context of government during the early twenty-first century.

Thus, Patton suggests that the call by queer activists for queers to come out of the closet, to identify themselves publicly as queers, is not an invocation of an essential queer identity so much as it is a call to moral and political commitment. Halley reviewed the implications of Stone's footnote four to suggest that, given Stone's primary concern with the legitimacy of the political process, and therefore with the possibility of restricting minorities' access to it, he was mistaken to specify "discrete and insular" minorities as those most likely to need the Court's protection from tyrannical majorities. Members of a readily identifiable group do not have the luxury, if such it is, of hiding. Benefiting as a free rider from the political work of others in the group is more difficult. This is so in part because one cannot escape discrimination by hiding until those who choose not to hide manage to eliminate discrimination and in part because activists in the group can more easily identify persons on whom they can exert pressure to contribute to group efforts. Discrete and insular minorities are more likely to be geographically concentrated and therefore able to elect one of their own to legislative bodies, where stopping legislation is usually easier than passing it in U.S. institutions. Anonymous, diffuse minorities—queers—may actually face greater difficulties organizing in the realm of political democracy than do discrete and insular minorities.[48] On this logic, queers have at least as strong a claim to equal protection from the courts as do African Americans.

But law, as Backer noted, is an object as well as a tool. It may necessarily be an object before it is a tool. African American civil rights activists had to fight, and at times defy, an overtly and deliberately exclusive system of laws in order to achieve the measure of formal equality that they now enjoy.[49] But queers should be wary of accepting the African American example as anything other than inspiration. The processes of identity formation for race and sexuality, while undoubtedly intertwined and probably susceptible to similar modes of analysis, are likely very different. Further, although the establishment of a civil rights tradition in the United States has proven an enormous boon to queer activists in most respects—providing an existing story into which they may fit the logic and goals of their activism—in some ways conservative opponents of queer civil rights still seem to draw their inspiration not only from their sincere desire to restrict the rights of queers but also from a continuing sense that now is the time to slam the gate shut. Despite conservatives' best efforts, black folks made it, at least in principle, into the garden of formal equality, so all the more reason to ensure that queers do not follow in their footsteps. Those who remain unreconciled at least to the federal mechanisms for civil rights enforcement and at most to the very idea of equality for African Americans can use their opposition to queer equality as a proxy for opposition to civil rights policies *tout court* at a time when political reality dictates at least lip service to the idea that racial discrimination is unjust.[50]

Queers must tell their own stories, and in at least two senses. We must have a story of changing (evolving?) U.S. identity such that queer equality is not a step in the wrong direction, away from tradition and morality, but a step in the right direction, toward a moral tradition of recognizing the legitimate claims of oppressed minorities in terms of the ideals of U.S. government: liberty and equality. The point is not necessarily to suggest that U.S. liberalism is the best possible government ever conceived. It is to acknowledge that, whatever its failings, U.S. liberalism is what we have, and we are far more likely to achieve demonstrable results through reform—or, as Backer would have it, subversion—within this system than we are by proposing or demanding some entirely new system.[51]

But queers must also tell the stories of specific queer persons to find out why these persons do or do not become activists and to find out how those who become activists succeed—or fail—in their activism. At one level, this approach responds to the most recent strategy of the far Right—the "ex-gay" movement. It is sometimes difficult to avoid the paranoid fantasy that conservative activists finally read *Madness and Civilization*[52] and figured out in the process how to deploy categories of mental illness for political purposes. Clearly, the primary goal of trumpeting the "ex-gay" movement in major media outlets is to deny queers the authority to speak truthfully about their own experiences. Why should the U.S. public listen to the political demands of mentally ill persons? Better to help them by "curing" their "illness," as the charmed few who have survived the therapeutic process without backsliding are only too happy to assert. The only true story of gay identity, on this view, is one that ends with conversion to "ex-gay" identity. Conservative activists have always proven more rhetorically astute than their progressive opponents.

Even if they have read *Madness and Civilization*, however, conservative activists apparently stopped before they got to *The History of Sexuality*. They missed the point that they cannot control unilaterally the discourses that they invoke. Relying as they do on the revealed wisdom of sacred text, conservative activists miss the empirical requirement inherent in modern discourses of mental illness and mental health. Only the most fervent true believers can long maintain commitment to a diagnosis of disease, "homosexuality," that completely lacks any signs or symptoms. The "ex-gay" movement has brought public attention to a debate in which queer activists can rely on the one realm of discourse that compares to religion in its capacity to convey truth in our culture—science.

But neither science nor law alone will solve the problems of violence and discrimination against queers. Patton argues that "the crucial battle now for 'minorities' and resistant subalterns is not achieving democratic representation but wresting control over the discourses concerning identity construction. The opponent is not the state as much as it is the other collectivities attempting to set the rules for identity constitution in something like 'civil society.'"[53] We derive our primary identities now not from an organic attachment usually defined primarily in geographical terms but through occupational and ethical networks in which we circulate and negotiate meanings and commitments. Patton, citing Sedgwick, described the essentialist and social constructionist positions as incommensurable. The stories of personal authenticity that queer activists rely on to motivate other queers and to authorize their stories in response to right-wing attacks constitute a strategic sort of essentialism that implicitly acknowledges the political, social, and cultural elements in the constitution of subjectivity by enlisting those elements in the service of Patton's "deontic closure," identification that spurs action.[54]

The Representation of Identity in Queer Politics

At the margin, queer politics remains a matter of survival for many people. Not surprisingly, the urgency of dead bodies leads critics of queer theory to ask questions about how books on the materiality of bodies will contribute to the goal of preventing queer deaths, whether by disease or by blunt force trauma. Pace Patton, one might argue, political organizing in the United States remains a matter of voting and lobbying, of involving warm bodies in the process of demanding representation. At its worst, queer theory undoubtedly will contribute little or nothing to this process. After a decade, the concept of queer theory has floated around universities long enough that mediocre professors and graduate students have undoubtedly used it to produce wooden, pedestrian readings of literary texts or historical interpretations that opponents of queer theory will point to in trumpeting its irrelevance.

But if violence is our litmus test, we would do better to consider the representational politics of a specific example to see where queer theory might contribute. There could be few better examples of identity formation and mobilization through practices of representation for political purposes than the death of gay college student Matthew Shepard in 1998. Following this tragedy, candlelight vigils took place in cities and towns across the nation.[55] The funeral made the national news. Suddenly, the long-running effort by queer activists to equate sexual orientation with race for purposes of civil rights legislation seemed to materialize in frequent comparisons between Shepard's death and that of James Byrd, a black man whom three white men dragged to death behind a pickup truck in Texas earlier the same year.[56] From the perspective of queer activists, the question had to be, Of the numerous queer deaths by violence that occur every year, why did this particular event cause such a flood of outrage and sympathy?

Responses to this question reflected efforts to manage the meaning of the story about Shepard's death. Queer activist Wayne Besen told reporters that "Matthew became a symbol because the boy next door was hung up like a scarecrow. People saw him as their son or little brother."[57] The event put anti-queer activist organizations on the defensive only three months after the triumph of their "Truth in Love" advertising campaign claiming that lesbians and gay men can be "cured." Many queers insisted that conservative activists' use of rhetorical violence in their anti-gay ad campaign along with repeated use of inflammatory anti-queer language in their fundraising campaigns contributed to the circumstances in which some persons could conclude that violence against queers was acceptable. Heather Farish, spokesperson for the Family Research Council, a leading sponsor of the ad campaign, illustrated both the organization's attempts to control the meaning of "homosexual" identity—including its relationship to this identity—and the political and rhetorical bind that Shepard's death put the organization in when she replied: "Don't blame [Alcoholics Anonymous] because a drunk was beat up."[58]

Patton argued that conservative and queer activists each define themselves in opposition to the other—the constitution of either identity requires the abjection of the opponent.[59] Shepard's death became a crystallizing moment in this process, with both sides deploying their carefully developed rhetorical/political strategies in order to persuade observers that their version of its meaning was the correct one. So far, the liberal politics of citizen mobilization have yet to match the representational politics of the Shepard incident. Predominantly Republican legislatures in Wyoming and Texas and the U.S. Congress have all refused to enact the hate crimes laws that activists demanded in response to not only Shepard's but also Byrd's death.[60] Hunkered down as they undoubtedly were during the onslaught of coverage from Wyoming, conservative activists continued to persuade many Americans that existing laws were sufficient to deal with the problem. It seems clear that persuading a large enough majority of the population to support such legislation and to articulate such support in a manner that will result in legislative action is a matter of constituting identities. It is a matter of persuading persons to identify with the queer story of justice and national purpose such that these persons achieve Patton's "deontic closure"—such that they act.

Cynical? I think queer theorists are simply realistic about the point that the representational codes—the stories and assumptions about identities and their politics—that persons have in their heads have an enormous impact on how these persons respond to political appeals. Consequently, mobilizing persons for political action entails astute management of these representational codes. If the simple logic of justice, of liberty and equality, fails to persuade the majority, as it manifestly has, then there must be some other explanation for the continuing struggles of queer politics, including violence against queer persons. Queer theorists would agree with Foucault that the best approach is to investigate "what thought silently thinks."

In some respects, the traditional liberal politics of public policy may also distract us from other important questions. Hate crimes laws may be important as indicators of the community's moral condemnation of violence motivated by hatred for identity characteristics, and they may help to prevent attacks. But they do little to help us understand the meanings that attackers associate with the identities that they hate and why they act on this hatred. This is a psychological question, but it is also a question of meaning and representation. Patton on the New

Right, Halley on Supreme Court decisions, Goldberg on Balboa, Sedg-wick on teen suicide, Butler on Plato's definition of matter and the per-sistence of scientific research aimed at grounding gender difference in anatomy serve to notify us that stories of gender and sexuality surround us on a daily basis and that the specific meanings of those stories are a matter of perpetual contest. Government is certainly a matter of state action, but it is also a matter of the daily actions of parents, teachers, professors, physicians, ministers, and psychologists. The specific topics that queer theorists read and write about matter less than their ability to help us notice codes of gender and sexuality, as others enforce them on us and as we enforce them on others, with the possibility that, whether pessimistically or optimistically, we will become hyperactive about contesting these codes in our politics, in our scholarship, and in all our relationships.

Notes

Introduction

Epigraph: Michel Foucault, *The Use of Pleasure: The History of Sexuality,* vol. 2, trans. Robert Hurley (Paris: Editions Gallimard, 1984; New York: Random House, 1985), 9.

1. Carol Marie Cropper, "Black Many Fatally Dragged in a Possible Racial Killing," *New York Times,* June 10, 1998, A:16; "Gay Student Dies of Head Injuries Days after Attack," *Nashville Tennessean,* October 13, 1998; David Firestone, "Murder Reveals Double Life of Being Gay in Rural South," *New York Times,* March 6, 1999.

2. The list, still in compilation as I write, came to me via an October 19, 1999, electronic mail message from Dede de Percin, who coordinates antiviolence projects for the lesbian/gay/bisexual/transgender civil rights group Equality Colorado.

3. Monica Whitaker, "Soldier's Death May be Hate Crime," *Nashville Tennessean,* July 13, 1999, 1A–2A; idem., "Soldier First Visited Gay Club with Man Charged in Death," *Nashville Tennessean,* July 21, 1999; Kathy Carlson, "Memorial for Slain Soldier Calls for Hate-Crimes Bill," *Nashville Tennessean,* July 22, 1999; Monica Whitaker, "Revenge May Have Led to Slaying, Servicemen Say," *Nashville Tennessean,* August 10, 1999; Steve Friess, "Insult and Injury: As Journalists Struggle with Gender Issues, Murdered Pfc. Barry Winchell's Girlfriend Mourns Her Loss," *The Advocate,* February 1, 2000, 22–23; Mary Sanchez, "Parents of Slain Soldier Take on an Activist Role," *Nashville Tennessean,* March 19, 2000, 14A. My knowledge of this particular incident stems in large measure from my direct participation, as Co-chair of Tennessee's Lesbian and Gay Coalition for Justice, in bringing this incident to public attention. The striking complexities of queer political work became clear to us as the hearings for Winchell's murderers took place at Fort Campbell in August 1999. Highly sympathetic reporters struggled to understand Calpernia's transgender identity, yet still referred to her as "he" in their stories. A national transgender activist group chastised my LGCJ Co-chair, Rhonda White, and me for calling this an "anti-gay" crime when, in their view, Winchell was not gay because he was dating a

woman. I maintain that, in order to convey the point that Winchell's death was a hate crime, a crime motivated primarily by the perpetrator's hatred for his identity, it was necessary to use the term "gay" because reporters, especially broadcast but print as well, simply did not have the time and the background information necessary to elucidate in detail the distinctions between gay identity and transgender identity.

4. The Department of Defense's own research demonstrates the absurdity of its policy on openly lesbian and gay soldiers. See Kate Dyer, ed., *Gays in Uniform: The Pentagon's Secret Reports* (Boston: Alyson Publications, 1990), and the National Defense Research Institute report *Sexual Orientation and U.S. Military Policy: Options and Assessment* (Santa Monica: RAND, 1993).

5. Judith Butler, *Bodies that Matter: On the Discursive Limits of "Sex"* (New York: Routledge, 1993).

6. Michel Foucault, *The History of Sexuality*, Volume 1: *An Introduction*, trans. Robert Hurley (Paris: Editions Gallimard, 1976; New York: Vintage Books, 1990).

7. Dinitia Smith, "'Queer Theory' Is Entering the Literary Mainstream," *New York Times*, January 17, 1998, A13, A15; quotation, A15.

8. Lisa Duggan, "Theory in Practice: The Theory Wars, or, Who's Afraid of Judith Butler?" *Journal of Women's History* 10/1 (Spring 1998): 13. Duggan identified herself as an activist in this article, and I feel compelled to follow her, if only to help stem the tide of denunciation that my defense of Butler will likely unleash. As a university professor who writes about queer theory, no doubt I eliminate the possibility for political reform as surely as Butler has, at least if we accept the arguments of Martha Nussbaum (see the text that follows) and others. Regrettably for this philosophically consistent, rational argument, I am the single most politically involved university professor I know. I currently serve in my fourth year as volunteer cochair of the Lesbian and Gay Coalition for Justice, Tennessee's lesbian/gay/bisexual/transgender (lgbt) civil rights group, and in May 1999 I won the "Most Supportive" award from the student lgbt group Lambda at Middle Tennessee State University (not to mention my stints with the short-lived Nashville chapters of Queer Nation and ACT-UP during 1991 and 1992) (see Knight Stivender, "Out, Proud, and Arguing: As Nashville's Gay Community Grows, So Do the Disagreements among Some of Its Factions," and "Support for Gay, Lesbian, Bi and Transgendered Nashvillians," *Nashville Tennessean*, October 17, 1999, 17A, 20A). My appreciation for the problem of queers' attachments to their identities in the face of significant discrimination, including violence, stems from concrete experience working to achieve just the sort of political and institutional change that Nussbaum applauds, and my understanding of how best to achieve such change depends, among other things, on my readings of Foucault, Butler, and other queer theorists.

9. Martha C. Nussbaum, "The Professor of Parody: The Hip Defeatism of Judith Butler," *New Republic*, February 22, 1999: 37–45.

10. Ibid., 37.

11. Ibid.

12. Michael Warner, Introduction to *Fear of a Queer Planet: Queer Politics and Social Theory*, ed. Michael Warner (Minneapolis: University of Minnesota Press,

1993), vii. I thank Robert Hood for expressing dissatisfaction with Warner's failure to answer his own question.

13. Michel Foucault, *The Order of Things: An Archaeology of the Human Sciences*, trans. Alan Sheridan (Paris: Editions Gallimard, 1966; New York: Vintage Books, 1973); idem., *Discipline and Punish: The Birth of the Prison*, trans. Alan Sheridan (Paris: Editions Gallimard, 1975; New York: Vintage Books, 1979).

14. Foucault, *The Order of Things*, p. xxii.

15. Elizabeth Cady Stanton, "Declaration of Sentiments," in *Early American Women: A Documentary History, 1600–1900*, ed. Nancy Woloch (Belmont, Calif.: Wadsworth Publishing, 1992), 350.

16. Betty Friedan, *The Feminine Mystique*, 2d ed. (with a new introduction and epilogue by the author) (New York: Dell Publishing, 1983), ix–xxviii.

17. Alice Echols, *Daring to Be Bad: Radical Feminism in America, 1967–1975*. (Minneapolis: University of Minnesota Press, 1989), especially 103–137.

18. Hugh Davis Graham usefully reviews the history of the ERA in *The Civil Rights Era: Origins and Development of National Policy* (New York: Oxford University Press, 1990), especially 206–8. For a more detailed discussion, see the contributions to Joan Hoff-Wilson, ed., *Rights of Passage: The Past and Future of the ERA* (Bloomington: Indiana University Press, 1986). On conservative women who opposed the ERA, see Donald G. Mathews and Jane Sherron De Hart, *Sex, Gender, and the Politics of ERA: A State and the Nation* (New York: Oxford University Press, 1990); and Rebecca E. Klatch, *Women of the New Right* (Philadelphia: Temple University Press, 1987), especially 136–41, 148–49.

19. Klatch, *Women of the New Right*, 148.

20. Michel Foucault, "The Subject and Power," afterword to *Michel Foucault: Beyond Structuralism and Hermeneutics*, 2d ed., by Hubert L. Dreyfus and Paul Rabinow (Chicago: University of Chicago Press, 1983), 212.

21. Klatch, *Women of the New Right*, 148.

22. On white feminists and the African American civil rights movement, see Sara Evans, *Personal Politics: The Roots of Women's Liberation in the Civil Rights Movement and the New Left* (New York: Knopf, 1979); see also Echols, *Daring to Be Bad*.

23. bell hooks, *Feminist Theory from Margin to Center* (Boston: South End Press, 1984), 2 (hooks chooses not to capitalize the initial letters of her name).

24. Echols, *Daring to Be Bad*, 210–41; Elizabeth Spelman, *Inessential Woman: Problems of Exclusion in Feminist Thought* (Boston: Beacon Press, 1988); Nancy Myron and Charlotte Bunch, eds., *Lesbianism and the Women's Movement* (Baltimore: Diana Press, 1975). See also Anonymous (interview with Anne Koedt), "Loving Another Woman," 85–93; Radicalesbians, "The Woman Identified Woman," 240–45; and Anne Koedt, "Lesbianism and Feminism," 246–58 (all in *Radical Feminism*, ed. Anne Koedt, Ellen Levine, and Anita Rapone[New York: Quadrangle Books, 1973]).

25. See various selections in Cherrie Moraga and Gloria Anzaldúa, eds., *This Bridge Called My Back: Writings by Radical Women of Color* (Latham, N.Y.: Kitchen Table Women of Color Press, 1983).

26. Elizabeth Lapovsky Kennedy and Madline Davis, "The Reproduction of Butch-Fem Roles: A Social Constructionist Approach," in *Passion and Power: Sexuality in History*, ed. Kathy Peiss and Christina Simmons with Robert Padgug

(Philadelphia: Temple University Press, 1989), 241–56; Esther Newton, "The Mythic Mannish Lesbian," in *Hidden from History: Reclaiming the Gay and Lesbian Past*, ed. Martin Bauml Duberman, Martha Vicinus, and George Chauncey Jr. (New York: New American Library, 1989), 281–93; John D'Emilio, *Sexual Politics, Sexual Communities: The Making of a Homosexual Minority in the United States, 1940–1970* (Chicago: University of Chicago Press, 1983), 92–107.

27. Ronald Bayer, *Homosexuality and American Psychiatry: The Politics of Diagnosis* (New York: Basic Books, 1981); and Terry Stein, "Out of Madness: A History of Homosexuality and American Psychiatry," in *Creating Change: Public Policy, Civil Rights, and Sexuality*, ed. John D'Emilio, William B. Turner, and Urvashi Vaid (New York: St. Martin's Press, 2000).

28. Anne Koedt, "The Myth of the Vaginal Orgasm," in Koedt, Levine, and Rapone, *Radical Feminism*; Rosalind Rosenberg, *Beyond Separate Spheres: Intellectual Roots of Modern Feminism* (New Haven: Yale University Press, 1982); Barbara Ehrenreich and Deirdre English, *For Her Own Good: 150 Years of the Experts' Advice to Women* (New York: Anchor Books, 1979); Bayer, *Homosexuality and American Psychiatry*; Jonathan Ned Katz, "Treatment," in *Gay American History: Lesbians and Gay Men in the USA. A Documentary History* (New York: Meridien, 1976; rev. ed., 1992).

29. For the opinion of Public Health Service physicians that they could spot "homosexuals" who were unaware of their own perversion, see "Report of the Public Health Service on the Medical Aspects of H.R. 2379, a Bill to Revise the Laws Relating to Immigration, Naturalization, and Nationality, and for Other Purposes," in U.S. House Report 1365 to the McCarran-Walter Act, *U.S. Code Congressional and Administrative News*, 82d Congress (1952), 2d Session, 1701.

30. The best evidence comes from that avatar of eighteenth-century political and scientific reason, Thomas Jefferson, who claimed in the *Notes on the State of Virginia* that, although some African American slaves kept company with the most cultivated white persons in North America, they never seemed to pick up on any of the intellectual and cultural sophistication around them, thus justifying claims to their intellectual and political inferiority. Thomas Jefferson, *Notes on the State of Virginia*, ed. William Peden (New York: W. W. Norton, 1972), 137–43, especially 140, 143.

31. Take, for example, the basic freedom to move about as one wishes. On one hand, in the 1990s African Americans as a class are no longer slaves and certainly enjoy greater freedom of movement than their slave ancestors did. On the other hand, numerous civil rights organizations have begun to refer to the "offense" of "driving while black or brown"—that is, while black and Hispanic persons constitute a small percentage of the total population, in some states they constitute a large majority of persons whom law enforcement officers stop while driving. Or take the case of my good friend, a highly competent painting professor who will pay movers to transport her belongings from Tennessee to Maryland rather than risk breaking down alone in a rented truck, because her experiences with routine, casual surveillance by ordinary men as she walks along the streets of Murfreesboro, Tennessee, lead her to fear for her safety. These are some examples of the ways in which assumptions about identity, and practices based on those assumptions, have an impact on the rights of individuals at the most basic level. I discuss the issue of practices in more detail in the next chapter.

32. "Liberalism," along with "middle class" and "postmodernism" (on which see the text that follows), must occupy the pantheon of words that have come to have so many meanings that, without further stipulation, they come to mean virtually nothing. Having already qualified my meaning by specifying "the U.S. liberalism of the twentieth century," let me further clarify. I mean the basic impulse of the founders in 1789 to achieve a balance of government specified in a constitution and designed to check the worst impulses of the citizenry in the name of individual liberty while preventing the government itself from becoming a threat to that liberty. In the twentieth century, various reformers then modified the basic framework during the Progressive, New Deal, and Great Society periods under the belief that government intervention, especially in the economy but also in areas where economic and social practice overlap (discrimination in public accommodations and employment, for example), is sometimes necessary to achieve the goal of liberty for all. For discussion of these issues, see Alonzo L. Hamby, *Liberalism and Its Challengers: FDR to Reagan* (New York: Oxford University Press, 1985); Graham, *The Civil Rights Era*; Allen J. Matusow, *The Unraveling of America: A History of Liberalism in the 1960s* (New York: Harper and Row, 1984); Louis Galambos and Joseph Pratt, *The Rise of the Corporate Commonwealth: United States Business and Public Policy in the Twentieth Century* (New York: Basic Books, 1988); Edward D. Berkowitz, *America's Welfare State: From Roosevelt to Reagan* (Baltimore: Johns Hopkins University Press, 1991); and Anthony J. Badger, *The New Deal: The Depression Years, 1933–1940* (New York: Noonday Press, 1989).

33. Quite literally, with one very important exception, the history of lesbian, gay, bisexual, transgender civil rights activity in the post–World War II period has yet to be written; but I and several others are working on it at the moment. See John D'Emilio, William B. Turner, and Urvashi Vaid, eds., *Creating Change: Public Policy, Civil Rights, and Sexuality* (New York: St. Martin's Press, forthcoming); see also D'Emilio's *Sexual Politics, Sexual Communities*, the definitive account of lesbian/gay political organizing in the period between the end of World War II and the Stonewall Riots.

34. Michel Foucault, foreword to *The Order of Things: An Archaeology of the Human Sciences*, trans. Alan Sheridan (New York: Vintage Books, 1973), xiv.

35. Foucault, *The Order of Things*, especially xiv; Gerard Lebrun, "Notes on Phenomenology in *Les Mots et les Choses* [the French title for *The Order of Things*]," in *Michel Foucault, Philosopher*, trans. Timothy J. Armstrong (New York: Routledge, 1992), 20–37.

36. Michel Foucault, *The Archaeology of Knowledge*, trans. A. M. Sheridan Smith (New York: Pantheon Books, 1972).

37. See Claude Lévi-Strauss, "Structural Analysis," 31–54; and, for a discussion of cooking terms, his "Postscripts to Chapters III and IV," 81–97 (both in *Structural Anthropology*, vol. 1, trans. Claire Jacobson and Brooke Grundfest Schoepf [New York: Basic Books, 1963]).

38. Jacques Derrida, "Structure, Sign, and Play in the Discourse of the Human Sciences," in *The Language of Criticism and the Sciences of Man: The Structuralist Controversy*, ed. Richard Macksey and Eugenio Donato (Baltimore: Johns Hopkins University Press, 1970), 251–52.

39. Lebrun, "Notes on Phenomenology," 21–25.

40. Derrida, "Structure, Sign, and Play," 249.

41. Charles E. Scott, *The Language of Difference* (Atlantic Highlands, N.J.: Humanities Press International, 1987).

42. Lévi-Strauss, *Structural Anthropology*, 33. See the dedication for a reference to the book as it originally appeared in 1958.

43. Jean-François Lyotard, *The Postmodern Condition: A Report on Knowledge*, trans. Geoff Bennington and Brian Massumi (foreword by Frederic Jameson) (Minneapolis: University of Minnesota Press, 1984).

44. See the introduction to Andrew Barry, Thomas Osborne, and Nikolas Rose, eds., *Foucault and Political Reason: Liberalism, Neo-Liberalism, and the Rationalities of Government* (Chicago: University of Chicago Press, 1996), 2–7.

45. Kenneth Cmiel, "History against Itself," *Journal of American History: A Special Issue on the Practice of American History* 81 (1994): 1169–74.

46. Ibid., 1169.

47. See Margaret L. Andersen, "Changing the Curriculum in Higher Education," 222–54; and Susan Hardy Aiken et al., "Trying Transformations: Curriculum Integration and the Problem of Resistance," 255–75 (both in *Signs* 12 [1987]).

48. Michel Foucault, "Two Lectures," in *Power/Knowledge: Selected Interviews and Other Writings by Michel Foucault, 1972–1977*, ed. Colin Gordon, trans. Colin Gordon et al. (New York: Pantheon Books, 1980), 80.

49. Joyce Appleby, Lynn Hunt, and Margaret Jacob, *Telling the Truth about History* (New York: W. W. Norton, 1994). I hope that I prove more rhetorically circumspect in my criticisms of this book than Appleby, Hunt, and Jacob are in their efforts to critique "postmodern" philosophers. I cannot help but note, however, that their scholarly practice undermines the very notions of "science" and "objectivity" that they claim to defend. Whatever utility "postmodernism" may have for designating a group of philosophers, or scholars more generally, any intellectual category that contains Jacques Derrida and Michel Foucault as its originary exemplars but also includes Jean-François Lyotard, F. R. Ankersmit, and Bruno Latour wants much more rigorous justification than Appleby, Hunt, and Jacob offer (see chap. 6, "Postmodernism and the Crisis of Modernity," 198–237). Further, while I cannot claim extensive knowledge of the other thinkers listed above, I must state unequivocally on the basis of my own reading of Foucault's work that Appleby, Hunt, and Jacob's account of his thought is, at best, a caricature that fundamentally fails to engage with the basic issues that Foucault raised even as it creates significant suspicions about their accounts of other thinkers. Appleby, Hunt, and Jacob may well wish to disagree with Foucault's account of power and knowledge, but their disagreement will become compelling only insofar as they bother to understand that account first. By way of illustration, I would point to what is perhaps an even more vigorous denunciation of the impact that the work of Foucault and other poststructuralist scholars has had on historical inquiry: Bryan D. Palmer, *Descent into Discourse: The Reification of Language and the Writing of Social History* (Philadelphia: Temple University Press, 1990). While I disagree with Palmer's diagnosis of the baleful impact of the "linguistic turn" on social history, if only because I would dispute his assumption of some necessary disjunction between language and matter

(since when is language itself not material?), his book reflects precisely the careful, sustained engagement with his intellectual opponents that *Telling the Truth about History* lacks.

50. The theme of scientific history and the unfolding of U.S. democracy as mutually reinforcing phenomena recurs throughout Appleby, Hunt, and Jacob's *Telling the Truth about History*. See especially 11, 33, and the last chapter, "The Future of History," 271–309, where the authors place themselves in the contradictory position of insisting (1) that U.S. national identity rests on, and is best served by, a complete freedom of inquiry, as opposed to a deliberate withholding of historical information in the service of patriotism (307–8) and (2) that members of minority groups should take care not to assert pride in their minority identity at the expense of pride in national identity because "the two stand or fall together. It is the nation that sustains and protects the array of particular identities in the United States" (p. 301). Compare to Lyotard's *The Postmodern Condition:* "The explicit appeal to narrative in the problematic of knowledge is concomitant with the liberation of the bourgeois classes from the traditional authorities. Narrative knowledge makes a resurgence in the West as a way of solving the problem of legitimating the new authorities. It is natural in a narrative problematic for such a question to solicit the name of a hero as its response: *Who* has the right to decide for society? Who is the subject whose prescriptions are norms for those they obligate? This way of inquiring into sociopolitical legitimacy combines with the new scientific attitude: the name of the hero is the people, the sign of legitimacy is the people's consensus, and their mode of creating norms is deliberation. The notion of progress is a necessary outgrowth of this. It represents nothing other than the movement by which knowledge is presumed to accumulate—but this movement is extended to the new sociopolitical subject" (p. 30).

51. Foucault, *The Order of Things*. For the section on man as "empirico-transcendental doublet," see 318–22; for references to Comte and Marx, see 320.

52. Murray G. Murphey, *Philosophical Foundations of Historical Knowledge* (Albany: State University of New York Press, 1994).

53. For Lyotard's account of modern science as claiming self-justification, see *The Postmodern Condition*, 29. For Murphey's claims, see *Philosophical Foundations*, xii.

54. Murphey, *Philosophical Foundations*, 19.

55. See, for example, Owen Flanagan, *Consciousness Reconsidered* (Cambridge, Mass.: MIT Press, 1992); Richard F. Thompson, *The Brain: A Neuroscience Primer*, 2d ed. (New York: W. H. Freeman, 1993); and Dominick P. Purpura, "Then and Now," introduction to *Neuroscience: From the Molecular to the Cognitive*, ed., Floyd E. Bloom, *Progress in Brain Research* 100 (Amsterdam: Elsevier, 1994).

56. Donald G. Stein, "Brain Damage and Recovery," and A. Claudio Cuello, "Trophic Factor Therapy in the Adult CNS: Remodeling of Injured Basalo-cortical Neurons" (both in Bloom, *Neuroscience*).

57. Teresa de Lauretis, "Queer Theory, Lesbian and Gay Sexualities: An Introduction," *differences: A Journal of Feminist Cultural Studies* 3/2 (Summer 1991; special issue): iii–xviii.

58. Brett Beemyn and Mickey Eliason, eds., *Queer Studies: A Lesbian, Gay, Bisexual, and Transgender Anthology* (New York: New York University Press, 1996).

59. Ki Namaste, "'Tragic Misreadings': Queer Theory's Erasure of Transgender Subjectivity," in ibid., 183–203.

60. Sarah D. Fox, report on survey of employment discrimination among lesbians and gay men, July 13, 1999. Contact sarah@gender.org.

61. Judith Butler, "Against Proper Objects," introduction to "More Gender Trouble: Feminism Meets Queer Theory," *differences: A Journal of Feminist Cultural Studies* 6, no.2/3 (Summer–Fall 1994; special issue): 1–26.

62. Eve Kosofsky Sedgwick, *Tendencies* (Durham, N.C.: Duke University Press, 1993), xii; David Halperin, *Saint Foucault* (New York: Oxford University Press, 1993), 63.

Chapter One

Epigraph: Michel Foucault, "Politics and Reason," in *Michel Foucault: Politics, Philosophy, Culture. Interviews and Other Writings, 1977–1984*, ed. Lawrence D. Kritzman (New York: Routledge, 1988), 71.

1. Insofar as Foucault stated his differences with the philosophical tradition in which he was trained, he usually did so in interviews and lectures, not in his books. My discussion depends heavily on these interviews and lectures. See Michel Foucault, *Remarks on Marx: Conversations with Duccio Trombadori*, trans. R. James Goldstein and James Cascaito (New York: Semiotext[e], 1991); Colin Gordon, ed., *Power/Knowledge: Selected Interviews and Other Writings by Michel Foucault, 1972–1977*, trans. Colin Gordon et al. (New York: Pantheon Books, 1980); Donald F. Bouchard, ed., *Language, Counter-Memory, Practice: Selected Essays and Interviews by Michel Foucault* (Ithaca, N.Y.: Cornell University Press, 1977); Lawrence D. Kritzman, ed., *Michel Foucault: Politics, Philosophy, Culture. Interviews and Other Writings, 1977–1984* (New York: Routledge, 1988); Michel Foucault, *"The Subject and Power,"* and *"On the Genealogy of Ethics: An Overview of Work in Progress,"* in *Michel Foucault: Beyond Structuralism and Hermeneutics*, 2d ed., by Hubert L. Dreyfus and Paul Rabinow (Chicago: University of Chicago Press, 1983); and Sylvere Lotringer, ed., *Foucault Live (Interviews, 1966–84)*, trans. John Johnston (New York: Semiotext[e], 1989). Another important collection, with two lectures by and an interview with Michel Foucault, is Graham Burchell, Colin Gordon, and Peter Miller, eds., *The Foucault Effect: Studies in Governmentality* (Chicago: University of Chicago Press, 1991). A comprehensive collection of Foucault's interviews and shorter writings that has appeared in French in four volumes under the general direction of Daniel Defert and François Ewald is *Dits et écrits par Michel Foucault, 1954–1988* (Paris: Editions Gallimard, 1994); Paul Rabinow has edited two of three volumes consisting of selections from *Dits et écrits*, under the general title *The Essential Works of Michel Foucault, 1954–1984* (New York: New Press, 1997). A useful compilation of other views of Foucault's work is Barry Smart, ed., *Michel Foucault: Critical Assessments*, 7 vols. (New York: Routledge, 1995).

2. Simone de Beauvoir, *The Second Sex*, ed. and trans. H. M. Parshley (New York: Vintage Books, 1989), xix.

3. The best biography of Foucault to date is Didier Eribon, *Michel Foucault*, trans. Betsy Wing (Cambridge, Mass.: Harvard University Press, 1991). See also

David Macey, *The Lives of Michel Foucault* (New York: Pantheon, 1993). James Miller's *The Passion of Michel Foucault* (New York: Simon and Schuster, 1993) offers a grossly reductive attempt to explain all of Foucault's life and work in terms of his desire for "limit-experiences," especially through sadomasochism. See Lisa Duggan's review, "Biography = Death," *Village Voice*, May 4, 1993, 90–91. See also David Halperin's extensive discussion of the ways in which biographical information in the hands of those who wish to dismiss Foucault's work has had precisely the normalizing effects that Foucault described during his life: David Halperin, "The Describable Life of Michel Foucault," *Saint Foucault: Towards a Gay Hagiography* (New York: Oxford University Press, 1995), 126–85. Eribon has also discussed his differences with Miller in *Michel Foucault et ses contemporains* (Paris: Fayard, 1994), 17–67.

4. Michel Foucault, *Madness and Civilization: A History of Insanity in the Age of Reason*, trans. Richard Howard (Paris: Librarie Plon, 1961; New York: Vintage Books, 1988).

5. Foucault, "The 'History of Truth,'" in *Remarks on Marx*, 64.

6. Ibid., 62.

7. Michel Foucault, *An Introduction*, vol. 1 of *The History of Sexuality*, trans. Robert Hurley (New York: Vintage Books, 1990). To some extent, this is the point of the whole book, but see especially p. 11. (Note that, throughout the text, I use *The History of Sexuality* to refer exclusively to Volume 1 of this series.)

8. Foucault, "On the Genealogy of Ethics," 229.

9. For references to "techniques of the self," see ibid., 229–52. For the largely ignored theme of "government" in Foucault's work of the 1970s, see the very important work of Burchell, Gordon, and Miller, *The Foucault Effect*; and Andrew Barry, Thomas Osborne, and Nikolas Rose, eds. *Foucault and Political Reason: Liberalism, Neo-Liberalism, and the Rationalities of Government* (Chicago: University of Chicago Press, 1996).

10. Foucault, "On the Genealogy of Ethics," 231–32.

11. Michel Foucault, *Folie et deraison: Histoire de la folie à l'age classique* (Paris: Plon, 1961), 58.

12. Foucault, "Politics and Reason," in Kritzman, *Michel Foucault*, 71; see also Foucault, "Critical Theory/Intellectual History," in Kritzman, *Michel Foucault*, 43.

13. This is the point of Joan W. Scott's brilliant essay "'Experience,'" in *Feminists Theorize the Political*, ed. Judith Butler and Joan W. Scott (New York: Routledge, 1992), 22–40. I discuss this essay in Chapter Three.

14. Michel Foucault, *The Order of Things: An Archaeology of the Human Sciences*, trans. Alan Sheridan (New York: Vintage Books, 1973), xv.

15. Michel Foucault, "Politics and the Study of Discourse," in Burchell, Gordon, and Miller, *The Foucault Effect*, 64–65.

16. Ibid., 69.

17. Michel Foucault, "Nietzsche, Genealogy, History," in Bouchard, *Language, Counter-Memory, Practice*, 140.

18 Michel Foucault, *Discipline and Punish: The Birth of the Prison* (Paris: Editions Gallimard, 1975; trans. Alan Sheridan, New York: Vintage Books, 1979).

19. Foucault, *The History of Sexuality*, 94.

20. Ibid., 94–95.

21. Michel Foucault,"Friendship as a Way of Life," trans. John Johnston, in *Ethics, Subjectivity, and Power,* vol. 1 of Rabinow, *The Essential Works of Michel Foucault,* 135–40.

22. See especially "The Incitement to Discourse," in Foucault, *The History of Sexuality,* 17–35.

23. Ibid., 55–56.

24. Michel Foucault, *The Birth of the Clinic: An Archaeology of Medical Perception,* trans. A. M. Sheridan Smith (Paris: Presses Universitaires de France, 1963; New York: Vintage Books, 1975).

25. Friedrich Nietzsche, *On the Genealogy of Morals,* trans. Walter Kaufmann and R. J. Hooingdale (1967; New York: Vintage Books, 1989), 77.

26. Foucault, "The Subject and Power," in Dreyfus and Rabinow, *Michel Foucault,* 212.

27. This observation offers an interesting point of comparison to the discussion of representation via Diego Velázquez's painting *Las Meninas* at the beginning of *The Order of Things* and in the section on "The Analytic of Finitude," pp. 312–18: Velázquez can represent representation only by painting as if from the king's perspective; similarly, the moral subject of sexuality takes over from the king as the observer and guarantor of his own productivity and sexual, which is to say moral and political, restraint.

28. Michel Foucault, *The Archaeology of Knowledge,* trans. A. M. Sheridan Smith (Paris: Editions Gallimard, 1969; New York: Pantheon Books, 1972).

29. Foucault, *The History of Sexuality,* 154.

30. I thank Cindy Patton for first pointing this out to me.

31. Dreyfus and Rabinow, *Michel Foucault,* 120–21; Gilles Deleuze, "What Is a *Dispositif?*" in *Michel Foucault: Philosopher,* trans. Timothy J. Armstrong (New York: Routledge, 1992), 159.

32. Michel Foucault, "Prison Talk," interview by J. J. Brochier, in Gordon, *Power/Knowledge,* 38.

33. Gordon, *Power/Knowledge,* 195–96.

34. See, for example, ibid., 52.

35. A cogent statement of this objection appears in Peter Dews, *Logics of Disintegration: Post-structuralist Thought and the Claims of Critical Theory* (London: Verso, 1987), 163–64.

36. Todd May suggests that "the juridical model of power—the liberal concept of power as a limit on freedom produced by the interplay of law and right—was, during the ascendancy of sovereign monarchy, an enlightening description of the functioning of power. However, it is no longer" (*Between Genealogy and Epistemology: Psychology, Politics, and Knowledge in the Thought of Michel Foucault* [University Park: Penn State University Press, 1993], 51). This looks like an accurate reading of Foucault's discussion of monarchies, the early modern state, and resistance to them in *The History of Sexuality,* except that it still fails to recognize the limitations on the availability of the critique—that only certain types of persons were free and able to critique and resist. This is probably more a failing of Foucault's account than of May's reading, however.

37. Foucault, *The History of Sexuality,* 101.

38. And this actually happened. See Ronald Bayer, *Homosexuality and American Psychiatry: The Politics of Diagnosis* (New York: Basic Books, 1981).

39. For accounts of Hooker's work, see ibid., 49–53; and Francis Mark Mondimore, *A Natural History of Homosexuality* (Baltimore: Johns Hopkins University Press, 1996), 90–94.

40. Foucault, *The History of Sexuality*, 43.

41. Herbert Marcuse, *Eros and Civilization: a Philosophical Inquiry into Freud* (Boston: Beacon Press, 1966).

42. Max Horkheimer and Theodor Adorno, *Dialectic of Enlightenment* (1944; rev. ed., New York: Herder and Herder, 1972), x.

43. Michel Foucault, "Adorno, Horkheimer, and Marcuse: Who Is a 'Negator of History'?" in *Remarks on Marx*, 120–21.

44. Habermas's most thoroughly developed critique of Foucault appears in *The Philosophical Discourse of Modernity*, trans. Frederick Lawrence (Cambridge, Mass.: MIT Press, 1987); the chapters on Foucault and related articles appear in Michael Kelly, ed., *Critique and Power: Recasting the Foucault/Habermas Debate* (Cambridge, Mass.: MIT Press, 1994).

45. Jürgen Habermas, *Reason and the Rationalization of Society*, trans. Thomas McCarthy, vol. 1 of *The Theory of Communicative Action* (Boston: Beacon Press, 1984); idem, *Lifeworld and System: A Critique of Functionalist Reason*, trans. Thomas McCarthy, vol. 2 of *The Theory of Communicative Action* (Boston: Beacon Press, 1987); see also, Arie Brand, *The Force of Reason: An Introduction to Habermas' Theory of Communicative Action* (Boston: Allen and Unwin, 1990).

46. Jürgen Habermas, "Modernity versus Postmodernity," *New German Critique* 22 (1981): 13.

47. Michel Foucault, "What Is Enlightenment?" in *The Foucault Reader*, ed. Paul Rabinow (New York: Pantheon Books, 1984), 32–50.

48. Jürgen Habermas, "Taking Aim at the Heart of the Present: On Foucault's Lecture on Kant's *What Is Enlightenment?*" in Kelly, *Critique and Power*, 152.

49. Foucault, "What Is Enlightenment?" 42.

50. Ibid., 43.

51. Habermas, *Theory of Communicative Action*, 397–98.

52. On Habermas's frustration with the failure of German authorities to heed his call for a discussion of German identity during the process of reunification, see Max Pensky, "Universalism and the Situated Critic," in *The Cambridge Companion to Habermas*, ed. Stephen K. White (New York: Cambridge University Press, 1995), 67–94.

53. Foucault, "What Is Enlightenment?" 45–46.

54. Michel Foucault, "Two Lectures," in Gordon, *Power/Knowledge*, 84.

Chapter Two

1. Jonathan Ned Katz, "The Invention of Heterosexuality," *Socialist Review* 20 (1990): 9.

2. Lisa Duggan, "Making It Perfectly Queer," *Socialist Review* 22 (1992): 22; Arthur N. Gilbert, "Review of *The History of Sexuality, Volume One: An Introduction*," *American Historical Review* 84 (1979): 1020–21.

3. See, for example, Torie Osborn, *Coming Home to America: A Roadmap to Gay and Lesbian Empowerment* (New York: St. Martin's Press, 1996). Osborn is a former executive director of both the Los Angeles Lesbian and Gay Community Center, the largest of its kind in the nation, and the National Gay and Lesbian Task Force.

4. Ibid., 3–13.

5. Jonathan Ned Katz, *Gay American History: Lesbians and Gay Men in the USA. A Documentary History* (New York: Meridien, 1976; rev. ed., 1992).

6. Ibid., 7.

7. Ibid., 1–9.

8. Jonathan Ned Katz, *Gay/Lesbian Almanac: A New Documentary* (New York: Harper and Row, 1983).

9. Ibid., 14, 16.

10. Ibid., 18.

11. Ibid., 18–19; Katz, *Gay American History*, 8.

12. Katz, *Gay/Lesbian Almanac*, 19.

13. Jeffrey Weeks, *Coming Out: Homosexual Politics in Britain from the Nineteenth Century to the Present* (New York: Quartet Books, 1977; rev. ed., 1990), 7.

14. E. P. Thompson, *The Making of the English Working Class* (New York: Vintage Books, 1966).

15. Mary McIntosh, "The Homosexual Role," *Social Problems* 16 (1968): 182–92.

16. Weeks, *Coming Out*, 4.

17. Ibid., xi.

18. Jeffrey Weeks, *Sexuality and Its Discontents: Meanings, Myths, and Modern Sexualities* (London: Routledge and Kegan Paul, 1985), 6.

19. Ibid., 260.

20. Ibid., 242.

21. Ibid., 210.

22. Ibid., 209.

23. Ibid., 260.

24. Michel Foucault, *The History of Sexuality*, Volume 1: *An Introduction*, trans. Robert Hurley (New York: Vintage Books, 1990), 159.

25. Weeks, *Sexuality and Its Discontents*, 260.

26. John D'Emilio, *Sexual Politics, Sexual Communities: The Making of a Homosexual Minority in the United States, 1940–1970*. (Chicago: University of Chicago Press, 1983); idem, "Dreams Deferred: The Birth and Betrayal of America's First Gay Liberation Movement," in *Making Trouble: Essays on Gay History, Politics, and the University* (New York: Routledge, 1992), 17–56.

27. John D'Emilio, "Capitalism and Gay Identity," in *Powers of Desire: The Politics of Sexuality*, ed. Ann Snitow, Christine Stansell, and Sharon Thompson (New York: Monthly Review Press, 1983), 100-13; reprinted in D'Emilio, *Making Trouble*, 3–16.

28. Foucault, *The History of Sexuality*, 113, 119–22.

29. D'Emilio, "Capitalism and Gay Identity," in Snitow, Stansell, and Thompson, *Powers of Desire*, 8; D'Emilio, *Sexual Politics*, 10.

30. Jonathan Ned Katz, *The Invention of Heterosexuality* (New York: Dutton, 1995), 13.

31. Robert A. Padgug, "Sexual Matters: On Conceptualizing Sexuality in History," *Radical History Review* 20 (1979): 3–23; reprinted in *Passion and Power: Sexuality in History*, ed. Kathy Peiss and Christina Simmons, with Robert Padgug (Philadelphia: Temple University Press, 1989), 14–31.

32. Ibid., 17–19, 25.

33. This tradition goes back to Charlotte Perkins Gilman, *Women and Economics* (Boston: Small, Maynard, 1911) and the birth control advocacy of Emma Goldman, Ben Reitman, and Margaret Sanger in her early, radical phase, on which see Linda Gordon, *Woman's Body, Woman's Right: A Social History of Birth Control in America* (New York: Penguin Books, 1976), 206–45. Note, also, that Goldman was probably the first well-known, public advocate of equal treatment for "homosexuals" in the United States.

34. Foucault, *The History of Sexuality*, 108–14, 119–21.

35. Padgug, "Sexual Matters," 22.

36. Martin Bauml Duberman, Martha Vicinus, and George Chauncey Jr., eds., *Hidden from History: Reclaiming the Gay and Lesbian Past* (New York: New American Library, 1989), 17–64; Eve Kosofsky Sedgwick, *Epistemology of the Closet* (Berkeley and Los Angeles: University of California Press, 1990), 44–48; Duggan, "Making It Perfectly Queer."

37. David Halperin, "One Hundred Years of Homosexuality," in Duberman, Vicinus, and Chauncey, *Hidden from History*, 37–53; David Halperin, *One Hundred Years of Homosexuality and Other Essays on Greek Love* (New York: Routledge, 1990), 26.

38. David Halperin, "One Hundred Years of Homosexuality," in *One Hundred Years of Homosexuality*, 27, 30–31.

39. John Boswell, "Revolutions, Universals, and Sexual Categories," in Duberman, Vicinus, and Chauncey, *Hidden from History*, 27–88 and n. 25, emphasis added. See also his discussion of "decorous" versus "indecorous" sexual roles for Roman free adult males (p. 33); again, Halperin's explanation in terms of a status taxonomy that includes sexual acts makes more sense than Boswell's explanation in terms of a sexual taxonomy the elements of which are the same as the modern except in emphasis.

40. Halperin, "One Hundred Years of Homosexuality," in *One Hundred Years of Sexuality*, 27.

41. Boswell, "Revolutions, Universals, and Sexual Categories," 21.

42. Halperin, "One Hundred Years of Homosexuality," in *One Hundred Years of Sexuality*, 29.

43. Ibid.

44. Boswell, "Revolutions, Universals, and Sexual Categories," 22.

45. Ibid., 23.

46. Ibid., 17–18.

47. John Boswell, *Christianity, Social Tolerance, and Homosexuality: Gay People in Western Europe from the Beginning of the Christian Era to the Fourteenth Century* (Chicago: University of Chicago Press, 1980).

48. John Boswell, *Same-Sex Unions in Premodern Europe* (New York: Villard Books, 1994).

49. Kenneth L. Woodward, "Do You, Paul, Take Ralph . . . ," *Newsweek*, June 20, 1994, 76–77.

50. Sedgwick, *Epistemology of the Closet*, 46.

51. Foucault, *The History of Sexuality*, 43; Halperin, *One Hundred Years of Homosexuality*, 9.

52. McIntosh, "The Homosexual Role," 187; Weeks, *Coming Out*, 36–37; Randolph Trumbach, "London's Sodomites: Homosexual Behavior and Western Culture in the Eighteenth Century," *Journal of Social History* 11 (1977): 1–33; Randolph Trumbach "The Birth of the Queen: Sodomy and the Emergence of Gender Equality in Modern Culture, 1660–1750," in Duberman, Vicinus, and Chauncy, *Hidden from History*, 129–40.

53. Alan Bray, *Homosexuality in Renaissance England* (London: Gay Men's Press, 1982), 134–37, n. 18.

54. Ibid., 76–80.

55. Ibid., 105–6.

56. Sedgwick, *Epistemology of the Closet*, 46–47.

57. Bray, *Homosexuality in Renaissance England*, 104.

58. Sedgwick, *Epistemology of the Closet*, 47. Indeed, it seems in the 1990s that religiously motivated opponents of lesbian/gay civil rights claims have hit on the psychopathology model as their most likely avenue for winning the political debate by making the issue of lesbian/gay identity a matter of moralized medical treatment rather than political contest. This allows them to portray their support for discrimination as compassion for mentally ill people while disqualifying those "ill people" from any contribution to the political debate about their own situation. See, for example, the article by charismatic Episcopal priest David Foster, "A Look at Male Homosexuality from the Inside," which combines exhortations to follow Jesus with a reductive, psychoanalytic account of the etiology of lesbian/gay identity (*Nashville Net*, Spring 1997, 34–36). And during the summer of 1998 a major controversy erupted when several right-wing groups paid for full-page advertisements in several major newspapers featuring a woman who claimed that her faith in Jesus "cured" her of her "homosexuality" (John Leland and Mark Miller, "Can Gays 'Convert'?" 46–50; and Marc Peyser, "Battling Backlash," 50–52, both in *Newsweek*, August 17, 1998).

59. Foucault, *The History of Sexuality*, 101.

60. Sedgwick, *Epistemology of the Closet*, 44.

61. George Chauncey, "From Sexual Inversion to Homosexuality: The Changing Medical Conceptualization of Female 'Deviance,'" *Salmagundi* 58–59 (1982–83); reprinted in Peiss and Simmons, *Passion and Power*, 87–117.

62. George Chauncey, *Gay New York: Gender, Urban Culture, and the Making of the Gay Male World, 1890–1940*. (New York: Basic Books, 1994), 27.

63. Chauncey, *"From Sexual Inversion to Homosexuality,"* 103.

Chapter Three

1. Michel Foucault, *The History of Sexuality*, Volume 1: *An Introduction*, trans. Robert Hurley (Paris: Editions Gallimard, 1976; New York: Vintage Books, 1990).

2. Carroll Smith-Rosenberg, "The Female World of Love and Ritual: Relations Between Women in Nineteenth-Century America," *Signs* 1 (1975): 1–30; reprinted in *Disorderly Conduct: Visions of Gender in Victorian America* (New York: Oxford University Press, 1985), 53–76.

3. Joan Wallach Scott, introduction to *Feminism and History*, ed. Joan Wallach Scott (New York: Oxford University Press, 1996), 1–13.

4. Irene Diamond and Lee Quinby, introduction to *Feminism and Foucault: Reflections on Resistance*, ed. Irene Diamond and Lee Quinby (Boston: Northeastern University Press, 1988), ix.

5. Smith-Rosenberg, "The Female World of Love and Ritual," 53–76.

6. Ibid., 53–54, 58.

7. Blanche Wiesen Cook, "Female Support Networks and Political Activism: Lillian Wald, Crystal Eastman, Emma Goldman," *Chrysalis* 3 (1977); reprinted in *Women's America: Refocusing the Past*, 2d ed., ed. Linda K. Kerber and Jane DeHart-Mathews (New York: Oxford University Press, 1987), 273–94; Blanche Wiesen Cook, "The Historical Denial of Lesbianism," *Radical History Review* 20 (1979): 60–65.

8. Lillian Faderman, "The Morbidification of Love between Women," *Journal of Homosexuality* 4 (1978): 73–90.

9. Editorial, Sex and Sexuality, *Signs* 5 (1980; special issue on sex and sexuality): 570.

10 Many of the papers at this conference, as well as a description of the controversy surrounding it, appear in Carol S. Vance, ed., *Pleasure and Danger: Exploring Female Sexuality* (New York: Routledge, 1984); see also Estelle B. Freedman and Barrie Thorne, "Introduction to 'The Feminist Sexuality Debates,'" *Signs* 10 (1984): 102–5. In *Feminist Studies* 9/1 (Spring 1983), the editors state, "Due to reflection on the part of the editors, we have chosen to excise pages 177–82." These pages originally contained the leaflets, including names of specific women accused of "antifeminist" sexual practices. In *Feminist Studies* 9/3: 589–602, various observers and participants castigated the editors for having published the leaflets in the first place.

11. Gayle Rubin, "Thinking Sex: Notes for a Radical Theory of the Politics of Sexuality," in Vance, *Pleasure and Danger*, 267–319.

12. Ibid., 275.

13. Ibid., 280–81.

14. Gayle Rubin, "Sexual Traffic," interview by Judith Butler, in "More Gender Trouble: Feminism Meets Queer Theory," *differences: A Journal of Feminist Cultural Studies* 6/2–3 (Summer–Fall 1994; special issue): 62–99, especially 83, 70.

15. Rubin, "Thinking Sex," 276–77.

16. Michel Foucault, *Madness and Civilization: A History of Insanity in the Age of Reason*, trans. Richard Howard (New York: Random House, 1965).

17. Rubin, "Thinking Sex," 309.

18. Irene Diamond and Lee Quinby, "American Feminism in the Age of the Body," *Signs* 10 (1984): 119–25.

19. Colin Gordon, ed., *Power/Knowledge: Selected Interviews and Other Writings by Michel Foucault, 1972–1977.* (New York: Pantheon, 1980).

20. Diamond and Quinby, "American Feminism," 121.

21. Ibid., 122.

22. Ibid., 121, 122.

23. Biddy Martin, "Feminism, Criticism, and Foucault," *New German Critique* 27 (1982): 3–30; reprinted in Diamond and Quinby, *Feminism and Foucault*, 3–19.

24. Lois McNay, *Foucault and Feminism: Power, Gender, and the Self* (Boston: Northeastern University Press, 1992), 4.

25. Ibid., 59–60, 66.

26. Sandra Lee Bartky, "Foucault, Femininity, and the Modernization of Patriarchal Power," 61–86; and Susan Bordo, "Anorexia Nervosa: Psychopathology as the Crystallization of Culture," 61–86 (both in Diamond and Quinby, *Feminism and Foucault*).

27. Bartky, "Foucault, Femininity, and Patriarchal Power," 74.

28. Ibid., 66–68.

29. Ibid., 75.

30. Ibid., 76.

31. Michel Foucault, *Discipline and Punish: The Birth of the Prison*, trans. Alan Sheridan (New York: Vintage Books, 1979): 200–209.

32. Bartky, "Foucault, Femininity, and Patriarchal Power," 81.

33. Martin, "Feminism, Criticism, and Foucault," 13.

34. Diamond and Quinby, introduction to Diamond and Quinby, *Feminism and Foucault*, x.

35. Linda Alcoff, "Cultural Feminism versus Poststructuralism: The Identity Crisis in Feminist Theory," *Signs* 13 (1988): 405.

36. Ibid., 431.

37. Nancy Fraser, "Foucault on Modern Power: Empirical Insights and Normative Confusions," in *Unruly Practices: Power, Discourse, and Gender in Contemporary Social Theory* (Minneapolis: University of Minnesota Press, 1989), 33.

38. Nancy Fraser, "Foucault: A 'Young Conservative'?" in Fraser, *Unruly Practices*, 47.

39. Foucault, *Discipline and Punish*, 30; and idem, "Two Lectures," in *Power/Knowledge: Selected Interviews and Other Writings by Michel Foucault, 1972–1977*, ed. Colin Gordon, trans. Colin Gordon et al. (New York: Pantheon Books, 1980), especially 81–82. On the Group d'Information sur les Prisons, see Didier Eribon, *Michel Foucault*, trans. Betsy Wing (Cambridge, Mass.: Harvard University Press, 1991), 224–34.

40. I take my description of this debate from Monique Plaza, "Our Damages and Their Compensation. Rape: The Will Not to Know of Michel Foucault," *Feminist Issues* 1 (1981): 25–35. Note that in Plaza's title, "the will not to know" is a play on the French title for *The History of Sexuality: La Volonte de savoir*, or "the will to knowledge."

41. Ibid., pp. 28–29. For Foucault's description of sex as constituting women's bodies, see Michel Foucault, *The History of Sexuality*, Volume 1: *An Introduction* (New York: Vintage Books, 1990), 153. Plaza quoted the passage on p. 28 of her article.

42. Winifred Woodhull, "Sexuality, Power, and the Question of Rape," in Diamond and Quinby, *Feminism and Foucault*, 167–76.

43. Plaza, "Our Damages and Their Compensation," 29.

44. Susan Brownmiller, *Against Our Will: Men, Women, and Rape* (New York: Bantam, 1975), 4; quoted in Woodhull, "Sexuality, Power, and Rape," 170.

45. Woodhull, "Sexuality, Power, and Rape," 171.

46. Foucault, *The History of Sexuality*, 31.

47. Kate Soper, "Productive Contradictions," in *Up against Foucault: Explorations of Some Tensions between Foucault and Feminism*, ed. Caroline Ramazanoglu (New York: Routledge, 1993), 42–44.

48. Ibid., 43.

49. Foucault, *The History of Sexuality*, 32.

50. Rubin, "Thinking Sex," 270–73.

51. Diamond and Quinby, introduction to *Feminism and Foucault*, xv.

52. Peggy Kamuf, "Penelope at Work: Interruptions in *A Room of One's Own*," in Diamond and Quinby, *Feminism and Foucault*, 157. See Virginia Woolf's *A Room of One's Own* (London: Harcourt, Brace, and World, 1929), 5–7, for her description of how a fascinating thought caused her to rise from the riverbank at Oxbridge. She walked across the grass only to have a beadle remind her that fellows and scholars alone might walk there. When she arrived at the library, its guardian then pointed out that ladies were admitted only in the company of a fellow or with a letter of introduction.

53. Michel Foucault, "The Subject and Power," afterword to *Michel Foucault: Beyond Structuralism and Hermeneutics*, 2d ed., by Hubert L. Dreyfus and Paul Rabinow (Chicago: University of Chicago Press, 1983), 220.

54. Joan Wallach Scott, "'Experience,'" in *Feminists Theorize the Political*, ed. Judith Butler and Joan W. Scott (New York: Routledge, 1992), 22–40. This article first appeared in *Critical Inquiry* 17 (1991): 773–97.

55. Ibid., 25.

56. Michel Foucault, "Nietzsche, Genealogy, History," in *Language, Counter-Memory, Practice: Selected Essays and Interviews by Michel Foucault*, ed. Donald F. Bouchard (Ithaca, N.Y.: Cornell University Press, 1977), 151–52.

57. Scott, "'Experience,'" 34.

Chapter Four

1. Allan Berube and Jeffrey Escoffier, "Queer/Nation," *OutLook: National Lesbian and Gay Quarterly* 11 (Winter 1991): 12.

2. Teresa de Lauretis, "Queer Theory, Lesbian and Gay Sexualities: An Introduction," *differences: A Journal of Feminist Cultural Studies* 3/2 (Summer 1991; special issue): iii.

3. I should point out that I served as chair of Queer Nation Nashville during its very brief existence in the second half of 1991. We took our lead from Queer Nation Atlanta, which was unusual in conceding a bit to organizational hierarchy by designating one person as "chair."

4. Michel Foucault, *The History of Sexuality*, Volume 1: *An Introduction*, trans. Robert Hurley (Paris: Editions Gallimard, 1976; New York: Vintage Books, 1990).

5 Judith Butler, *Gender Trouble: Feminism and the Subversion of Identity* (New York: Routledge, 1990), 5, emphasis in original.

6. Ibid., 106–11.

7. Ibid., 140.

8. Michel Foucault, ed., *Herculine Barbin, Being the Recently Discovered Memoirs of a Nineteenth Century Hermaphrodite*, trans. Richard McDongall (New York: Colophon, 1980). For Butler's discussion of this text, see her *Gender Trouble*, 93–106.

9. Butler, *Gender Trouble*, 130–33; quotation 130.

10. Judith Butler, *Bodies That Matter: On the Discursive Limits of 'Sex'* (New York: Routledge, 1993.

11. Butler, *Gender Trouble*, 134.

12. Judith Butler, *Bodies That Matter: On the Discursive Limits of "Sex"* (New York: Routledge, 1993), ix.

13. Ibid., 67–69.

14. Ibid., 6.

15. Judith Butler, *The Psychic Life of Power* (Stanford: Stanford University Press, 1997).

16. Judith Butler, "Sexual Inversions," in *Discourses of Sexuality: From Aristotle to AIDS*, ed. Domna C. Stanton (Ann Arbor: University of Michigan Press, 1992), 344–61.

17. Foucault, *The History of Sexuality*, 137.

18. Butler, "Sexual Inversions," 348.

19. Foucault, *The History of Sexuality*, 142; quoted in Butler, "Sexual Inversions," 347.

20. Butler, "Sexual Inversions," 346. Note, too, that Foucault made no such claim. Although he referred to "epidemics" generally, which have continued to occur throughout the intervening centuries, he also clearly named the plague, a very specific epidemic that had far-reaching consequences for most of western Europe between 1348 and the eighteenth century; see Emmanuel Le Roy Ladurie, *The Mind and Method of the Historian*, trans. Sian Reynolds and Ben Reynolds (Chicago: University of Chicago Press, 1981), 28–83.

21. Allan Megill, "The Reception of Foucault by Historians," *Journal of the History of Ideas* 48 (1987): 117–41.

22. For a description of this process, see Randy Shilts, *And the Band Played On: People, Politics, and the AIDS Epidemic* (1987; New York: Penguin Books, 1988). Note that the political inadequacy of the Reagan administration's response to AIDS in no way vitiates my point. One of Shilts's major themes involves the way in which the political preferences of the Reagan administration clashed with the professional commitments of the bureaucrats at the Centers for Disease Control (CDC)—including, in some cases, Reagan appointees—who first recognized the existence of a new epidemic. The health bureaucracy was trying to function properly even as Reaganite political interference prevented it from doing so. Whether Reagan's policies in these matters indicate the beginning of a significant shift away from the administrative apparatus that began to emerge in the late eighteenth century is a different question.

23. Butler, *Bodies That Matter*, 282 n. 8.

24. Butler, "Sexual Inversions," 348.

25. Butler, *Bodies That Matter*, 234.

26. Michel Foucault, "Nietzsche, Genealogy, History," in *Language, Counter-Memory, Practice: Selected Essays and Interviews by Michel Foucault*, ed. Donald F. Bouchard (Ithaca, N.Y.: Cornell University Press, 1977), 147–48.

27. See the Gayatri Chakravorty Spivak quotation in Butler, *Bodies That Matter*, 27.

28. Judith Butler, *The Psychic Life of Power* (Stanford, Calif.: Stanford University Press, 1997), 42.

29. Introduction to *Feminists Theorize the Political*, ed. Judith Butler and Joan W. Scott (New York: Routledge, 1992), xiii.

30. For a useful overview of the process by which researcher Evelyn Hooker demonstrated the empirical vacuity of "homosexuality" as a diagnosis, see Francis Mark Mondimore, *A Natural History of Homosexuality* (Baltimore: Johns Hopkins University Press, 1996), 89–95.

31. Butler, *Psychic Life of Power*, 93.

32. Ibid., 94.

33. See Howell Rains, *My Soul Is Rested: The Story of the Civil Rights Movement in the Deep South* (1977; New York: Penguin, 1983), 40–42, for Parks's own understanding of why she refused to move.

34. Michel Foucault, *The Order of Things: An Archaeology of the Human Sciences*, trans. Alan Sheridan (New York: Vintage Books, 1973), 373–86.

35. Foucault, *The History of Sexuality*, 150.

36. John Forrester, "Michel Foucault and the History of Psychoanalysis," *History of Science* 18 (1980): 286–303.

37. Foucault, *The Order of Things*, xi, emphasis in original.

38. See Judith Butler, "Critically Queer," in *Bodies That Matter*, chap. 8, 223–42.

39. Judith Butler, "The Lesbian Phallus and the Morphological Imaginary," *Bodies That Matter*, 57–91.

40. Teresa de Lauretis, "The Technology of Gender," in *Technologies of Gender: Essays on Theory, Film, and Fiction* (Bloomington: Indiana University Press, 1987), 13.

41. Ibid., 15.

42. Ibid., 22–24.

43. Teresa de Lauretis, *Alice Doesn't: Feminism, Semiotics, Cinema* (Bloomington: University of Indiana Press, 1984), 3–7.

44. Ibid., 86.

45. Teresa de Lauretis, *The Practice of Love: Lesbian Sexuality and Perverse Desire* (Bloomington: Indiana University Press, 1994), 4–6, 75.

46. Ibid.; see especially chaps. 3 and 5.

47. Ibid., 155–57.

48. Ibid., 301.

49. Ibid., 303.

50. Ibid., 310.

51. Ibid., 311.

52. Eve Kosofsky Sedgwick, *Epistemology of the Closet* (Berkeley and Los Angeles: University of California Press, 1990).

53. Ibid., 22–27.

54. Eve Kosofsky Sedgwick, *Between Men: English Literature and Male Homosocial Desire* (New York: Columbia University Press, 1985), 5.

55. Sedgwick, *Epistemology of the Closet*, 3.

56. Ibid., 43.

57. Ibid., 40–43.

58. Ibid., 40.

59. Ibid., 4–8.

60. See Butler, "Critically Queer."

61. Sedgwick, *Epistemology of the Closet*, 9–11.

62. Ibid., 12.

63. Ibid., 52.

64. Ibid., 53, emphasis in original.

65. Eve Kosofsky Sedgwick, "Queer and Now," in *Tendencies* (Durham, N.C.: Duke University Press, 1993), 9, 11.

66. David Blanton, comp., *Queer Notions: A Fabulous Collection of Gay and Lesbian Wit and Wisdom* (Philadelphia: Running Press, 1996). This book may represent a certain apotheosis in the mainstreaming of everything lesbian/gay, even queer. Note that the copyright page includes a list of "other [much more prosaic] books in this series," including *Medical Wit and Wisdom*, *The Quotable Cat*, and *Gardens*.

67. Lauretis, "Queer Theory," iv.

68. Sedgwick, "Queer and Now," 8.

69. Ibid., 14.

70. David Halperin, "The Queer Politics of Michel Foucault," in *Saint Foucault* (New York: Oxford University Press, 1995), 63, emphasis in original.

71. Here I should clarify that I count myself among such activists. The connection between scholarship and politics remains murky even for those of us who do both.

72. Sedgwick, "Queer and Now," 3. For more information about lesbian/gay teen suicide, including the infamous report that the Bush administration tried to suppress in order to appease right-wing members of Congress, see Gary Remafei, ed., *Death by Denial: Studies of Suicide in Gay and Lesbian Teenagers* (Boston: Alyson Publications, 1994).

73. Ibid., 3.

74. "How to Bring Your Kids up Gay," in *Fear of a Queer Planet: Queer Politics and Social Theory*, ed. Michael Warner (Minneapolis: University of Minnesota Press, 1993), 69–81.

75. Sedgwick, *Epistemology of the Closet*, 69–70; quoted in Halperin, "Queer Politics," 36–37.

76. For example, as I witnessed myself, in justifying a bill that would prohibit the state of Tennessee from recognizing same-sex marriages, one Representative Peach argued simultaneously that same-sex relationships are "unnatural" and that legalizing such marriages would imperil the species by significantly reducing the rate of reproduction.

77. Halperin, "Queer Politics," 38.

78. Sedgwick, "Queer and Now," 4.

Chapter Five

1. David Halperin, *Saint Foucault: Towards a Gay Hagiography* (New York: Oxford University Press, 1995), 3–8; quotation, 6.

2. The anthology is Brett Beemyn and Mickey Eliason, eds., *Queer Studies: A Lesbian, Gay, Bisexual, and Transgender Anthology* (New York: New York University Press, 1996).

3. Eve Kosofsky Sedgwick, *Epistemology of the Closet* (Berkeley and Los Angeles: University of California Press, 1990); Michael Warner, introduction to *Fear of a Queer Planet: Queer Politics and Social Theory*, ed. Michael Warner (Minneapolis: University of Minnesota Press, 1993), xiii.

4. I mention being from Oklahoma simply because, as friends and advisers have noted, I take a certain sort of pride in being a fourth-generation Oklahoman myself and because Michael Moon takes his childhood in Oklahoma as the starting point for a reflection on queer identities in "Whose History? The Case of Oklahoma" (in *A Queer World: The Center for Lesbian and Gay Studies Reader*, ed. Martin Bauml Duberman [New York: New York University Press, 1997], 24–34).

5. Richard D. Mohr, *Gay Ideas: Outing and Other Controversies* (New York: Beacon, 1992), 142.

6. Donald Morton, "A Note on Cultural Studies," in *The Material Queer: A Les-BiGay Cultural Studies Reader*, ed. Donald Morton (Boulder, Colo.: Westview Press, 1996), xv.

7. Michel Foucault, *Discipline and Punish: The Birth of the Prison*, trans. Alan Sheridan (New York: Vintage Books, 1979).

8. Michel Foucault, *The History of Sexuality*, Volume 1: *An Introduction*, trans. Robert Hurley (Paris: Editions Gallimard, 1976; New York: Vintage Books, 1990).

9. Steven Seidman, "Identity and Politics in a 'Postmodern' Gay Culture: Some Historical and Conceptual Notes," in Warner, *Fear of a Queer Planet*, 132.

10. Ibid., 136–37.

11. On race, see Richard Mohr, "Black Law and Gay Law: Do Civil Rights Have a Future?" 54–86; on a God's-eye view and the possibility for culturally neutral definitions of "homosexuality," see Richard Mohr, "The Thing of It Is: Some Problems with Models for the Social Construction of Homosexuality," 221–42 (both in *Gay Ideas*).

12. Ibid., 251–56.

13. Frank Browning, *A Queer Geography: Journeys toward a Sexual Self*, rev. ed. (New York: Noonday Press, 1998), 12.

14. For the widget comparison, see Mohr, *Gay Ideas*, 236–37.

15. Mohr, *Gay Ideas*, p. 235.

16. For further discussion of "gender identity disorder," see Susan Coates, "Gender Identity Disorder in Boys: The Search for a Constitutional Factor," in Duberman, *A Queer World*, 108–33.

17. If only to forestall the accusation that this scenario constitutes nothing other than activist hysteria, I cite Leroy Aarons, *Prayers for Bobby: A Mother's Coming to Terms with the Suicide of Her Gay Son* (New York: HarperCollins, 1995). Marc Adams, a former student and employee at Jerry Falwell's Liberty University, has developed

an outreach program specifically designed to help lesbians and gay men at conservative, religious colleges and universities. He explains that, at Liberty University and other such institutions, students often have a written obligation to report anyone they even suspect of being gay. Authorities then require the suspect to call her or his parents and inform them either that the student is leaving the school because of her/his identity or is undergoing "therapy" to "cure" the identity. Not surprisingly, this process often leads the suspect to commit suicide. Adams describes his own experiences in *The Preacher's Son* (Seattle: Window Books, 1996). The uniform resource locator (URL) for Adams's web site is www.heartstrong.org. His e-mail address is MarcAdams@heartstrong.org.

18. Eve Kosofsky Sedgwick, "Queer and Now," in *Tendencies* (Durham, N.C.: Duke University Press, 1993), 4.

19. Halperin, "Queer Politics," 18–26.

20. See the web site for the New York chapter of ACT-UP, www.actupny.org.

21. The reference to "Lick Bush" comes from the foreword by Eve Kosofsky Sedgwick, "T-times," in *Tendencies*, xi.

22. Lauren Berlant and Elizabeth Freeman, "Queer Nationality," in Warner, *Fear of a Queer Planet*, 193–229.

23. Alexander S. Chee, "A Queer Nationalism," *OutLook* 11 (Winter 1991): 17.

24. Jonathan Goldberg, *Sodometries: Renaissance Texts, Modern Sexualities* (Stanford, Calif.: Stanford University Press, 1992); idem, ed., *Queering the Renaissance* (Durham, N.C.: Duke University Press, 1994); and idem, ed., *Reclaiming Sodom* (New York: Routledge, 1994).

25. *Bowers v. Hardwick*, 478 U.S. 186 (1986).

26. Janet Halley, "*Bowers v. Hardwick* in the Renaissance," in *Queering the Renaissance*, ed Jonathan Goldberg (Durham, N.C.: Duke University Press, 1994), 15–39

27. Jonathan Goldberg, *Sodometries: Renaissance Texts, Modern Sexualities* (Stanford: Stanford University Press, 1992), 20.

28. *The Nation*, June 30, 1997, 7.

29. Jeffrey N. Cox and Larry J. Reynolds, introduction to *New Historical Literary Study: Essays on Reproducing Texts, Representing History*, ed. Jeffrey N. Cox and Larry J. Reynolds (Princeton, N.J.: Princeton University Press, 1993), 3–38; Joseph Litvak, "Back to the Future: A Review Article on the New Historicism, Deconstruction, and Nineteenth-Century Fiction," *Texas Studies in Language and Literature* 30 (1988): 120–49.

30. Goldberg, *Queering the Renaissance*, 380.

31. Goldberg, *Sodometries*, 179–249.

32. Ibid., 184.

33. Michel Foucault, "Nietzsche, Genealogy, History," in *Language, Counter-Memory, Practice: Selected Essays and Interviews by Michel Foucault*, ed. Donald Bouchard (Ithaca: Cornell University Press, 1977), 139–64.

34. Ibid., 140.

35. *Bowers v. Hardwick* 478 U.S. 186 (1986), 190.

36. Derrick Sherwin Bailey, *Homosexuality and the Western Christian Tradition* (New York: Longmans, 1955).

37. *Bowers v. Hardwick*, 196–97. Boswell described his approach to Bailey's work in *Christianity, Social Tolerance, and Homosexuality: Gay People in Western Europe from the Beginning of the Christian Era to the Fourteenth Century* (Chicago: University of Chicago Press, 1980), 4 n. 3.

38. *Bowers v. Hardwick*, 197.

39. See my article, "Lesbian/Gay Rights and Immigration Policy: Lobbying to End the Medical Model," *Journal of Policy History* 7 (1995): 208–25.

40. Foucault, *The History of Sexuality*, 100–102.

41. *Romer v. Evans* 116 S. Ct. 1620 (1996).

42. Matt Coles, telephone conversation with author, February 1998.

43. *Able v. U.S.A.*, U.S. District Court for the Eastern District of New York, July 2, 1997. The text of the decision is available from the Lambda Legal Defense and Education Fund web site, www.lambdalegal.org. For references to Boswell and Halperin, see sec. III.A.

44. Valerie Traub, "The (In)Significance of 'Lesbian' Desire in Early Modern England," in Goldberg, *Queering the Renaissance*, 70.

45. Ibid., 64.

46. Alan Bray, "Homosexuality and the Signs of Male Friendship in Elizabethan England," in Goldberg, *Queering the Renaissance*, 40–61.

47. Sedgwick, *Epistemology of the Closet*, 7.

48. Quoted in ibid., 6.

49. Lee Edelman, "Capitol Offenses: Sodomy in the Seat of American Government," in *Homographesis: Essays in Gay Literary and Cultural Theory* (New York: Routledge, 1994), 129–37.

50. Goldberg, *Sodometries*, 11.

51. Michel Foucault, "Nietzsche, Genealogy, History," in *Language, Counter-Memory, Practice: Selected Essays and Interviews*, ed. Donald F. Bouchard (Ithaca, N.Y.: Cornell University Press, 1977), 153.

52. *Jantz v. Muci* 759 F. Supp. 1543 (D. Kan, 1991).

53. Janet Halley, "The Construction of Heterosexuality," in Warner, *Fear of a Queer Planet*, 95.

54. Cindy Patton, "Tremble, Hetero Swine!" in Warner, *Fear of a Queer Planet*, 173.

55. Ibid., 162.

56. Judith Butler, "Against Proper Objects," introduction to "More Gender Trouble: Feminism Meets Queer Theory," *differences: A Journal of Feminist Cultural Studies* 6, no. 2/3 (Summer–Fall 1994; special issue): 1–26.

57. Henry Abelove, Michele Aina Barale, and David Halperin, introduction to *The Lesbian and Gay Studies Reader*, ed. Henry Abelove, Michele Aina Barale, and David Halperin (New York: Routledge, 1993), xv–xviii.

58. Butler, "Against Proper Objects," 15.

59. Ibid., 5.

60. Valerie Traub, "Mapping the Terms of 'Lesbian' Studies in the Early Modern Period" (draft manuscript in my possession), 6–10.

61. Butler, "Against Proper Objects," 16–20.

62. Ibid., 20–21.

63. Laura Alexander Harris, "Queer Black Feminism: The Pleasure Principle," *Feminist Review* 54 (Autumn 1996): 3–30, 20.

64. Teresa de Lauretis, "Queer Theory, Lesbian and Gay Studies: An Introduction" *differences: A Journal of Feminist Cultural Studies* 3/2 (Summer 1991; special issue): iv, viii–ix.

65. Evelynn Hammonds, "Black (W)holes and the Geometry of Black Female Sexuality," *differences: A Journal of Feminist Cultural Studies* 6/2–3 (Summer–Fall 1994): 126–45, 129.

66. Ibid., 130–39.

67. Ibid., 140–41.

68. Ibid., 13.

69. Harris, "Queer Black Feminism," 13.

70. Ibid., 16, emphasis in original.

71. Foucault, *Discipline and Punish*, 31.

72. Foucault, "Nietzsche, Genealogy, History."

73. Ibid., 139.

Conclusion

Epigraphs: Melissa Etheridge, "Silent Legacy," song 4 on the album *Yes I Am*, New York, Island Records, 1993; Michel Foucault, "The Subject and Power," afterword to *Michel Foucault: Beyond Structuralism and Hermeneutics*, 2d ed., by Hubert L. Dreyfus and Paul Rabinow (Chicago: University of Chicago Press, 1983), 210.

1. Because much of women's history over the past three decades or so has this effect, rather than attempt an exhaustive list here, I mention two prominent examples: (1) Carroll Smith-Rosenberg, "The Abortion Movement and the AMA, 1850–1880," in *Disorderly Conduct: Visions of Gender in Victorian America* (New York: Oxford University Press, 1985), 217–44. This article demonstrated that state laws prohibiting abortion in the United States were the product of a specific campaign spearheaded by the American Medical Association beginning in the late 1850s that shifted the logic of such laws from regulation in the interest of maternal health to prohibition in the interest of reversing a trend toward smaller families among the middle and upper classes—that is, toward requiring supposedly lazy, irresponsible women to do their duty for the race and for the nation. (2) Stephanie Coontz, *The Social Origins of Private Life: A History of American Families, 1600–1900* (New York: Verso, 1988), who states flatly that "cross-culturally, families vary so greatly in their gender, marital, and child-rearing arrangements that it is not possible to argue that they are based on universal psychological or biological relations" (p. 8) or, she need not have added, universal moral principles grounded in revealed wisdom.

2. See the cover story by John Leland and Mark Miller, "Can Gays 'Convert'?" 46–50; and Marc Peyser, "Battling Backlash," 50–52 (both in *Newsweek*, August 17, 1998).

3. See John D'Emilio, *Sexual Politics, Sexual Communities: The Making of a Homosexual Minority in the United States, 1945–1970.* (Chicago: University of Chicago

Press, 1983); Stuart Timmons, *The Trouble with Harry Hay, Founder of the Modern Gay Movement* (Boston: Alyson Press, 1990); and Franklin E. Kameny, "Government vs. Gays: Two Sad Stories with Two Happy Endings, Civil Service Employment and Security Clearances," in *Creating Change: Public Policy, Civil Rights, and Sexuality*, ed. John D'Emilio, William B. Turner, and Urvashi Vaid (New York: St. Martin's Press, forthcoming).

4. *Bowers v. Hardwick*, 478 US 1986, 199.

5. Ibid., 190.

6. Michel Foucault, *The Use of Pleasure: The History of Sexuality*, vol. 2 (Paris: Editions Gallimard, 1984; trans. Robert Hurley, New York: Random House, 1985), 5; idem., *The Care of the Self: The History of Sexuality*, vol. 3 (Paris: Editions Gallimard, 1984; trans. Robert Hurley, New York: Random House, 1986).

7. Foucault, *The Use of Pleasure*, 4.

8. Joan Wallach Scott, "'Experience,'" in *Feminists Theorize the Political*, ed. Judith Butler and Joan W. Scott (New York: Routledge, 1992), 22–40.

9. Judith Butler, *Gender Trouble: Feminism and the Subversion of Identity* (New York: Routledge, 1990), 107–10.

10. Simon LeVay, "A Difference in Hypothalmic Structure between Heterosexual and Homosexual Men," *Science* 253 (1991): 1034–37.

11. Simon LeVay, *The Sexual Brain* (Cambridge: MIT Press, 1993), 1.

12. Bonnie Zimmerman, "The Politics of Transliteration: Lesbian Personal Narratives," *Signs* 9 (1983): 663–82.

13. Anne Fausto-Sterling, *Myths of Gender: Biological Theories about Women and Men*, rev. ed. (New York: Basic Books, 1992), 256.

14. Michel Foucault, "Two Lectures," in *Power/Knowledge: Selected Interviews and Other Writings by Michel Foucault, 1972–1977*, ed. Colin Gordon, trans. Colin Gordon et al. (New York: Pantheon Books, 1980), 85.

15. Irene Diamond and Lee Quinby, "American Feminism in the Age of the Body," *Signs* 10 (1984): 119–25; reprinted in *Feminism and Foucault: Reflections on Resistance*, ed. Irene Diamond and Lee Quinby (Boston: Northeastern University Press, 1988), 193–206.

16. In 1995 in Wilson County, Tennessee, county commissioners cited the biblical story of Sodom and Gomorrah in a resolution stating that "acceptance of, and practice of homosexual behavior has brought about the destruction of major civilizations throughout history"; Warren Duzak, "Commission Cites Bible in Gay Vote: Denounces NEA on History Month," *Nashville Tennessean*, November 21, 1995, Local News Section, 1. In June 1998, Pat Robertson "warned" the city of Orlando, Florida, that, simply by flying rainbow flags—a symbol of gay liberation—during Disney World's annual Gay Day, they opened themselves to God's wrath in the form of hurricanes, other severe weather, and even terrorist attacks. For an amusing comparison of Orlando's and North Carolina's fates during the fall 1999 hurricane season as an indication that God is more upset with North Carolina for returning Jesse Helms to the Senate than with Disney World for sponsoring Gay Day, see Mike Thomas, "The Melody Theory of Hurricane Paths," *Orlando Sentinel*, September 25, 1999.

17. *The Advocate*, May 27, 1997.

18. Eve Kosofsky Sedgwick, *Epistemology of the Closet* (Berkeley and Los Angeles: University of California Press, 1990), 1.

19. Max Pensky, "Universalism and the Situated Critic," in *The Cambridge Companion to Habermas*, ed. Stephen K. White (New York: Cambridge University Press, 1995), 67–94.

20. Jürgen Habermas, "Modernity versus Postmodernity," *New German Critique* 22 (1981): 13.

21. Hans Johnson, "The 'Pink Nazis,'" *Harvard Gay and Lesbian Review* 2 (1995): 1, 49–50.

22. Ibid., 1.

23. Michel Foucault, "How Much Does It Cost for Reason to Tell the Truth?" in *Foucault Live (Interviews, 1966–84)*, ed. Sylvere Lotringer, trans. Dudley M. Marchi (New York: Semiotext[e], 1989), 233–55; quotation, 254.

24. Michel Foucault, *The History of Sexuality*, trans. Robert Hurley (New York: Vintage Books, 1990), 135–59; idem, "The Politics of Health in the Eighteenth Century," in Gordon, *Power/Knowledge*, 166–82.

25. For a specific example, see Sara Miles, "He Kissed a Girl: How a Journey through the Heyday of Gay Identity Politics Led to a Straight Romance," *Out* (July 1999): 51–53, 94–96.

26. Foucault, *The Use of Pleasure*, 9.

27. John Boswell, *Christianity, Social Tolerance, and Homosexuality: Gay People in Western Europe from the Beginning of the Christian Era to the Fourteenth Century* (Chicago: University of Chicago Press, 1980).

28 Richard Plant, *The Pink Triangle: The Nazi War against Homosexuals* (New York: Henry Holt, 1986), 181.

29. Nancy Fraser, "Foucault: A 'Young Conservative'?" in *Unruly Practices: Power, Discourse, and Gender in Contemporary Social Theory* (Minneapolis: University of Minnesota Press, 1989), 47, emphasis in original.

30. Plant, *The Pink Triangle*, 13–19.

31. D'Emilio, *Sexual Politics, Sexual Communities*.

32. David Halperin, *Saint Foucault: Towards a Gay Hagiography* (New York: Oxford University Press, 1995), 134.

33. Larry Cata Backer, "Queering Theory: An Essay on the Conceit of Revolution in Law," in *Legal Queeries: Lesbian, Gay, and Transgender Legal Studies*, ed. Leslie J. Moran, Daniel Monk, and Sarah Beresford (New York: Cassell, 1998), 185–203; quotation, 188, emphasis in original.

34. See Nancy D. Polikoff, "Raising Children: Lesbian and Gay Parents Face the Public and the Courts," in D'Emilio, Turner, and Vaid, *Creating Change*.

35. See Linda Gordon, *Heroes of Their Own Lives: The Politics and History of Family Violence* (New York: Viking Penguin, 1988); and U.S. Commission on Civil Rights, *Battered Women: Issues of Public Policy* (Washington, D.C.: U.S. Commission on Civil Rights, 1978). The latter is especially interesting: a "consultation" sponsored by the Civil Rights Commission on battered women—domestic violence as a civil rights issue.

36. *Bowers v. Hardwick*, 190.

37. Ibid., 200.

38. Ibid., 194–95.

39. Janet Halley, "The Politics of the Closet: Towards Equal Protection for Gay, Lesbian, and Bisexual Identity," in *Reclaiming Sodom*, ed. Jonathan Goldberg (New York: Routledge, 1994), 145–204, 145.

40. *United States v. Carolene Products*, 304 U.S. 144, 152 n.4.

41. Halley, *Politics of the Closet*, 146.

42. Evan Gerstmann, *The Constitutional Underclass: Gays, Lesbians, and the Failure of Class-Based Equal Protection* (Chicago: University of Chicago Press, 1999).

43. See Scalia's dissent in *Romer v. Evans*, 116 S. Ct. 1620 (1996), especially sec. II; Halley's discussion of this problem in "The Politics of the Closet," 147–48; and Gestmann's discussion in *The Constitutional Underclass*, xx.

44. *Romer v. Evans*, xx.

45. Leland and Miller, "Can Gays 'Convert'?"

46. Halley, "The Politics of the Closet," 150–57.

47. Cindy Patton, "Tremble, Hetero Swine!" in *Fear of a Queer Planet: Queer Politics and Social Theory*, ed. Michael Warner (Minneapolis: University of Minnesota Press, 1993), 143–77, especially 166.

48. Halley, "The Politics of the Closet," 154–57.

49. See John Hope Franklin and Genna Rae McNeil, eds., *African-Americans and the Living Constitution* (Washington, D.C.: Smithsonian Institution Press, 1995); and Richard Bardolph, ed., *The Civil Rights Record: Black Americans and the Law, 1849–1970.* (New York: Thomas Y. Crowell, 1970).

50. For my discussion of the ways in which general support for civil rights in the Carter administration and general opposition to civil rights in the Reagan administration had a substantial impact on the fortunes of lesbian/gay civil rights activists, see William B. Turner, "Mirror Images: Lesbian/Gay Civil Rights in the Carter and Reagan Administrations," in D'Emilio, Turner, and Vaid, *Creating Change*. Patton, on the other hand, describes the ways in which the New Right strives to grant some legitimacy to African American civil rights gains while insisting that lesbian/gay attempts to extend the basic logic of civil rights to include sexual minorities constitutes a horrific perversion of the civil rights tradition; "Tremble, Hetero Swine!" 151–53.

51. Backer, "Queering Theory," 194–97.

52. Michel Foucault, *Madness and Civilization: A History of Insanity in the Age of Reason*, trans. Richard Howard (New York: Vintage Books, 1988).

53. Patton, "Tremble, Hetero Swine!" 173.

54. Ibid., 147–48, 162, 165.

55. In the interest of full disclosure, I should mention that I participated in organizing the candlelight vigil in Shepard's memory in Nashville; see Rob Moritz, "Vigil Honors Slain Gay Student: Speakers Urge Crowd to Fight Hate Crimes," *Nashville Tennessean*, October 19, 1998, 2B. At the vigil, I spoke about rights and urged participants to support the hate crimes bill that at the time the lesbian/gay/bisexual/transgender civil rights organization that I cochair, the Lesbian and Gay Coalition for Justice, was working to introduce in the Tennessee General Assembly.

56. For an article that illustrates all these points, see Brooks Egerton, "Outpouring: From Grief to Anger to Hate, No Gay Victim Has Inspired the Reaction

Matthew Has," *Dallas Morning News;* reprinted in Nashville *Tennessean*, October 18, 1998, 1D, 3D.

57. Quoted in ibid., 3D.

58. Quoted in ibid.

59. Patton, "Tremble, Hetero Swine!" 144–45.

60. On the demise of the Hate Crimes Prevention Act in conference commit-tee, see the October 18, 1999, press release from Parents, Family, and Friends of Lesbians and Gays (PFLAG). For overviews of legislative activity in Texas and Wyoming, see National Gay and Lesbian Task Force, *Capital Gains and Losses: A State by State Review of Gay, Lesbian, Bisexual, Transgender, and HIV/AIDS–Related Legislation in 1998* (Washington, D.C.: National Gay and Lesbian Task Force Pol-icy Institute, 1998), 84, 93.

Bibliography

Aarons, Leroy. *Prayers for Bobby: A Mother's Coming to Terms with the Suicide of Her Gay Son.* New York: HarperCollins, 1995.

Abelove, Henry, Michele Aina Barale, and David Halperin. Introduction to *The Lesbian and Gay Studies Reader,* ed. Henry Abelove, Michele Aina Barale, and David Halperin. New York: Routledge, 1993.

———, eds. *The Lesbian and Gay Studies Reader.* New York: Routledge, 1993.

Adams, Marc. *The Preacher's Son.* Seattle: Window Books, 1996.

Aiken, Susan Hardy, Karen Anderson, Myra Dinnerstein, Judy Lensink, and Patricia MacCorquodale. "Trying Transformations: Curriculum Integration and the Problem of Resistance." *Signs* 12 (1987): 255–75.

Alcoff, Linda. "Cultural Feminism versus Poststructuralism: The Identity Crisis in Feminist Theory." *Signs* 13 (1988): 405–36.

Appleby, Joyce, Lynn Hunt, and Margaret Jacob. "Response." *Journal of the History of Ideas* 56 (1995): 677–68.

———. *Telling the Truth about History.* New York: W. W. Norton, 1994.

Arac, Jonathan, ed. *After Foucault: Humanistic Knowledge, Postmodern Challenges.* New Brunswick, N.J.: Rutgers University Press, 1988.

Backer, Larry Cata. "Queering Theory: An Essay on the Conceit of Revolution in Law." In *Legal Queeries: Lesbian, Gay, and Transgender Legal Studies,* ed. Leslie J. Moran, Daniel Monk, and Sarah Beresford. New York: Cassell, 1998.

Badger, Anthony J. *The New Deal: The Depression Years, 1933–1940.* New York: Noonday Press, 1989.

Bailey, Derrick Sherwin. *Homosexuality and the Western Christian Tradition.* New York: Longmans, 1955.

Bardolph, Richard, ed. *The Civil Rights Record: Black Americans and the Law, 1849–1970.* New York: Thomas Y. Crowell, 1970.

Barker, Philip. *Michel Foucault: Subversions of the Subject.* New York: St. Martin's Press, 1993.

Barry, Andrew, Thomas Osborne, and Nikolas Rose, eds. *Foucault and Political Reason: Liberalism, Neo-Liberalism, and the Rationalities of Government.* Chicago: University of Chicago Press, 1996.

229

Bartky, Sandra Lee. *Femininity and Domination: Studies in the Phenomenology of Oppression*. New York: Routledge, 1990.

———. "Foucault, Femininity, and the Modernization of Patriarchal Power." In *Feminism and Foucault: Reflections on Resistance*, ed. Irene Diamond and Lee Quinby. Boston: Northeastern University Press, 1988.

Bayer, Ronald. *Homosexuality and American Psychiatry: The Politics of Diagnosis*. New York: Basic Books, 1981.

Beauvoir, Simone de. *The Second Sex*. Ed. and trans. H. M. Parshley. New York: Vintage Books, 1989.

Beemyn, Brett, and Mickey Eliason, eds. *Queer Studies: A Lesbian, Gay, Bisexual, and Transgender Anthology*. New York: New York University Press, 1996.

Berkowitz, Edward D. *America's Welfare State: From Roosevelt to Reagan*. Baltimore: Johns Hopkins University Press, 1991.

Berlant, Lauren, and Elizabeth Freeman. "Queer Nationality." In *Fear of a Queer Planet: Queer Politics and Social Theory*, ed. Michael Warner. Minneapolis: University of Minnesota Press, 1993.

Bernauer, James. "America's Foucault." *Man and World* 16 (1983): 389–405.

Bernstein, Richard J. "Foucault: Critique as a Philosophical Ethos." In *Critique and Power: Recasting the Foucault/Habermas Debate*, ed. Michael Kelly. Cambridge, Mass.: MIT Press, 1994.

Berube, Allan. *Coming Out under Fire: The History of Gay Men and Women in World War Two*. New York: Free Press, 1990. Reprint, New York: Plume, 1991.

Berube, Allan, and Jeffrey Escoffier. "Queer/Nation." *Outlook: National Lesbian and Gay Quarterly* 11 (Winter 1991): 12–14.

Blanton, David, comp. *Queer Notions: A Fabulous Collection of Gay and Lesbian Wit and Wisdom*. Philadelphia: Running Press, 1996.

Bloom, Floyd E., ed. *Neuroscience: From the Molecular to the Cognitive. Progress in Brain Research* 100. Amsterdam: Elsevier, 1994.

Bordo, Susan. "Anorexia Nervosa: Psychopathology as the Crystallization of Culture." In *Feminism and Foucault: Reflections on Resistance*, ed. Irene Diamond and Lee Quinby. Boston: Northeastern University Press, 1988.

Boswell, John. *Christianity, Social Tolerance, and Homosexuality: Gay People in Western Europe from the Beginning of the Christian Era to the Fourteenth Century*. Chicago: University of Chicago Press, 1980.

———. "Revolutions, Universals, and Sexual Categories." In *Hidden from History: Reclaiming the Gay and Lesbian Past*, ed. Martin Bauml Duberman, Martha Vicinus, and George Chauncey Jr. New York: New American Library, 1989.

———. *Same-Sex Unions in Premodern Europe*. New York: Villard Books, 1994.

Bouchard, Donald F., ed. *Language, Counter-Memory, Practice: Selected Essays and Interviews by Michel Foucault*. Ithaca, N.Y.: Cornell University Press, 1977.

Bowers v. Hardwick. 478 US 186 (1986).

Brand, Arie. *The Force of Reason: An Introduction to Habermas' Theory of Communicative Action*. Boston: Allen and Unwin, 1990.

Bray, Alan. *Homosexuality in Renaissance England*. London: Gay Men's Press, 1982.

———— "Homosexuality and the Signs of Male Friendship in Elizabethan England." In *Queering the Renaissance*, ed., Jonathan Goldberg. Durham, N.C.: Duke University Press, 1994.

Browning, Frank. *A Queer Geography: Journeys toward a Sexual Self*. Rev. ed. New York: Noonday Press, 1998.

Brownmiller, Susan. *Against Our Will: Men, Women, and Rape*. New York: Bantam, 1975.

Buell, Lawrence. "The Historicist Explosion in Recent Literary Studies." *Intellectual History Newsletter* 12 (1990): 22–26.

Burchell, Graham, Colin Gordon, and Peter Miller, eds. *The Foucault Effect: Studies in Governmentality*. Chicago: University of Chicago Press, 1991.

Butler, Judith. "Against Proper Objects." Introduction to "More Gender Trouble: Feminism Meets Queer Theory." *differences: A Journal of Feminist Cultural Studies* 6/2–3 (Summer–Fall 1994; special issue): 1–26.

————. *Bodies That Matter: On the Discursive Limits of "Sex."* New York: Routledge, 1993.

————. "Contingent Foundations: Feminism and the Question of 'Postmodernism.'" In *Feminists Theorize the Political*, ed. Judith Butler and Joan W. Scott. New York: Routledge, 1992.

————. *Gender Trouble: Feminism and the Subversion of Identity*. New York: Routledge, 1990.

————. *The Psychic Life of Power*. Stanford: Stanford University Press, 1997.

————. "Sexual Inversions." In *Discourses of Sexuality: From Aristotle to AIDS*, ed. Domna C. Stanton. Ann Arbor: University of Michigan Press, 1992.

Butler, Judith, and Joan W. Scott. Introduction to *Feminists Theorize the Political*, ed. Judith Butler and Joan W. Scott. New York: Routledge, 1992.

————, eds. *Feminists Theorize the Political*. New York: Routledge, 1992.

Caraway, Nancie. *Segregated Sisterhood: Racism and the Politics of American Feminism*. Knoxville: University of Tennessee Press, 1991.

Chauncey, George. "From Sexual Inversion to Homosexuality: The Changing Medical Conceptualization of Female 'Deviance.'" In *Passion and Power: Sexuality in History*, ed. Kathy Peiss and Christina Simmons with Robert Padgug. Philadelphia: Temple University Press, 1989.

————. *Gay New York: Gender, Urban Culture, and the Making of the Gay Male World, 1890–1940*. New York: Basic Books, 1994.

Chee, Alexander S. "A Queer Nationalism." *Outlook* 11 (Winter 1991): 15–19.

Christian, Barbara. "The Race for Theory." *Feminist Studies* 14 (1988): 67–80.

Cmiel, Kenneth. "History against Itself." *Journal of American History* 81 (1994; special issue on the practice of American history): 1169–74.

Coates, Susan. "Gender Identity Disorder in Boys: The Search for a Constitutional Factor." In *A Queer World: The Center for Lesbian and Gay Studies Reader*, ed. Martin Bauml Duberman. New York: New York University Press, 1997.

Collins, Patricia Hill. *Black Feminist Thought: Knowledge, Consciousness, and the Politics of Empowerment*. New York: Routledge, 1991.

Cook, Blanche Wiesen. "Female Support Networks and Political Activism: Lillian Wald, Crystal Eastman, Emma Goldman." *Chrysalis* 3 (1977). Reprinted in

Women's America: Refocusing the Past, 2d ed., ed. Linda K. Kerber and Jane DeHart-Mathews. New York: Oxford University Press, 1987.

———. "The Historical Denial of Lesbianism." *Radical History Review* 20 (1979): 60–65.

Coontz, Stephanie. *The Social Origins of Private Life: A History of American Families, 1600–1900*. New York: Verso, 1988.

Cox, Jeffrey N., and Larry J. Reynolds, eds. Introduction to *New Historical Literary Study: Essays on Reproducing Texts, Representing History*. Princeton, N.J.: Princeton University Press, 1993.

———. *New Historical Literary Study: Essays on Reproducing Texts, Representing History*. Princeton, N.J.: Princeton University Press, 1993.

Carol Marie Cropper. "Black Many Fatally Dragged in a Possible Racial Killing." *New York Times*, June 10, 1998, A:16.

Cuello, A. Claudio. "Trophic Factor Therapy in Adult CNS: Remodeling of Injured Basalo-cortical Neurons." In *Neuroscience: From the Molecular to the Cognitive*, ed. Floyd E. Bloom. *Progress in Brain Research* 100. Amsterdam: Elsevier, 1994.

DeHart, Jane, and Donald Mathews. "The Cultural Politics of the ERA's Defeat." In *Rights of Passage: The Past and Future of the ERA*, ed. Joan Hoff-Wilson. Bloomington: Indiana University Press, 1986.

Deleuze, Gilles. "What Is a *Dispositif*?" In *Michel Foucault: Philosopher*, trans. Timothy J. Armstrong. New York: Routledge, 1992.

D'Emilio, John. "Capitalism and Gay Identity." In *Powers of Desire: The Politics of Sexuality*, ed. Ann Snitow, Christine Stansell, and Sharon Thompson. New York: Monthly Review Press, 1983.

———. "Dreams Deferred: The Birth and Betrayal of America's First Gay Liberation Movement." In *Making Trouble: Essays on Gay History, Politics, and the University*. New York: Routledge, 1992.

———. *Making Trouble: Essays on Gay History, Politics, and the University*. New York: Routledge, 1992.

———. *Sexual Politics, Sexual Communities: The Making of a Homosexual Minority in the United States, 1940–1970*. Chicago: University of Chicago Press, 1983.

D'Emilio, John, and Estelle B. Freedman. *Intimate Matters: A History of Sexuality in America*. New York: Harper and Row, 1988.

D'Emilio, John, William B. Turner, and Urvashi Vaid, eds. *Creating Change: Public Policy, Civil Rights, and Sexuality*. New York: St. Martin's Press, forthcoming.

Derrida, Jacques. "Structure, Sign, and Play in the Discourse of the Human Sciences." In *The Languages of Criticism and the Sciences of Man: The Structuralist Controversy*, ed. Richard Macksey and Eugenio Donato. Baltimore: Johns Hopkins University Press, 1970.

Dews, Peter. *Logics of Disintegration: Post-structuralist Thought and the Claims of Critical Theory*. London: Verso, 1987.

Diamond, Irene, and Lee Quinby. "American Feminism in the Age of the Body." *Signs* 10 (1984): 119–25.

———. Introduction to *Feminism and Foucault: Reflections on Resistance*, ed. Irene Diamond and Lee Quinby. Boston: Northeastern University Press, 1988.

———, ed. *Feminism and Foucault: Reflections on Resistance*. Boston: Northeastern University Press, 1988.

Dollimore, Jonathan. *Sexual Dissidence: Augustine to Wilde, Freud to Foucault*. New York: Oxford University Press, 1991.

Dreyfus, Hubert L., and Paul Rabinow. *Michel Foucault: Beyond Structuralism and Hermeneutics*. 2d ed. Chicago: University of Chicago Press, 1983.

Duberman, Martin Bauml. *About Time: Exploring the Gay Past*. Rev. ed. New York: Meridien, 1991.

———. *Cures: A Gay Man's Odyssey*. New York: Dutton, 1991.

———. *Stonewall*. New York: Dutton, 1993.

———, ed. *A Queer World: The Center for Lesbian and Gay Studies Reader*. New York: New York University Press, 1997.Duberman, Martin Bauml, Martha Vicinus, and George Chauncey Jr., eds. *Hidden from History: Reclaiming the Gay and Lesbian Past*. New York: New American Library, 1989.

Duggan, Lisa. "Biography = Death." *Village Voice*. May 4, 1993, 90–91.

———. "Making It Perfectly Queer." *Socialist Review* 22 (1992): 11–31.

———. "Theory in Practice: The Theory Wars, or, Who's Afraid of Judith Butler?" *Journal of Women's History* 10/1 (Spring 1998): 9–19.

Duzak, Warren. "Commission Cites Bible in Gay Vote: Denounces NEA on History Month." *Nashville Tennessean*, November 21, 1995, Local News Section, 1.

Echols, Alice. *Daring to Be Bad: Radical Feminism in America, 1967–1975*. Minneapolis: University of Minnesota Press, 1989.

Edelman, Lee. "Capitol Offenses: Sodomy in the Seat of American Government." In *Homographesis: Essays in Gay Literary and Cultural Theory*. New York: Routledge, 1994.

———. *Homographesis: Essays in Gay Literary and Cultural Theory*. New York: Routledge, 1994.

Editorial, *Signs* 5 (1980; special issue on sex and sexuality): 570.

Egerton, Brooks. "Outpouring: From Grief to Anger to Hate, No Gay Victim Has Inspired the Reaction Matthew Has." *Dallas Morning News*. Reprinted in *Nashville Tennessean*, October 18, 1998, 1D–3D.

Ehrenreich, Barbara, and Deirdre English. *For Her Own Good: 150 Years of the Experts' Advice to Women*. New York: Anchor Books, 1979.

Eribon, Didier. *Michel Foucault*. Trans. Betsy Wing. Cambridge, Mass.: Harvard University Press, 1991.

Evans, Sara. *Personal Politics: The Roots of Women's Liberation in the Civil Rights Movement and the New Left*. New York: Knopf, 1979.

Faderman, Lillian. "The Morbidification of Love between Women." *Journal of Homosexuality* 4 (1978): 73–90.

Fausto-Sterling, Anne. *Myths of Gender: Biological Theories about Women and Men*. Rev. ed. New York: Basic Books, 1992.

Ferguson, Anne. "Patriarchy, Sexual Identity, and the Sexual Revolution." *Signs* 7 (1981): 158–72.

Firestone, David. "Murder Reveals Double Life of Being Gay in Rural South." *New York Times*, March 6, 1999, A1, A9.

Flanagan, Owen. *Consciousness Reconsidered*. Cambridge, Mass.: MIT Press, 1992.

Forrester, John. "Michel Foucault and the History of Psychoanalysis." *History of Science* 18 (1980): 286–303.

Foster, David. "A Look at Male Homosexuality from the Inside." *Nashville Net* (Spring 1997): 34–36.

Foucault, Michel. "Adorno, Horkheimer, and Marcuse: Who Is a 'Negator of History'?" In *Remarks on Marx: Conversations with Duccio Trombadori*, trans. R. James Goldstein and James Cascaito. New York: Semiotext(e), 1991.

———. *The Archaeology of Knowledge*. Trans. A. M. Sheridan Smith. New York: Pantheon Books, 1972.

———. *The Birth of the Clinic: An Archaeology of Medical Perception*. Trans. A. M. Sheridan Smith. New York: Random House, 1973.

———. *The Care of the Self: The History of Sexuality*, Vol. 3. Trans. Robert Hurley. New York: Random House, 1986. Paris: Editions Gallimard, 1984.

———. "Critical Theory/Intellectual History." In *Michel Foucault: Politics, Philosophy, Culture. Interviews and Other Writings, 1977–1984*, ed. Lawrence D. Kritzman. New York: Routledge, 1988.

———. *Discipline and Punish: The Birth of the Prison*. Trans. Alan Sheridan. New York: Vintage Books, 1979. Paris: Editions Gallimard, 1975.

———. "The Discourse of History." Interview by Raymond Bellour. In *Foucault Live (Interviews, 1966–84)*, ed. Sylvere Lotringer, trans. John Johnston. New York: Semiotext(e), 1989.

———. *Dits et écrits par Michel Foucault, 1954–1988*. Ed. Daniel Defert and Francis Ewald. 4 vols. Paris: Editions Gallimard, 1994.

———. "The End of the Monarchy of Sex." Interview by Bernard-Henri Levy. In *Foucault Live (Interviews, 1966–84)*, ed. Sylvere Lotringer, trans. Dudley M. Marchi. New York: Semiotext(e), 1989.

———. *The Essential Works of Michel Foucault, 1954–1984*. Ed. Paul Rabinow. 2 vols. New York: New Press, 1997.

———. *Folie et deraison: Histoire de la folie à l'age classique*. Paris: Plon, 1961.

———. "Friendship as a Way of Life." In *Ethics, Subjectivity, and Power*, trans. John Johnston. Vol 1 of *The Essential Works of Michel Foucault, 1954–1984*, ed. Paul Rabinow. New York: New Press, 1997.

———. "The History of Sexuality." Interview by Lucette Finas. In *Power/Knowledge: Selected Interviews and Other Writings by Michel Foucault, 1972–1977*, ed. Colin Gordon, trans. Colin Gordon, Leo Marshall, John Mepham, and Kate Soper. New York: Pantheon Books, 1980.

———. *The History of Sexuality*. Volume 1: *An Introduction*. Trans. Robert Hurley. New York: Vintage Books, 1990.

———. "How Much Does It Cost for Reason to Tell the Truth?" In *Foucault Live (Interviews, 1966–84)*, ed. Sylvere Lotringer, trans. Dudley M. Marchi. New York: Semiotext(e), 1989.

———. *Madness and Civilization: A History of Insanity in the Age of Reason*. Trans. Richard Howard. New York: Random House, 1965.

———. "Nietzsche, Freud, Marx." In *Transforming the Hermeneutic Context: From Nietzsche to Nancy*, ed. Gayle L. Ormiston and Alan D. Schrift. Albany: State University of New York Press, 1990.

———. "Nietzsche, Genealogy, History." In *Language, Counter-Memory, Practice: Selected Essays and Interviews by Michel Foucault*, ed. Donald F. Bouchard. Ithaca, N.Y.: Cornell University Press, 1977.

————. "On the Genealogy of Ethics: An Overview of Work in Progress." In *Michel Foucault: Beyond Structuralism and Hermeneutics*, 2d ed., by Hubert L. Dreyfus and Paul Rabinow. Chicago: University of Chicago Press, 1983.

————. *The Order of Things: An Archaeology of the Human Sciences*. Trans. Alan Sheridan. New York: Vintage Books, 1973.

————. "Politics and Reason." In *Michel Foucault: Politics, Philosophy, Culture. Interviews and Other Writings, 1977–1984*, ed. Lawrence D. Kritzman. New York: Routledge, 1988.

————. "Politics and the Study of Discourse." In *The Foucault Effect: Studies in Governmentality*, ed. Graham Burchell, Colin Gordon, and Peter Miller. Chicago: University of Chicago Press, 1991.

————. "The Politics of Health in the Eighteenth Century." In *Power/Knowledge: Selected Interviews and Other Writings by Michel Foucault, 1972–1977*, ed. Colin Gordon, trans. Colin Gordon, Leo Marshall, John Mepham, and Kate Soper. New York: Pantheon Books, 1980.

————. "Power, Moral Values, and the Intellectual." Interview by Michael Bess. *History of the Present* 4 (1988): 1.

————. "Prison Talk." Interview by J. J. Brochier. In *Power/Knowledge: Selected Interviews and Other Writings by Michel Foucault, 1972–1977*, ed. Colin Gordon, trans. Colin Gordon, Leo Marshall, John Mepham, and Kate Soper. New York: Pantheon Books, 1980.

————. "Questions on Geography." Interview by the editors of *Herodote*. In *Power/Knowledge: Selected Interviews and Other Writings by Michel Foucault, 1972–1977*, ed. Colin Gordon, trans. Colin Gordon, Leo Marshall, John Mepham, and Kate Soper. New York: Pantheon Books, 1980.

————. *Remarks on Marx: Conversations with Duccio Trombadori*. Trans. R. James Goldstein and James Cascaito. New York: Semiotext(e), 1991.

————. "The Subject and Power." Afterword to *Michel Foucault: Beyond Structuralism and Hermeneutics*, 2d ed., by Hubert L. Dreyfus and Paul Rabinow. Chicago: University of Chicago Press, 1983.

————. "Truth and Power." Interview by Alessandro Fontana and Pasquale Pasquino. In *Power/Knowledge: Selected Interviews and Other Writings by Michel Foucault, 1972–1977*, ed. Colin Gordon, trans. Colin Gordon, Leo Marshall, John Mepham, and Kate Soper. New York: Pantheon Books, 1980.

————. "Two Lectures." In *Power/Knowledge: Selected Interviews and Other Writings by Michel Foucault, 1972–1977*, ed. Colin Gordon, trans. Colin Gordon, Leo Marshall, John Mepham, and Kate Soper. New York: Pantheon Books, 1980.

————. *The Use of Pleasure: The History of Sexuality*. Vol. 2. Trans. Robert Hurley. New York: Random House, 1985. Paris: Editions Gallimard, 1984.

————. "What Is an Author?" In *Language, Counter-Memory, Practice: Selected Essays and Interviews by Michel Foucault*, ed. Donald F. Bouchard. Ithaca, N.Y.: Cornell University Press, 1977.

————. "What Is Enlightenment?" In *The Foucault Reader*, ed. Paul Rabinow. New York: Pantheon Books, 1984.

————, ed. *Herculine Barbin, Being the Recently Discovered Memoirs of a Nineteenth Century Hermaphrodite*. Trans. Richard McDongall. New York: Colophon, 1980.

Franklin, John Hope, and Genna Rae McNeil, eds. *African Americans and the Living Constitution*. Washington, D.C.: Smithsonian Institution Press, 1995.

Fraser, Nancy. "Foucault: A 'Young Conservative'?" In *Unruly Practices: Power, Discourse, and Gender in Contemporary Social Theory*. Minneapolis: University of Minnesota Press, 1989.

———. "Foucault on Modern Power: Empirical Insights and Normative Confusions." In *Unruly Practices: Power, Discourse, and Gender in Contemporary Social Theory*. Minneapolis: University of Minnesota Press, 1989.

———. "Foucault's Body Language: A Posthumanist Political Rhetoric?" In *Unruly Practices: Power, Discourse, and Gender in Contemporary Social Theory*. Minneapolis: University of Minnesota Press, 1989.

———. *Unruly Practices: Power, Discourse, and Gender in Contemporary Social Theory*. Minneapolis: University of Minnesota Press, 1989.

Freedman, Estelle B., and Barrie Thorne. "Introduction to 'The Feminist Sexuality Debates.'" *Signs* 10 (1984): 102–5.

Friedan, Betty. *The Feminine Mystique*. 2d ed. New York: Dell Publishing, 1983.

Fuss, Diana. *Essentially Speaking: Feminism, Nature, and Difference*. New York: Routledge, 1989.

Gadamer, Hans-Georg. *Truth and Method*. Rev. ed. Rev. trans. Joel Weinsheimer and Donald G. Marshall. New York: Crossroad Publishing, 1990.

Galambos, Louis, and Joseph Pratt. *The Rise of the Corporate Commonwealth: United States Business and Public Policy in the Twentieth Century*. New York: Basic Books, 1988.

Gandal, Keith. "Michel Foucault: Intellectual Work and Politics." *Telos* 67 (1986): 121–34.

"Gay Student Dies of Head Injuries Days after Attack." *Nashville Tennesean*, October 13, 1998.

Gerstmann, Evan. *The Constitutional Underclass: Gays, Lesbians, and the Failure of Class-Based Equal Protection*. Chicago: University of Chicago Press, 1999.

Gilbert, Arthur N. "Review of *The History of Sexuality, Volume One: An Introduction*." *American Historical Review* 84 (1979): 1020–21.

Gilman, Charlotte Perkins. *Women and Economics*. Boston: Small, Maynard, 1911.

Goldberg, Jonathan. *Sodometries: Renaissance Texts, Modern Sexualities*. Stanford, Calif.: Standford University Press, 1992.

———, ed. *Queering the Renaissance*. Durham, N.C.: Duke University Press, 1994.

———, ed. *Reclaiming Sodom*. New York: Routledge, 1994.

Gordon, Colin, ed. *Power/Knowledge: Selected Interviews and Other Writings by Michel Foucault, 1972–1977*. Trans. Colin Gordon, Leo Marshall, John Mepham, and Kate Soper. New York: Pantheon Books, 1980.

Gordon, Linda. *Heroes of Their Own Lives: The Politics and History of Family Violence*. New York: Viking Penguin, 1988.

———. "A Socialist View of Women's Studies: A Reply to the Editorial, Volume 1, Number 1." *Signs* 1 (1975): 559–66.

———. *Woman's Body, Woman's Right: A Social History of Birth Control in America*. New York: Penguin Books, 1976.

Graham, Hugh Davis. *The Civil Rights Era: Origins and Development of National Policy*. New York: Oxford University Press, 1990.

Grimshaw, Jean. "Practices of Freedom." In *Up against Foucault: Explorations of Some Tensions between Foucault and Feminism*, ed. Caroline Ramazanoglu. New York: Routledge, 1993.

Habermas, Jürgen. *Lifeworld and System: A Critique of Functionalist Reason*. Trans. Thomas McCarthy. Vol. 2 of *The Theory of Communicative Action*. Boston: Beacon Press, 1987.

———. "Modernity versus Postmodernity." *New German Critique* 22 (1981): 3–14.

———. *The Philosophical Discourse of Modernity*. Trans. Frederick Lawrence. Cambridge, Mass.: MIT Press, 1987.

———. *Reason and the Rationalization of Society*. Trans. Thomas McCarthy. Vol. 1 of *The Theory of Communicative Action*. Boston: Beacon Press, 1984.

———. "Taking Aim at the Heart of the Present: On Foucault's Lecture on Kant's *What Is Enlightenment?*" In *Critique and Power: Recasting the Foucault/Habermas Debate*, ed. Michael Kelly. Cambridge, Mass.: MIT Press, 1995.

Halley, Janet. "*Bowers v. Hardwick* in the Renaissance." *Queering the Renaissance*. Ed Jonathan Goldberg. Durham, N.C.: Duke University Press, 1994, 15–39.

———. "The Construction of Heterosexuality." In *Fear of a Queer Planet: Queer Politics and Social Theory*, ed. Michael Warner. Minneapolis: University of Minnesota Press, 1993.

———. "The Politics of the Closet: Towards Equal Protection for Gay, Lesbian, and Bisexual Identity." In *Reclaiming Sodom*, ed. Jonathan Goldberg. New York: Routledge, 1994.

Halperin, David. "The Describable Life of Michel Foucault." *Saint Foucault: Towards a Gay Hagiography*. New York: Oxford University Press, 1995.

———. "One Hundred Years of Homosexuality." In *Hidden from History: Reclaiming the Gay and Lesbian Past*, ed. Martin Bauml Duberman, Martha Vicinus, and George Chauncy Jr. New York: New American Library, 1989.

———. "One Hundred Years of Homosexuality." In *One Hundred Years of Homosexuality and Other Essays on Greek Love*. New York: Routledge, 1990.

———. *One Hundred Years of Homosexuality and Other Essays on Greek Love*. New York: Routledge, 1990.

———. "The Queer Politics of Michel Foucault." In *Saint Foucault: Towards a Gay Hagiography*. New York: Oxford University Press, 1995.

———. *Saint Foucault: Towards a Gay Hagiography*. New York: Oxford University Press, 1995.

Hammonds, Evelynn. "Black (W)holes and the Geometry of Black Female Sexuality." *differences: A Journal of Feminist Cultural Studies* 6/2–3 (Summer–Fall 1994): 126–45.

Hanby, Alonzo L. *Liberalism and Its Challengers: FDR to Reagan*. New York: Oxford University Press, 1985.

Harris, Laura Alexandra. "Queer Black Feminism: The Pleasure Principle." *Feminist Review* 54 (Autumn 1996): 3–30.

Harvey, David. *The Condition of Postmodernity: An Inquiry into the Origins of Cultural Change*. Oxford: Basil Blackwell, 1989.

Hiley, David R. "Foucault and the Analysis of Power: Political Engagement without Liberal Hope or Comfort." *Praxis International* 4 (1984): 192–207.

Hoff-Wilson, Joan, ed. *Rights of Passage: The Past and Future of the ERA.* Bloomington: Indiana University Press, 1986.

Hollinger, David. "Banality and Enigma." *Journal of American History* 81 (1994; special issue on the practice of American history): 1152–56.

Honneth, Axel. "Foucault's Theory of Society: A Systems-Theoretic Dissolution of the *Dialectic of Enlightenment.*" In *Critique and Power: Recasting the Foucault/Habermas Debate,* ed. Michael Kelly. Cambridge, Mass.: MIT Press, 1994.

hooks, bell. *Feminist Theory from Margin to Center.* Boston: South End Press, 1984.

Horkheimer, Max, and Theodore Adorno. *Dialectic of Enlightenment.* New York: Herder and Herder, 1972.

Hoy, David Couzens, ed. *Foucault: A Critical Reader.* New York: Basil Blackwell, 1986.

Hull, Gloria T., Patricia Bell Scott, and Barbara Smith, eds. *All the Women Are White, All the Blacks Are Men, but Some of Us Are Brave: Black Women's Studies.* Old Westbury, N.Y.: Feminist Press, 1982.

Jameson, Frederic. *The Prison-House of Language: A Critical Account of Structuralism and Russian Formalism.* Princeton, N.J.: Princeton University Press, 1972.

Jefferson, Thomas. *Notes on the State of Virginia.* Ed. William Peden. New York: W. W. Norton, 1972.

Johnson, Hans. "The 'Pink Nazis.'" *Harvard Gay and Lesbian Review* 2 (1995): 1, 49–50.

Kameny, Franklin E. "Government vs. Gays: Two Sad Stories with Two Happy Endings. Civil Service Employment and Security Clearances." In *Creating Change: Public Policy, Civil Rights, and Sexuality,* ed. John D'Emilio, William B. Turner, and Urvashi Vaid. New York: St. Martin's Press, forthcoming.

Kamuf, Peggy. "Penelope at Work: Interruptions in *A Room of One's Own.*" In *Feminism and Foucault: Reflections on Resistance,* ed. Irene Diamond and Lee Quinby. Boston: Northeastern University Press, 1988.

Katz, Jonathan Ned. *Gay American History: Lesbians and Gay Men in the USA. A Documentary History.* New York: Meridien, 1976. Rev. ed., 1992.

———. *Gay/Lesbian Almanac: A New Documentary.* New York: Harper and Row, 1983.

———. "The Invention of Heterosexuality." *Socialist Review* 20 (1990): 5–34.

———. *The Invention of Heterosexuality.* New York: Dutton, 1995.

———. "Treatment." In *Gay American History: Lesbians and Gay Men in the USA. A Documentary History.* New York: Meridien, 1976. Rev. ed., 1992.

Keller, Evelyn Fox. *Reflections on Gender and Science.* New Haven: Yale University Press, 1985.

Kelly, Joan. *Women, History, and Theory: The Essays of Joan Kelly.* Chicago: University of Chicago Press, 1984.

Kelly, Michael, ed. *Critique and Power: Recasting the Foucault/Habermas Debate.* Cambridge, Mass.: MIT Press, 1994.

Kennedy, Elizabeth Lapovsky, and Madline Davis. "The Reproduction of Butch-Fem Roles: A Social Constructionist Approach." In *Passion and Power: Sexuality in History,* ed. Kathy Peiss and Christina Simmons with Robert Padgug. Philadelphia: Temple University Press, 1989.

Kerber, Linda K., and Jane DeHart-Mathews, eds. *Women's America: Refocusing the Past*. 2d ed. New York: Oxford University Press, 1987.

Klatch, Rebecca E. *Women of the New Right*. Philadelphia: Temple University Press, 1987.Koedt, Anne. "Lesbianism and Feminism." In *Radical Feminism*, ed. Anne Koedt, Ellen Levine, and Anita Rapone. New York: Quadrangle Books, 1973.

———. "The Myth of the Vaginal Orgasm." In *Radical Feminism*, ed. Anne Koedt, Ellen Levine, and Anita Rapone. New York: Quandrangle Books, 1973.

Koedt, Anne, Ellen Levine, and Anita Rapone, eds. *Radical Feminism*. New York: Quadrangle Books, 1973.

Kritzman, Lawrence D., ed. *Michel Foucault: Politics, Philosophy, Culture. Interviews and Other Writings, 1977–1984*. New York: Routledge, 1988.

Ladurie, Emmanuel Le Roy. *The Mind and Method of the Historian*. Trans. Sian Reynolds and Ben Reynolds. Chicago: University of Chicago Press, 1981.

Landry, Donna, and Gerald Maclean. *The Spivak Reader*. New York: Routledge, 1996.

Laqueur, Thomas. *Making Sex: Body and Gender from the Greeks to Freud*. Cambridge, Mass.: Harvard University Press, 1990.

Lauretis, Teresa de. *Alice Doesn't: Feminism, Semiotics, Cinema*. Bloomington: Indiana University Press, 1984.

———. *The Practice of Love: Lesbian Sexuality and Perverse Desire*. Bloomington: Indiana University Press, 1994.

———. "Queer Theory, Lesbian and Gay Studies: An Introduction." *differences: A Journal of Feminist Cultural Studies* 3/2 (Summer 1991; special issue): iii–xviii.

———. *Technologies of Gender: Essays on Theory, Film, and Fiction*. Bloomington: Indiana University Press, 1987.

———. "The Technology of Gender." In *Technologies of Gender: Essays on Theory, Film, and Fiction*. Bloomington, Indiana University Press, 1987.

Lebrun, Gerard. *Michel Foucault, Philosopher*. Trans. Timothy J. Armstrong. New York: Routledge, 1992.

———. "Notes on Phenomenology in *Les Mots et Les Choses*." In *Michel Foucault, Philosopher*, trans. Timothy J. Armstrong. New York: Routledge, 1992.

Leland, John, and Mark Miller. "Can Gays 'Convert'?" *Newsweek*, August 17, 1998, 46–50.

LeVay, Simon. "A Difference in Hypothalmic Structure between Heterosexual and Homosexual Men." *Science* 253 (1991): 1034–37.

———. *The Sexual Brain*. Cambridge, Mass.: MIT Press, 1993.

Lévi-Strauss, Claude. "Postscripts to Chapters III and IV." In *Structural Anthropology*, vol. 1, trans. Claire Jacobson and Brooke Grundfest Schoepf. New York: Basic Books, 1963.

———. "Structural Analysis." In *Structural Anthropology*, vol. 1, trans. Claire Jacobson and Brooke Grundfest Schoepf. New York: Basic Books, 1963.

———. *Structural Anthropology*. Vol. 1. Trans. Claire Jacobson and Brooke Grundfest Schoepf. New York: Basic Books, 1963.

Litvak, Joseph. "Back to the Future: A Review Article on the New Historicism, Deconstruction, and Nineteenth-Century Fiction." *Texas Studies in Language and Literature* 30 (1988): 120–49.

Longino, Helen. "To See Feelingly: Reason, Passion, and Dialogue in Feminist Philosophy." In *Feminisms in the Academy*, ed. Domna C. Stanton and Abigail J. Stewart. Ann Arbor: University of Michigan Press, 1995.

Lotringer, Sylvere, ed. *Foucault Live (Interviews, 1966–84)*. Trans. John Johnston and Dudley M. March. New York: Semiotext(e), 1989.

Lyotard, Jean-François. *The Postmodern Condition: A Report on Knowledge*. Trans. Geoff Bennington and Brian Massumi. Foreword by Frederic Jameson. Minneapolis: University of Minnesota Press, 1984.

Macey, David. *The Lives of Michel Foucault*. New York: Pantheon Books, 1993.

Macksey, Richard, and Eugenio Donato, eds. *The Languages of Criticism and the Sciences of Man: The Structuralist Controversy*. Baltimore: Johns Hopkins University Press, 1970.

Marcuse, Herbert. *Eros and Civilization: a Philosophical Inquiry into Freud*. Boston: Beacon Press, 1966.

Margolis, Joseph. *The Flux of History and the Flux of Science*. Berkeley and Los Angeles: University of California Press, 1993.

Maroney, Thomas J. "*Bowers v. Hardwick*: A Case Study in Federalism, Legal Procedure, and Constitutional Interpretation." *Syracuse Law Review* 38 (1987): 1223–50.

Martin, Biddy. "Feminism, Criticism, and Foucault." *New German Critique* 27 (1982). Reprinted in *Feminism and Foucault: Reflections on Resistance*, ed. Irene Diamond and Lee Quinby. Boston: Northeastern University Press, 1988.

Martin, Luther H., Huck Gutman, and Patrick H. Hutton, eds. *Technologies of the Self: A Seminar with Michel Foucault*. Amherst: University of Massachusetts Press, 1988.

Mathews, Donald G., and Jane Sherron DeHart. *Sex, Gender and the Politics of ERA: A State and the Nation*. New York: Oxford University Press, 1990.

Matusow, Allen J. *The Unraveling of America: A History of Liberalism in the 1960s*. New York: Harper and Row, 1984.

May, Todd. *Between Genealogy and Epistemology: Psychology, Politics, and Knowledge in the Thought of Michel Foucault*. University Park: Penn State University Press, 1993.

McIntosh, Mary. "The Homosexual Role." *Social Problems* 16 (1968): 182–92.

McNay, Lois. *Foucault: A Critical Introduction*. New York: Continuum Publishing, 1994.

———. *Foucault and Feminism: Power, Gender, and the Self*. Boston: Northeastern University Press, 1992.

Megill, Allan. "The Reception of Foucault by Historians." *Journal of the History of Ideas* 48 (1987): 117–41.

Miles, Sara. "He Kissed a Girl: How a Journey through the Heydey of Gay Identity Politics Led to a Straight Romance." *Out* (July 1999): 51–53, 94–96.

Miller, James. *The Passion of Michel Foucault*. New York: Simon and Schuster, 1993.

Mohr, Richard. "Black Law and Gay Law: Do Civil Rights Have a Future?" In *Gay Ideas: Outing and Other Controversies*. New York: Beacon Press, 1992.

———. *Gay Ideas: Outing and Other Controversies*. New York: Beacon Press, 1992.

———. "The Thing of It Is: Some Problems with Models for the Social Constructions of Homosexuality." In *Gay Ideas: Outing and Other Controversies*. New York: Beacon Press, 1992.

Mondimore, Francis Mark. *A National History of Homosexuality*. Baltimore: Johns Hopkins University Press, 1966.

Moon, Michael. "Whose History? The Case of Oklahoma." In *A Queer World: The Center for Lesbian and Gay Studies Reader*, ed. Martin Bauml Duberman. New York: New York University Press, 1997.

Moraga, Cherrie, and Gloria Anzaldúa, eds. *This Bridge Called My Back: Writings by Radical Women of Color*. Latham, N.Y.: Kitchen Table Women of Color Press, 1983.

Moran, Leslie J., Daniel Mond, and Sarah Beresford, eds. *Legal Queeries: Lesbian, Gay, and Transgender Legal Studies*. New York: Cassell, 1998.

Moritz, Rob. "Vigil Honors Slain Gay Student: Speakers Urge Crowd to Fight Hate Crimes." *Nashville Tennessean*, October 19, 1998, 2B.

Morton, Donald. "A Note on Cultural Studies." In *The Material Queer: A LesBiGay Cultural Studies Reader*, ed. Donald Morton. Boulder, Colo.: Westview Press, 1996.

————, ed. *The Material Queer: A LesBiGay Cultural Studies Reader*. Boulder, Colo.: Westview Press, 1996.

Murphey, Murray G. *Philosophical Foundations of Historical Knowledge*. Albany: State University of New York Press, 1994.

Myron, Nancy, and Charlotte Bunch, eds. *Lesbianism and the Women's Movement*. Baltimore: Diana Press, 1975.

Namaste, Ki. "'Tragic Misreadings': Queer Theory's Erasure of Transgender Subjectivity." In *Queer Studies: A Lesbian, Gay, Bisexual, and Transgender Anthology*, ed. Brett Beemyn and Mickey Eliason. New York: New York University Press, 1996.

National Gay and Lesbian Task Force. *Capital Gains and Losses: A State by State Review of Gay, Lesbian, Bisexual, Transgender, and HIV/AIDS–Related Legislation in 1998*. Washington, D.C.: National Gay and Lesbian Task Force Policy Institute, 1998.

Newton, Esther. "The Mythic Mannish Lesbian." In *Hidden from History: Reclaiming the Gay and Lesbian Past*, ed. Martin Bauml Duberman, Martha Vicinus, and George Chauncey Jr. New York: New American Library, 1989.

Nietzsche, Friedrich. *On the Genealogy of Morals*. Trans. Walter Kaufmann and R. J. Hooingdale. New York: Vintage Books, 1989.

Nussbaum, Martha C. "The Professor of Parody: The Hip Defeatism of Judith Butler." *New Republic*, February 22, 1999, 37–45.

Ormiston, Gayle L., and Alan D. Schrift, eds. *Transforming the Hermeneutic Context: From Nietzsche to Nancy*. Albany: State University of New York Press, 1990.

Osborn, Torie. *Coming Home to America: A Roadmap to Gay and Lesbian Empowerment*. New York: St. Martin's Press, 1996.

Ostriker, Alicia. "The Thieves of Language: Women Poets and Revisionist Mythmaking." *Signs* 8 (1982): 68–90.

Padgug, Robert A. "Sexual Matters: On Conceptualizing Sexuality in History." *Radical History Review* 20 (1979): 3–23. Reprinted in *Passion and Power: Sexuality in History*, ed. Kathy Peiss and Christina Simmons with Robert Padgug. Philadelphia: Temple University Press, 1989.

Page, Carl. *Philosophical Historicism and the Betrayal of First Philosophy*. University Park: Pennsylvania State University Press, 1995.

Palmer, Bryan D. *Descent into Discourse: The Reification of Language and the Writing of Social History*. Philadelphia: Temple University Press, 1990.

Patton, Cindy. "Tremble, Hetero Swine!" In *Fear of a Queer Planet: Queer Politics and Social Theory*, ed. Michael Warner. Minneapolis: University of Minnesota Press, 1993.

Peiss, Kathy, and Christina Simmons, eds., with Robert Padgug. *Passion and Power: Sexuality in History*. Philadelphia: Temple University Press, 1989.

Pensky, Max. "Universalism and the Situated Critic." In *The Cambridge Companion to Habermas*, ed. Stephen K. White. New York: Cambridge University Press, 1995.

Person, Ethel Spector. "Sexuality as the Mainstay of Identity: Psychoanalytic Perspectives." *Signs* 5 (1980): 605–30.

Peyser, Marc. "Battling Backlash." *Newsweek*, August 17, 1998, 50–52.

Plant, Richard. *The Pink Triangle: The Nazi War against Homosexuals*. New York: Henry Holt, 1986.

Plaza, Monique. "Our Damages and Their Compensation. Rape: The Will Not to Know of Michel Foucault." *Feminist Issues* 1 (1981): 25–35.

Polikoff, Nancy D. "Raising Children: Lesbian and Gay Parents Face the Public and the Courts." In *Creating Change: Public Policy, Civil Rights, and Sexuality*, ed. John D'Emilio, William B. Turner, and Urvashi Vaid. New York: St. Martin's Press, forthcoming.

Purpura, Dominick P. "Then and Now." Introduction to *Neuroscience: From the Molecular to the Cognitive*, ed. Floyd E. Bloom. *Progress in Brain Research* 100. Amsterdam: Elsevier, 1994.

Rabinow, Paul, ed. *The Essential Works of Michel Foucault, 1954–1984*. New York: New Press, 1997.

———. *The Foucault Reader*. New York: Pantheon Books, 1984.

Radicalesbians. "The Woman Identified Woman." In *Radical Feminism*, ed. Anne Koedt, Ellen Levine, and Anita Rapone. New York: Quadrangle Books, 1973.

Rains, Howell. *My Soul Is Rested: The Story of the Civil Rights Movement in the Deep South*. 1977. Reprint, New York: Penguin, 1983.

Rajchman, John. *Michel Foucault: The Freedom of Philosophy*. New York: Columbia University Press, 1985.

Ramazanoglu, Caroline, ed. *Up against Foucault: Explorations of Some Tensions between Foucault and Feminism*. New York: Routledge, 1993.

Remafei, Gary, ed. *Death by Denial: Studies of Suicide in Gay and Lesbian Teenagers*. Boston: Alyson Publications, 1994.

"Report of the Public Health Service on the Medical Aspects of H.R. 2379, a Bill to Revise the Laws Relating to Immigration, Naturalization, and Nationality, and for Other Purposes." In U.S. House Report 1365 to the McCarran-Walter Act, *U.S. Code Congressional and Administrative News*, 82d Congress, 2d Session, 1701.

Rich, Adrienne. "Compulsory Heterosexuality and Lesbian Existence." In *The Lesbian and Gay Studies Reader*, ed. Henry Abelove, Michele Aina Barale, and David Halperin. New York: Routledge, 1993.

Rosaldo, M. Z. "The Use and Abuse of Anthropology: Reflections on Feminism and Cross-Cultural Understanding." *Signs* 5 (1980): 389–417.

Rosen, Stanley. "Review of *Philosophical Historicism and the Betrayal of First Philosophy*, by Carl Page." *History and Theory* 35 (1996): 410–11.

Rosenberg, Rosalind. *Beyond Separate Spheres: Intellectual Roots of Modern Feminism.* New Haven: Yale University Press, 1982.

Rosenman, Ellen Bayuk. "Sexual Identity and *A Room of One's Own*: 'Secret Economies' in Virginia Woolf's Feminist Discourse." *Signs* 14 (1989): 634–50.

Ross, Ellen, and Rayna Rapp. "Sex and Society: A Research Note from Social History and Anthropology." *Comparative Studies in Society and History* 23 (1981): 51–72.

Rothman, David J. *The Discovery of the Asylum: Social Order and Disorder in the New Republic.* Boston: Little, Brown, 1990.

Rubin, Gayle. "Sexual Traffic." Interview by Judith Butler. In "More Gender Trouble: Feminism Meets Queer Theory." *differences: A Journal of Feminist Cultural Studies* 6/2–3 (Summer–Fall 1994; special issue): 62–99.

———. "Thinking Sex: Notes for a Radical Theory of the Politics of Sexuality." In *Pleasure and Danger: Exploring Female Sexuality*, ed. Carole S. Vance. New York: Routledge, 1984.

Russett, Cynthia Eagle. *Sexual Science: The Victorian Construction of Womanhood.* Cambridge, Mass.: Harvard University Press, 1989.

Said, Edward. "Michel Foucault, 1926–1984." In *After Foucault: Humanistic Knowledge, Postmodern Challenges*, ed. Jonathan Arac. New Brunswick, N.J.: Rutgers University Press, 1988.

Sawicki, Jana. *Disciplining Foucault: Feminism, Power, and the Body.* New York: Routledge, 1991.

———. "Feminism and the Power of Foucaultian Discourse." In *After Foucault: Humanistic Knowledge, Postmodern Challenges*, ed. Jonathan Arac. New Brunswick, N.J.: Rutgers University Press, 1988.

Scott, Charles E. *The Language of Difference.* Atlantic Highlands, N.J.: Humanities Press International, 1987.

———. *The Question of Ethics: Nietzsche, Foucault, Heidegger.* Bloomington: University of Indiana Press, 1990.

Scott, Joan Wallach. "'Experience.'" *Critical Inquiry* 17 (1991): 773–97. Reprinted in *Feminists Theorize the Political*, ed. Judith Butler and Joan W. Scott. New York: Routledge, 1992.

———. *Gender and the Politics of History.* New York: Columbia University Press, 1988.

———. Introduction to *Feminism and History.* Ed. Joan Wallach Scott. New York: Oxford University Press, 1996.

———, ed. *Feminism and History.* New York: Oxford University Press, 1996.

Sedgwick, Eve Kosofsky. *Between Men: English Literature and Male Homosocial Desire.* New York: Columbia University Press, 1985.

———. *Epistemology of the Closet.* Berkeley and Los Angeles: University of California Press, 1990.

———. "Queer and Now." In *Tendencies.* Durham, N.C.: Duke University Press, 1993.

———. *Tendencies.* Durham, N.C.: Duke University Press, 1993.

Seidman, Steven. "Identity and Politics in a 'Postmodern' Gay Culture: Some Historical and Conceptual Notes." In *Fear of a Queer Planet: Queer Politics and Social Theory*, ed. Michael Warner. Minneapolis: University of Minnesota Press, 1993.

Shaffer, Elinor. "Review of *The History of Sexuality, Volume One: An Introduction*." *Signs* 5 (1980): 812–20.

Shilts, Randy. *And the Band Played On: People, Politics, and the AIDS Epidemic*. 1987. Reprint, New York: Penguin Books, 1988.

Showalter, Elaine. "Introduction: The Rise of Gender." In *Speaking of Gender*, ed. Elaine Showalter. New York: Routledge, 1989.

———, ed. *Speaking of Gender*. New York: Routledge, 1989.

Smart, Barry, ed. *Michel Foucault: Critical Assessments*. 7 vols. New York: Routledge, 1995.

Smith, Barbara, ed. *Home Girls: A Black Feminist Anthology*. New York: Kitchen Table Women of Color Press, 1983.

Smith, Bonnie. "Historiography, Objectivity, and the Case of the Abusive Widow." *History and Theory* 31 (1992): 15–32.

———. "Whose Truth, Whose History?" *Journal of the History of Ideas* 56 (1995): 661–63.

Smith, Dinitia. "'Queer Theory' Is Entering the Literary Mainstream." *New York Times*, January 17, 1998.

Smith-Rosenberg, Carroll. "The Abortion Movement and the AMA, 1850–1880." In *Disorderly Conduct: Visions of Gender in Victorian America*. New York: Oxford University Press, 1985.

———. *Disorderly Conduct: Visions of Gender in Victorian America*. New York: Oxford University Press, 1985.

———. "The Female World of Love and Ritual: Relations between Women in Nineteenth-Century America." *Signs* 1 (1975): 1–30. Reprinted in *Disorderly Conduct: Visions of Gender in Victorian America*. New York: Oxford University Press, 1985.

———. "Hearing Women's Words: A Feminist Reconstruction of History." In *Disorderly Conduct: Visions of Gender in Victorian America*. New York: Oxford University Press, 1985.

Snitow, Ann, Christine Stansell, and Sharon Thompson, eds. *Powers of Desire: The Politics of Sexuality*. New York: Monthly Review Press, 1983.

Soper, Kate. "Productive Contradictions." In *Up against Foucault: Explorations of Some Tensions between Foucault and Feminism*, ed. Caroline Ramazanoglu. New York: Routledge, 1993.

Spelman, Elizabeth. *Inessential Woman: Problems of Exclusion in Feminist Thought*. Boston: Beacon Press, 1988.

Spivak, Gayatri Chakravorty. "More on Power/Knowledge." In *The Spivak Reader*, ed. Donna Landry and Gerald Maclean. New York: Routledge, 1996.

———. "Subaltern Studies: Deconstructing Historiography." In *The Spivak Reader*, ed. Donna Landry and Gerald Maclean. New York: Routledge, 1996.

Stanton, Domna C., ed. *Discourses of Sexuality: From Aristotle to AIDS*. Ann Arbor: University of Michigan Press, 1992.

Stanton, Domna C., and Abigail J. Stewart. *Feminism in the Academy*. Ann Arbor: University of Michigan Press, 1995.

Stanton, Elizabeth Cady. "Declaration of Sentiments." In *Early American Women: A Documentary History, 1600–1900*, ed. Nancy Woloch. Belmont, Calif.: Wadsworth Publishing, 1992.

Stein, Donald G. "Brain Damage and Recovery." In *Neuroscience: From the Molecular to the Cognitive*, ed. Floyd E. Bloom. *Progress in Brain Research* 100. Amsterdam: Elsevier, 1994.

Stewart, Thomas A. "Gay in Corporate America." *Fortune*, December 16, 1991, 42–56.

Stivender, Knight. "Out, Proud and Arguing: As Nashville's Gay Community Grows, So Do the Disagreements among Some of Its Factions." *Nashville Tennessean*, October 17, 1999, 17A–20A.

———. "Support for Gay, Lesbian, Bi and Transgendered Nashvillians." *Nashville Tennessean*, October 17, 1999, 20A.

Strong, Tracy B., and Frank Andreas Sposito. "Habermas's Significant Other." In *The Cambridge Companion to Habermas*, ed. Stephen K. White. New York: Cambridge University Press, 1995.

Thomas, Mike. "The Melody Theory of Hurricane Paths." *Orlando Sentinel*, September 25, 1996.

Thompson, E. P. *The Making of the English Working Class.* New York: Vintage Books, 1966.

Thompson, Richard F. *The Brain: A Neuroscience Primer.* 2d ed. New York: W. H. Freeman, 1993.

Timmons, Stuart. *The Trouble with Harry Hay, Founder of the Modern Gay Movement.* Boston: Alyson Publications, 1990.

Traub, Valerie. "The (In)Significance of Lesbian Desire in Early Modern England." In *Queering the Renaissance*, ed. Jonathan Goldberg. Durham, N.C.: Duke University Press, 1994.

———. "Mapping the Terms of 'Lesbian' Studies in the Early Modern Period." Draft manuscript in my possession, 6–10.

Trumbach, Randolph. "The Birth of the Queen: Sodomy and the Emergence of Gender Equality in Modern Culture, 1660–1750." In *Hidden from History: Reclaiming the Gay and Lesbian Past*, ed. Martin Bauml Duberman, Martha Vicinus, and George Chauncey Jr. New York: New American Library, 1989.

———. "London's Sodomites: Homosexual Behavior and Western Culture in the Eighteenth Century." *Journal of Social History* 11 (1977): 1–33.

Turner, William B. "Lesbian/Gay Rights and Immigration Policy: Lobbying to End the Medical Model." *Journal of Policy History* 7 (1995): 208–25.

———. "Mirror Images: Lesbian/Gay Civil Rights in the Carter and Reagan Administrations." In *Creating Change: Public Policy, Civil Rights, and Sexuality*, ed. John D'Emilio, William B. Turner, and Urvashi Vaid. New York: St. Martin's Press, forthcoming.

U.S. Commission on Civil Rights. *Battered Women: Issues of Public Policy.* Washington, D.C.: U.S. Commission on Civil Rights, 1978.

Vance, Carole S., ed. *Pleasure and Danger: Exploring Female Sexuality.* New York: Routledge, 1984.

Veeser, H. Aram, ed. *The New Historicism.* New York: Routledge, 1989.

Walzer, Michael. "The Politics of Michel Foucault." In *Foucault: A Critical Reader,* ed. David Couzens Hoy. New York: Basil Blackwell, 1986.

Warner, Michael. Introduction to *Fear of a Queer Planet: Queer Politics and Social Theory,* ed. Michael Warner. Minneapolis: University of Minnesota Press, 1993.

———, ed. *Fear of a Queer Planet: Queer Politics and Social Theory.* Minneapolis: University of Minnesota Press, 1993.

Watney, Simon. "Practices of Freedom: 'Citizenship' and the Politics of Identity in the Age of AIDS." In *Practices of Freedom: Selected Writings on HIV/AIDS.* Durham, N.C.: Duke University Press, 1994.

———. *Practices of Freedom: Selected Writings on HIV/AIDS.* Durham, N.C.: Duke University Press, 1994.

———. "The Subject of AIDS." In *Practices of Freedom: Selected Writings on HIV/AIDS.* Durham, N.C.: Duke University Press, 1994.

Weeks, Jeffrey. *Coming Out: Homosexual Politics in Britain from the Nineteenth Century to the Present.* New York: Quartet Books, 1977. Rev. ed., 1990.

———. "Foucault for Historians." *History Workshop* 14 (1982): 106–19.

———. *Sex, Politics, and Society: The Regulation of Sexuality Since 1800.* London: Longman, 1981.

———. *Sexuality and Its Discontents: Meanings, Myths, and Modern Sexualities.* London: Routledge and Kegan Paul, 1985.

White, Stephen K. *The Cambridge Companion to Habermas.* New York: Cambridge University Press, 1995.

———. "Reason, Modernity, and Democracy." In *The Cambridge Companion to Habermas,* ed. Stephen K. White. New York: Cambridge University Press, 1995.

Wolin, Richard. "Foucault's Aesthetic Decisionism." *Telos* 67 (1986): 71–86.

Woloch, Nancy, ed. *Early American Women: A Documentary History, 1600–1900.* Belmont, Calif.: Wadsworth Publishing, 1992.

Woodhull, Winifred. "Sexuality, Power, and the Question of Rape." In *Feminism and Foucault: Reflections on Resistance,* ed. Irene Diamond and Lee Quinby. Boston: Northeastern University Press, 1988.

Woodward, Kenneth L. "Do You, Paul, Take Ralph. . . ." *Newsweek,* June 20, 1994, 76–77.

Woolf, Virginia. *A Room of One's Own.* London: Harcourt, Brace, and World, 1929.

Zimmerman, Bonnie. "The Politics of Transliteration: Lesbian Personal Narratives." *Signs* 9 (1983): 663–82.

Zinn, Maxine Baca, Lynn Weber Cannon, Elizabeth Higginbotham, and Bonnie Thornton Dill. "The Costs of Exclusionary Practices in Women's Studies." *Signs* 11 (1986): 290–303.

Index

AA (Alcoholics Anonymous), 198
abjection
  Butler's use of, 111, 182
  as constituting identity, 19, 182, 185, 186, 188, 189, 199
  defined, 111
Able v. USA, 158
Abortion, 91
  and conservative opposition, 13, 173
  of fetuses with "gay gene," 180
activism, 78, 180
  African American, 17
  feminist, 11–16, 18, 21, 189
    and scholarship, 6–8, 89–91
  Foucault's "hyper and pessimistic," 40
  lesbian/gay, 18, 134, 165, 174–75, 176, 179, 189
  queer, 10, 17, 123, 174–75
    and scholarship, 6–8, 141–42, 195–200
  right-wing, 165, 173–74, 181, 194
  transgender, 31
ACT-UP (AIDS Coalition to Unlease Power), 106, 169
  influence on Queer Nation, 145–46
Addams, Calpernia, 2
Adorno, Theodor, 55–57. *See also* Frankfurt School
African Americans
  area studies, 105
  civil rights movement of, 13, 120, 121
  critiques of white feminists, 13–14
  equal protection claims of, 195–96
  as historians, 26
  inclusion in U.S. history, 25–26
  and lesbian/gay civil rights movement, 17

  and queer scholarship, 168
  violent attacks on, 1
Against Our Will: Men, Women, and Rape (Brownmiller), 99
agency
  and feminist theory, 84, 92,
  Butler on, 109–10
  de Lauretis on, 126
  and queer theory, 168–69
AIDS (Acquired Immune Deficiency Syndrome)
  and development of queer theory, 30
  and genealogy, 115–16
  in queer black feminism, 169
Alcoff, Linda, 95–96, 173
Alice Doesn't: Feminism, Semiotics, Cinema (Lauretis), 124
ambiguity
  in definitions of queerness, 168
  in definitions of sodomy, 154
  of gender and sexuality, 5
  of literature as historical evidence, 146
  in morality of power, 176
Amendment Two (Colorado), 157, 175, 193
American Psychiatric Association, definition of "homosexuality" as mental illness by, 14–15, 135, 173
anal intercourse, as defining "homosexual" identity
  among medieval Muslims, 75
  in early modern Europe, 79
anatomy
  defining gender identity, 13, 28, 96, 109–10, 113, 166, 200
  defining sexual orientation, 184

and equal protection, 163–64, 191–93
Goldberg on, 149, 152, 154–55, 162–63
Halley on, 147, 153–55, 163–64
and historical change, 157
and knowledge/ignorance of "homosexuals," 160–64
and privacy rights, 162–63, 175
and queer politics, 157–58
as reinforcing connection between sodomy and "homosexual" identity, 147–49, 152, 153–54, 186
and renaissance England, 147
Sedgwick on, 160–64
Bray, Alan, 79–81, 160
Browning, Frank, 143
Brownmiller, Susan, 99
Brown v. Board of Education, 19
bureaucracy, and rationalization of identity, 172, 184
Burger, Warren, 153, 154
Butler, Judith, 128, 134, 142, 200
critique of Foucault, 111, 113–16
on feminist theory and activism, 109–110
as genealogist, 109
on individual identity as historical process, 131
as leading queer theorist, 3, 5–8, 34, 108
on materiality, 112
psychoanalysis in, 113–14, 115–23, 126
queer theory of, 109–23
on queer theory and feminist theory, 166–68
and the signification of gender, 110
and speech acts, 191
as threat to feminist political activism, 6–8
Byrd, James, 1, 33, 198, 199

Califia, Pat, 89
capitalism, and sexuality, 66, 68, 71
"Capitalism and Gay Identity" (D'Emilio), 71
The Care of the Self, vol. 3 of *The History of Sexuality* (Foucault), 175
categories
defining identities, 137–38
of gender and sexuality, 84
importance for queer theory, 2
as questions for queer theory, 4
reductiveness of, 137
Chauncey, George, 80–82
Chee, Alexander, 107
Cher, 170

child care
political issue for conservatives, 173
political issue for feminists, 95–96
Christian eschatology, 152
Christianity
and "ex-gay" movement, 174
recent opposition to "homosexuality" in, 77, 186
Christianity, Social Tolerance, and Homosexuality: Gay People in Western Europe from the Beginning of the Christian Era to the Fourteenth Century (Boswell), 77, 153, 158
Civil Rights Act (1964), 17, 19
class, absence of, in Foucault's work, 45–46
See also suspect class, lesbians and gay men as
closet
and *Bowers v. Hardwick*, 162
centrality to Western culture, 180
as defining gay oppression, 158
and disavowel of "homosexuality," 54
and knowledge about "homosexuality," 130, 132–33
and performativity, 133
and political action, 165, 182, 195
safety of, 139
Cmiel, Ken, 25
cognition, 28–29
Coles, Matthew, 157–58
colonialism, 20
Coming Out: Homosexual Politics in Britain from the Nineteenth Century to the Present (Weeks), 66, 67
communicative rationality, 57–59
Comte, August, 27
concentration camps, "homosexuals" in, 172, 186, 188
confession
connecting categories and consciousness, 73
and deployment of sexuality, 40, 49–50, 70
Congress, United States, 12, 173, 199
conscience
Butler on, 118–19, 121
as element of subjectivity, 13, 51
Constitution, United States, 90, 121, 153–54, 161, 191–93
contingency, of formal logic, 137
control
over bodies, 68, 89
in definition of subjectivity, 13, 51, 70